Writing a Cybersecurity Accreditation Package

A NIST-based CMMC Roadmap

+ Cybersecurity Maturity Model Capability (CMMC) Traceability Model Included

Mark A. Russo, Ph.D., CISSP-ISSAP
Former Chief Information Security Officer, Department of Education

Copyright 2021, Cybersentinel, LLC, All Rights Reserved
Washington, DC ∞ Tucson, AZ

DEDICATION

This book is dedicated to my continually supportive instructors and professors at the National Defense University, Washington, DC, and their daily efforts to train and teach the next generation of cyber-warriors of this great Nation.

This is also dedicated to my family, who have been supportive of my endeavors to plunge into writing as not just a hobby but a calling to make the world a better and more secure place.

Copyright 2021, Cybersentinel, LLC, All Rights Reserved
Washington, DC ∞ Tucson, AZ

Writing a Cybersecurity Accreditation Package by Mark A. Russo

Copyright © 2021 Cybersentinel LLC. All rights reserved.

Printed in the United States of America.

2020 March

Revision History for the First Edition:

March 2021 VERSION B

The Cybersentinel Logo is a registered trademark of Cybersentinel LLC. **Writing a Cybersecurity Accreditation Package.** *While the publisher and the authors have used good faith efforts to ensure that the information and instructions contained in this work are accurate, the publisher and the authors disclaim all responsibility for errors or omissions, including without limitation, responsibility for damages resulting from the use of or reliance on this work. The use of the information and instructions contained in this work is at your own risk. If any code samples or other technology this work has or describes is subject to open source licenses or the intellectual property rights of others, it is your responsibility to ensure that your use thereof complies with such licenses or rights.*

NOTE: Actual systems, software, or product names are provided only for added context. The mention of real solutions should NOT be construed as a suggestion or endorsement by the author. Always consult with your cybersecurity professionals and engineers for security product needs and requirements. Furthermore, refer to the discussion on FIPS140-2 standards for vetted products

Check Out the
<u>Most-Extensive</u> Cybersecurity Blog Site

This is the primary resource of everything, "Cyber."
"The good, the bad, and the ugly of cybersecurity all in one place."

Join us at https://cybersentinel.tech

This free resource is available to everyone interested in the fate and future of cybersecurity in the 21st Century

Copyright 2021, Cybersentinel, LLC, All Rights Reserved
Washington, DC ∞ Tucson, AZ

Writing a Cybersecurity Accreditation Package

Contents

Forward 17
Pathway to Creating a Comprehensive Cybersecurity Packet 19
Global Cybersecurity Policy (G-CSP) 24
Global Policy Introduction 26
Access Control (AC) 31
    [CMMC AC.1.001] 33
    [CMMC AC.1.002] 34
    [CMMC AC.2.016] 35
    [CMMC AC.3.017] 37
    [CMMC AC.2.007] 38
    [CMMC AC.2.008] 38
    [CMMC AC.3.018] 39
    [CMMC AC.2.009] 39
    [CMMC AC.2.005] 41
    [CMMC AC.2.010] 41
    [CMMC AC.3.019] 41
    [CMMC AC.2.013] 42
    [CMMC AC.3.014] 42
    [CMMC AC.2.015] 43
    [CMMC AC.3.021] 44
    [CMMC AC.2.011] 45
    [CMMC AC.3.012] 45
    [CMMC AC.3.020] 45
    [CMMC AC.3.022] 46
    [CMMC AC.1.003] 46
    [CMMC AC.2.006] 47

[CMMC AC.1.004] 48
Awareness and Training (AT) 49
   [CMMC AT.2.056] 49
   [CMMC AT.2.057] 50
   [CMMC AT.3.058] 50
Audit and Accountability (AU) 52
   [CMMC AU.2.042] 53
   [CMMC AU.2.041] 54
   [CMMC AU.3.045] 55
   [CMMC AU.3.046] 55
   [CMMC AU.3.051] 55
   [CMMC AU.3.052] 58
   [CMMC AU.2.043] 58
   [CMMC AU.3.049] 59
   [CMMC AU.3.50] 59
Configuration Management (CM) 60
   [CMMC CM.2.061] 61
   [CMMC CM.2.064] 63
   [CMMC CM.2.065] 63
   [CMMC CM.2.066] 63
   [CMMC CM.3.067] 64
   [CMMC CM.2.062] 64
   [CMMC CM.3.068] 65
   [CMMC CM.3.069] 65
   [CMMC CM.2.063] 67
Identification and Authentication (IA) 69
   [CMMC IA.1.076] 69
   [CMMC IA.1.077] 69
   [CMMC IA.3.083] 70
   [CMMC IA.3.084] 70
   [CMMC IA.3.085] 70
   [CMMC IA.3.086] 71
   [CMMC IA.2.078] 71
   [CMMC IA.2.079] 72

- [CMMC IA.2.080] 72
- [CMMC IA.2.081] 72
- [CMMC IA.2.082] 73

Incident Response (IR) 74
- [CMMC IR.2.092] 74
- [CMMC IA.3.098] 74
- [CMMC IA.3.099] 75

Maintenance (MA) 76
- [CMMC MA.2.111] 76
- [CMMC MA.2.112] 76
- [CMMC MA.3.115] 77
- [CMMC MA.3.116] 77
- [CMMC MA.2.113] 78
- [CMMC MA.2.114] 79

Media Protection (MP) 80
- [CMMC MP.2.119] 81
- [CMMC MP.2.120] 81
- [CMMC MP.1.118] 81
- [CMMC MP.3.122] 82
- [CMMC MP.3.124] 82
- [CMMC MP.3.125] 83
- [CMMC MP.2.121] 83
- [CMMC MP.3.123] 83
- [CMMC RE.2.138] 84

Personnel Security (PS) 85
- [CMMC PS.2.127] 85
- [CMMC PS.2.128] 86

Physical Protection (PP) 87
- [CMMC PE.1.131] 87
- [CMMC PE.2.135] 87
- [CMMC PE.1.132] 88
- [CMMC PE.1.133] 89
- [CMMC PE.1.134] 89
- [CMMC PE.3.136] 90

- Risk Assessment (RA) 91
  - [CMMC RM.2.141] 92
  - [CMMC RM.2.142] 93
  - [CMMC RM.2.143] 93
- Security Assessment (SA) 96
  - [CMMC CA.2.158] 96
  - [CMMC CA.2.159] 97
  - [CMMC CA.3.161] 100
  - [CMMC CA.2.157] 100
- System and Communications Protection (SC) 102
  - [CMMC SC.1.175] 102
  - [CMMC SC.3.180] 102
  - [CMMC SC.3.181] 105
  - [CMMC SC.3.182] 106
  - [CMMC SC.1.176] 107
  - [CMMC SC.3.183] 107
  - [CMMC SC.3.184] 108
  - [CMMC SC.3.185] 108
  - [CMMC SC.3.186] 109
  - [CMMC SC.3.187] 109
  - [CMMC SC.3.177] 109
  - [CMMC SC.2.178] 110
  - [CMMC SC.3.188] 110
  - [CMMC SC.3.189] 110
  - [CMMC SC.3.190] 111
  - [CMMC SC.3.191] 113
- System and Information Integrity (SI) 114
  - [CMMC SI.1.210] 114
  - [CMMC SI.1.211] 115
  - [CMMC SI.2.214] 115
  - [CMMC SI.1.212] 115
  - [CMMC SI.1.213] 116
  - [CMMC SI.2.216] 116
  - [CMMC SI.2.217] 116

ANNEX A – Acceptable Use Policy (AUP) 119
ANNEX B – System Administrator (SysAdmin) Guide [3.1.4] --RESERVED 124
ANNEX C – Controlled Unclassified Information (CUI)/Critical Defense Information (CUI) Marking, Handling & Storage Guide [3.1.9] 125
ANNEX D – Remote Access Procedures [3.1.12] 126
ANNEX E – Wireless Policy [3.1.16] 129
ANNEX F – Portable Storage Devices [3.1.21] -- RESERVED 135
ANNEX G – Publicly Accessible Information [3.1.22] –RESERVED 136
ANNEX H – Awareness and Training [3.2.1 – 3.2.3] 137
ANNEX I – Audit Policy and Procedure [3.3.1-3.3.9] --RESERVED 138
ANNEX J – Configuration Management Procedure [3.4.1-3.4.9] 139
    Introduction 140
    Roles and Responsibilities 140
    Configuration Control Board (CCB) 140
    Configuration Control (CC) 141
    Configuration Management Database (CMDB) 142
    Configuration Status Accounting 142
    Configuration Audits 143
ANNEX K – Multi-factor Authentication (MFA) Implementation [3.5.2] – RESERVED 146
ANNEX L – Password Policy [3.5.5, 3.5.7] 147
ANNEX M – Incident Response Plan (IRP) [3.6.1-3.6.3] 149
ANNEX N – Maintenance Procedures [3.7.1-3.7.5] – RESERVED 168
ANNEX O – Media Sanitization Procedures [3.8.3] 169
ANNEX P – Risk Assessment Procedure [3.11.1- 3.11.3] 171
    Risk Assessment Examples 173
ANNEX Q – Continuous Monitoring Procedure for NIST 800-171 Security Controls [3.12.1- 3.12.4] 179
ANNEX R – NIST 800-171 Compliance Checklist 189
    Access Control (AC) 190
    Awareness & Training (AT) 196
    Audit & Accountability (AU) 198
    Configuration Management (CM) 201
    Identification & Authentication (IA) 205
    Incident Response (IR) 208
    Maintenance (MA) 210

- Media Protection (MP) 212
- Personnel Security (PS) 214
- Physical Security (PP) 215
- Risk Assessments (RA) 217
- Security Assessments (SA) 219
- System & Communications Protection (SC) 221
- System & Information Integrity (SI) 226

ANNEX S – Acceptable Encryption Policy 228

ANNEX T – Separation of Duties for System Security Administration and Auditing 230

ANNEX U – Incident Response Procedures 233

ANNEX V – Disaster Recovery Procedures 236

ANNEX W – DEFENSE BUSINESS SOLUTION Architecture Documents (as of Jan 30, 20xx) 238

ANNEX X – Preliminary Security Assessment Report (July 20XX) 241

ANNEX Y – CUI Marking, Handling & Storage Guide 244

- Introduction 245
- CUI Banner Markings (Reference 32 CFR 2002.20(b)) 246
- CUI Banner Control Markings (Reference 32 CFR 2002.20(b)(1)) 248
- CUI Categories and Subcategories (Reference 32 CFR 2002.12) 249
- Banner Markings for Category and Subcategory Markings (Reference 32 CFR 2002.20(b)(2)) 250
- Banner Markings with Multiple of Subcategory Markings (Reference 32 CFR 2002.20) 252
- Banner Markings (Limited Dissemination Controls) (Reference 32 CFR 2002.20(b)(3)) 253
- Designation Indicator (Reference 32 CFR 2002.20(a)(3)(d)) 254
- Portion Markings (Reference 32 CFR 2002.20(f)) 255
- Portion Markings with Category Only (Reference 32 CFR 2002.20(f)) 258
- Portion Markings with Category and Dissemination Caveats (Reference 32 CFR 2002.20(f)) 258
- Marking of Multiple Pages (Reference 32 CFR 2002.20(c)) 259
- Required Indicators as directed by Authorities (Reference 32 CFR 2002.20 (b)(2)(iii)) 260
- Supplemental Administrative Markings (Reference 32 CFR 2002.20(l)) 261
- Common Mistakes for Supplemental Administrative Markings 263

 Electronic Media Storage and Marking Procedures (Reference 32 CFR 2002.20) 263
 Marking Forms (Reference 32 CFR 2002.20) 264
 CUI Coversheets (Reference 32 CFR 2002.32) 265
 Marking Transmittal Documents (Reference 32 CFR 2002.20) 267
 Alternate Marking Methods (Reference 32 CFR 2002.20) 267
 Room or Area Markings (Reference 32 CFR 2002.20) 268
 Container Markings (Reference 32 CFR 2002.20) 269
 Shipping and Mailing (Reference 32 CFR 2002.20) 269
 Re-marking Legacy Information (Reference 32 CFR 2002.36) 270
ANNEX Z--CUI MARKINGS IN CLASSIFIED ENVIRONMENTS. 273
 Marking Commingled Information (Reference 32 CFR 2002.20(g)) 273
 Commingling Example 1 275
 Commingling Example 2 277
 Commingling Example 3 277
 Commingling Portion Markings (Reference 32 CFR 2002.20(g)) 278
APPENDICES 280
 APPENDIX A -- RELEVANT REFERENCES 281
 APPENDIX B -- TERMS & GLOSSARY 282
 APPENDIX C – MANAGING THE LIFECYCLE OF A POAM 287
ABOUT THE AUTHOR 292

Forward

 One of the most common requests I receive from my readers is help in creating an effective Cybersecurity Policy (CSP). I initially was focused on the two major technical parts of the NIST 800-171 accreditation package, the System Security Plan (SSP) and Plans of Action and Milestones (POAM). I consider the CSP more a Human Resources effort that focuses on the people side of the People-Process-Technology Triad, but no less critical. Fortunately, I have recently been able to dedicate the time to develop what I describe as an *onion approach* to create a CSP. I define a GLOBAL CSP as a base document. The cybersecurity professional can strip out the SSP, the final CSP, and several other vital cybersecurity documents needed to manage any IT system.

I am introducing the **Security Authorization Development Package Model (SADP-M).** I hope this helps you create a fully auditable and complete package under the base NIST 800-171 and the Cybersecurity Maturity Model Certification (CMMC) process emerging from the Department of Defense (DOD). I have added CMMC control traceability for Levels 1 through 3 in this version. Again, I hope this gets you where you want and need to stop and defeat the "bad guys of cyberspace."

See the Cyber-Shop for the most current Templates....

Mark A. Russo
Mark A. Russo, CISSP-ISSAP

Pathway to Creating a Comprehensive Cybersecurity Packet

This model introduces the Global Cybersecurity Policy (G-CSP). It forms the starting point for required accreditation documentation under NIST 800-171, applicable to CMMC. This is a defined process to help create auditable packages for accreditation. The assigned IT professional or ISSO will subsequently populate and provide answers for the auditor in the G-CSP. After this work is completed, the ISSO will begin to "strip out" the other documents, including the SSP, CSP, POAM, etc.

"Onion Approach"

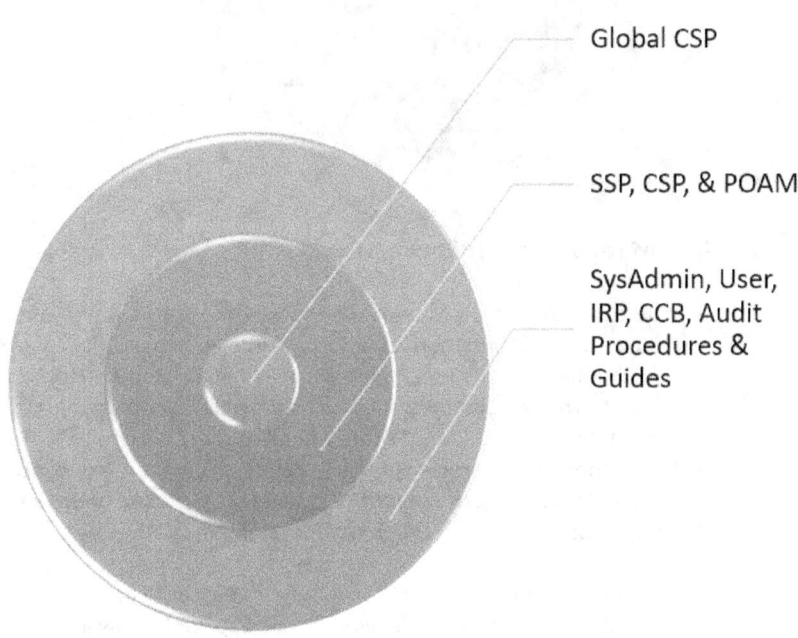

Global CSP

SSP, CSP, & POAM

SysAdmin, User, IRP, CCB, Audit Procedures & Guides

The SADP-M begins with an understanding of the People-Process-Technology (PPT) Triad. It requires active and regular participation from an organization's senior leadership to provide advocacy, support, and resourcing. Cybersecurity is no more than a one-time drill that will not protect the system or network during the lifecycle without engaged leadership. The modern-day cybersecurity challenges do not rest with the failures of cybersecurity personnel alone. They include leadership to devote the requisite care and attention to detect and PREVENT the next cyber-attack.

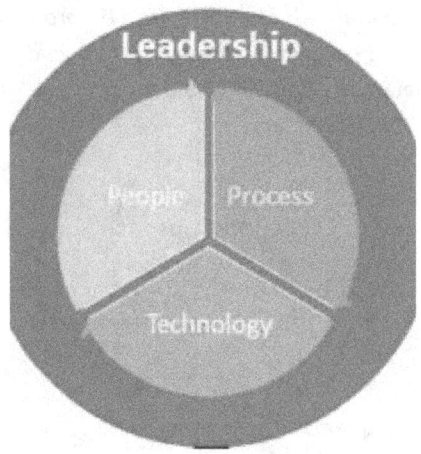

The SADP-M follows the following steps:

1. Populate all 110 controls (or more if following the CMMC framework) with how the company or organization will implement security controls applying technical and people solutions in an initial "global policy" document. This template provides that start-point. Additionally, it includes traceability to CMMC control families ONLY specific to NIST 800-171; those are addressed in the current version of ***Cybersecurity Maturity Model Certification (CMMC): Levels 1-3 Manual: Detailed Security Control Implementation Guidance*** on Amazon®.

2. Once every control is addressed then the other security accreditation documents can be split out. The workflow is depicted below in the Security Authorization Development Package Model (SADP-M).

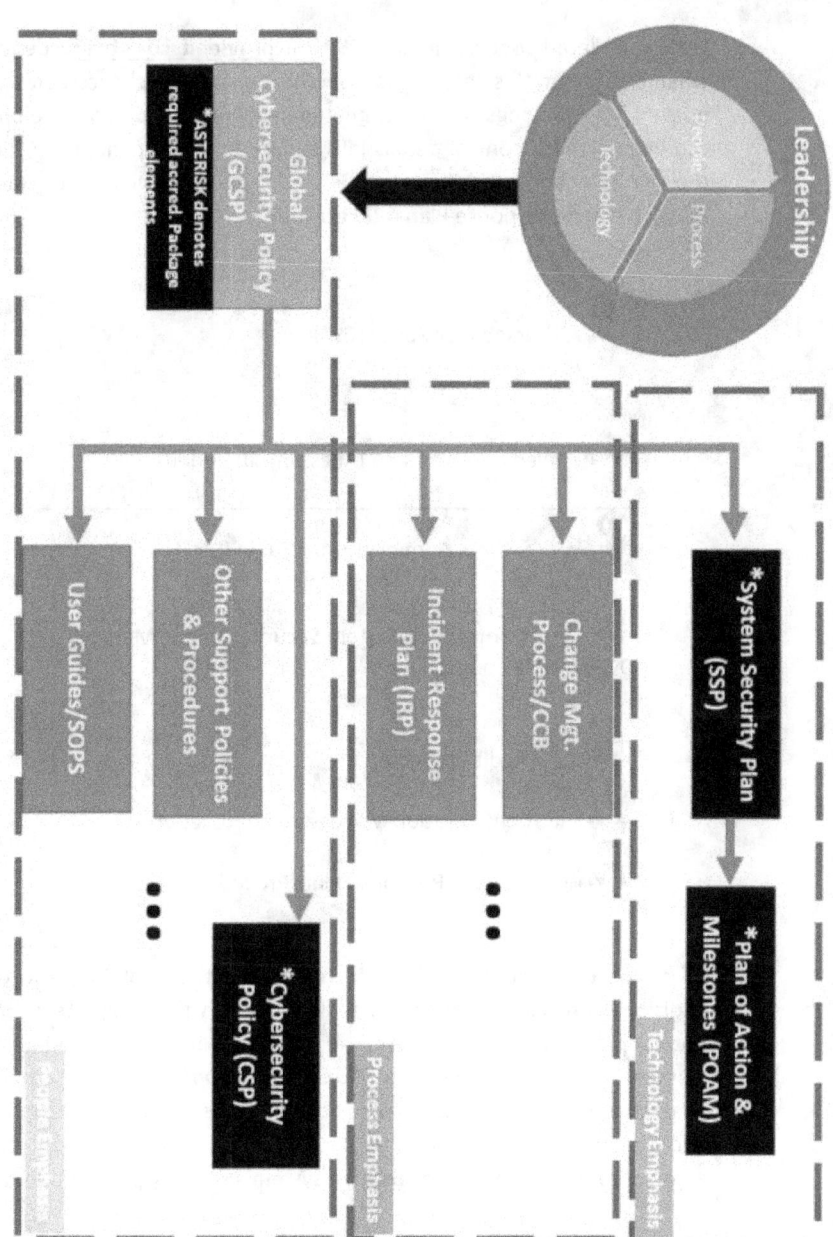

The Security Authorization Development Package Model (SADP-M) ©

3. Once completed populating the G-CSP, the **provided icons below** denote what document this information should be and which accreditation documents it belongs to. A designated cybersecurity policy developer can extract those control details into supporting documents to include the Plan of Action and Milestones (POAM), System Administrator Guide (SAG), Incident Response Plan (IRP) document, etc.

 Cybersecurity Policy (CSP)

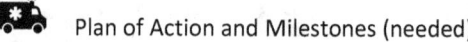 Plan of Action and Milestones (needed)

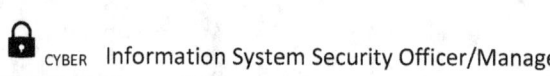 System Administrators Guide (SAG)

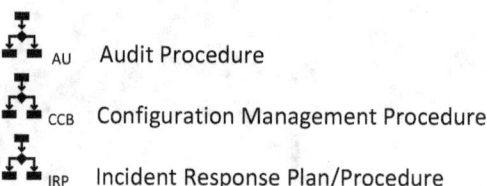

CYBER   Information System Security Officer/Manager Oversight Responsibility

AU   Audit Procedure

CCB   Configuration Management Procedure

IRP   Incident Response Plan/Procedure

4. **All of the controls created should remain for the final SSP, and the additional suggested artifact types are found in the template of this book's presentation.** Furthermore, after you have extracted these elements*, the System Security Plan (SSP) remains*. The SSP should possess both the technical and people procedures—duplication is encouraged, especially with the SSP. It is the crucial document that assessors will rely upon to evaluate a system's security protection level.

5. *The following is a detailed template based upon a notional standard Windows® based system deployed in a local IT environment with cloud solution components.*

Global Cybersecurity Policy (G-CSP)
[becomes the System Security Plan once completed]

---EXAMPLE—

DEFENSE BUSINESS SOLUTION System v1.0

[DATE]

Report Prepared By (ISSO)	
Approved By (System Owner)	

CHANGE RECORD

Date	Description	Editor
1/15/20XX	Initial edits	ABC

Global Policy Introduction

TITLE: Cybersecurity Policy for the DEFENSE BUSINESS SOLUTION (DBS) System

1. **REFERENCES:**

    a. Executive Order 12958, as Amended, Classified National Security Information.
    b. DoDI 8510.01, *Risk Management Framework for DoD Information Technology*, March 12, 2014 (and Change 1 effective 24 May 2016)
    c. DODD 8140, Cyberspace Workforce Management, July 31, 2017.
    d. DODI 5000.02, Defense Acquisition, November 26, 2013.
    e. NIST SP 800-53A Revision 4, *Assessing Security and Privacy Controls in Federal Information Systems and Organizations*, December 2014 (and 18 December 2014 updates).
    f. NIST SP 800-53 Revision 4, *Security and Privacy Controls for Federal Information Systems and Organizations*, April 2013 (and 22 January 2015 updates).
    g. NIST 800-171, revision 1, "Protecting Controlled Unclassified Information in Nonfederal Systems and Organizations."
    h. NIST Special Publication 800-137, *Information Security Continuous Monitoring (ISCM) for Federal Information Systems and Organizations*,
    i. NIST SP 800-92, Guide to Computer Security Log Management, February 2015.
    j. National Industrial Security Program Operating Manual (NISPOM), *DoD 5220.22-M*.
    k. Unicorn Red, Password Policy.
    l. Unicorn Red, Acceptable Encryption Policy.
    m. Unicorn Red, Access Control Policy.
    n. Unicorn Red, Authorized Wireless Policy
    o. Unicorn Red, Awareness, and Training Policy.
    p. Unicorn Red, Separation of Duties for System Security Administration and Auditing.
    q. Unicorn Red, Data Breach Plan.
    r. Unicorn Red, Disaster Recovery Plan/Policy.
    s. Unicorn Red, Identification, and Authentication (specific to NIST 800-171 related controls).
    t. Unicorn Red, Risk Assessment Procedures.
    u. **ClownCar LLC**, Standard Practices and Procedures (SPP), undated.

2. **PURPOSE**:

   a. This **System Security Plan (SSP) [or Cybersecurity Policy (CSP)]** is provided to meet requirements under the National Institute of Standards and Technology (NIST) Special Publication (SP) 800-171 version 1, *Protecting Controlled Unclassified Information in Nonfederal Systems and Organizations, [or Cybersecurity Maturity Model Certification (CMMC)]* and the Risk Management Framework (RMF).

   b. Compliance is in accordance with (IAW) applicable Federal Acquisition Regulation (FAR) and Defense Federal Acquisition Regulation Supplement (DFARS) 252.204-7012 clauses. It applies to Nonfederal System Owners (NSO) and Organizations conducting business with the US Government.

   c. It applies to Information Systems (IS) to include Local Area Networks, Wide Area Networks, and Interconnected Systems used in conducting authorized business activities with the federal government.

   d. This policy is specific to **Unicorn Red (UR)**[1] personnel security requirements for meeting NIST 800-171 (or the CMMC). Technical implementation of each control is more defined in the DEFENSE BUSINESS SOLUTION System Security Plan (SSP).

   e. **System Unique Identifier:** *DEFENSE BUSINESS SOLUTION System* (Contractor Developed/Contractor Operated (CDCO)).

   ---

   f. **The number of end-users and privileged users:**

User Roles and Number of Each Type

Overall User Numbers	Number of Administrators/ Privileged Users with Elevated Privileges
##	#

---

[1] UNICORN RED (UR) is the notional company executing the cybersecurity control effort under this vignette.

Responsible Organization: <u>Unicorn Red Solutions</u>

Name:	
Address:	
Phone:	

Information Owner[2]

Name:	
Title:	
Office Address:	
Work Phone:	
e-Mail Address:	

System Owner (Program Manager)

Name:	
Title:	
Office Address:	
Work Phone:	
e-Mail Address:	

Information System Security Officer/Engineer

Name:	
Title:	
Office Address:	
Work Phone:	
e-Mail Address:	

---

[2] This is usually the customer.

CHANGE SUMMARY: No changes.

CANCELLATION OF PREVIOUS: This is the first version of the policy.

NOTE: Actual systems, software, or products are provided only for added context. The mention of any products should NOT be construed as a suggestion or endorsement by the author. Always consult with your cybersecurity professionals and engineers for security product needs and requirements.

POLICIES & PROCEDURES

Access Control (AC)

UR GENERAL POLICY

Access control is IAW Unicorn Red's (UR) *Access Control Policy*.

Only authorized users are granted access to information systems, and users are limited to specific defined, documented, and approved applications and levels of access rights. Computer and communication system access control is achieved via user IDs unique to each user to provide individual accountability.

Who is Affected: This policy affects all employees of this UR and its subsidiaries and all contractors, consultants, temporary employees, and business partners? Employees who deliberately violate this policy will be subject to disciplinary action up to and including termination.

Affected Systems: This policy applies to all computer and communication systems owned or operated by UR and its subsidiaries. Similarly, this policy applies to all platforms (operating systems) and all application systems.

Entity Authentication: Any User (remote or internal) accessing UR networks and systems must be authenticated. The level of authentication must be appropriate to the data classification and transport medium.

Entity authentication includes but is not limited to:

- Automatic logoff
- And Unique user identifier
- At least one of the following:
    - Biometric identification
    - Password
    - Personal identification number
    - A telephone callback procedure
    - Token

Workstation Access Control System: All workstations used for UR business activities, no matter where they are located, must use an access control system approved by UR. Active workstations are not to be left unattended for prolonged periods, where appropriate. When a user leaves a workstation, that user will adequately log out of all applications and networks. Users will be held responsible for all actions taken under their sign-on.

Disclosure Notice: A notice warning that those who should only access the system with proper authority will be displayed initially before signing on to the system. The warning message will clarify that the system is a private network or application, and those unauthorized users should disconnect or log off immediately.

System Access Controls: Access controls will be applied to all computer-resident information based on its Data Classification to ensure that it is not improperly disclosed, modified, deleted, or rendered unavailable.

Access Approval: System access will not be granted to any user without appropriate approval. Management immediately notifies the Security Administrator (SysAdmin) and reports all significant end-user duties or employment status changes. User access is to be immediately revoked if the individual has been terminated. Also, user privileges are to be appropriately changed if the user is transferred to a different job.

Limiting User Access: UR-approved access controls, such as user logon scripts, menus, session managers, and other access controls, will be used to restrict user access to only those network applications and functions for which they have been authorized.

Need-to-Know: Users will be granted access to information on a "need-to-know" basis. Users will only receive access to the minimum applications and privileges required to perform their jobs.

Access for Non-Employees: Individuals who are not employees, contractors, consultants, or business partners must not be granted a user-ID or otherwise be given privileges to use the UR computers or information systems unless the written approval of the Department Head has first been obtained. Before any third party or business partner is given access to these UR computers or information systems, a chain of trust agreement defining the terms and conditions of such access must have been signed by a responsible manager at the third-party organization.

Unauthorized Access: Employees are prohibited from gaining unauthorized access to any other information systems or in any way damaging, altering, or disrupting the operations of these systems. System privileges allowing the modification of 'production data' must be restricted to 'production' applications.

[CMMC AC.1.001]

3.1.1 Limit system access to authorized users, processes acting on behalf of authorized users, and devices (including other systems).

👤 Authorized users, processes, and devices are managed and restricted by the DEFENSE BUSINESS SOLUTION (DBS) application. All users will abide by these restrictions based upon their duty position and role.

SSP ARTIFACT RECOMMENDATIONS: (CURRENT ARTIFACT DATE): Screen capture of all current and privileged users and their rights type and levels. (This information will come from the System Administrator [SysAdmin] or Network Administrator [NWA].)

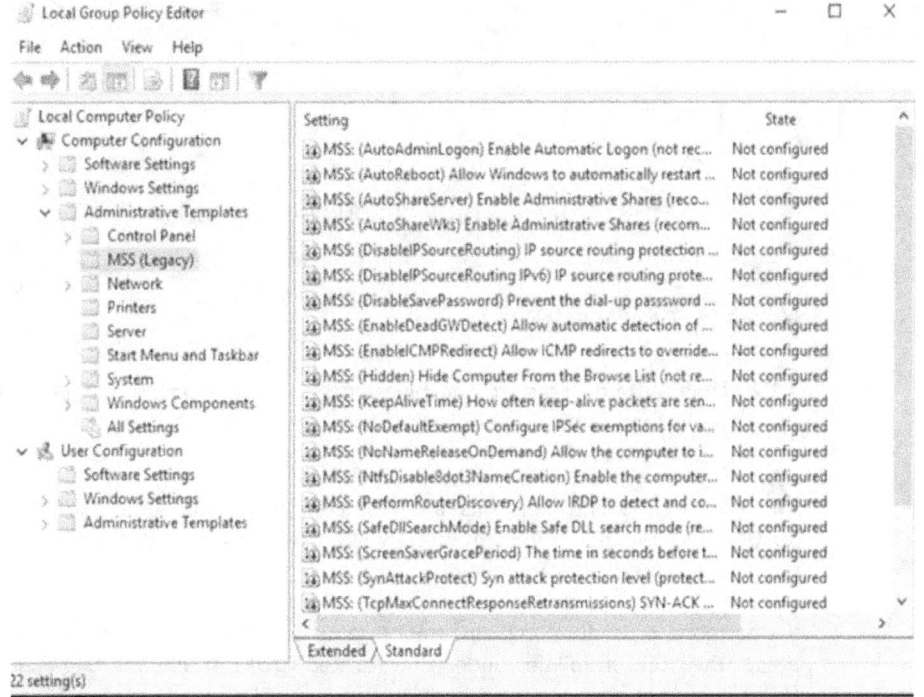

EXAMPLE ONLY ARTIFACT

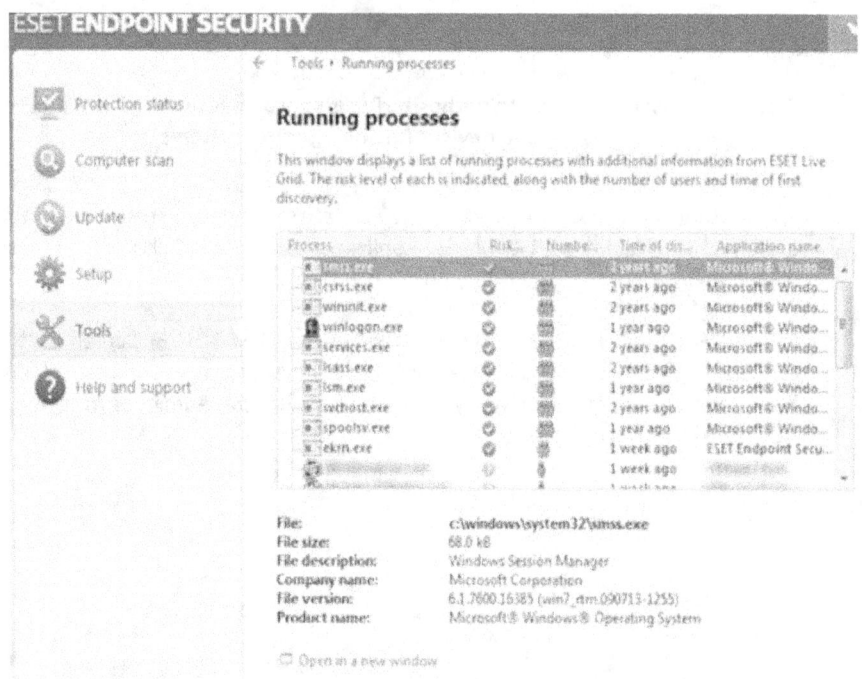

ESET EXAMPLE ONLY OF RUNNING PROCESSES

[CMMC AC.1.002]

3.1.2 Limit system access to the types of transactions and functions that authorized users are permitted to execute.

👤 Transactions and functions are restricted by the DEFENSE BUSINESS SOLUTION (DBS) application. All users will abide by these restrictions based upon their duty position and role(s).

Furthermore, procedural implementation requires DBS personnel to read and accept their responsibilities under **Unicorn Red's (UR)** Acceptable Use Policy (AUP) (See Annex A). Users and privileged users will be limited to only those transactions and functions required to accomplish their mission.

SSP ARTIFACT RECOMMENDATIONS: (CURRENT ARTIFACT DATE): Screen capture. Like 3.1.1.

[CMMC AC.2.016]

3.1.3 Control the flow of CUI in accordance with approved authorizations.

👤 The control of CUI flow will be IAW the approved Unicorn Red *CUI Guide*. The Confidentiality, Integrity, and Availability (CIA) will be maintained primarily by Data in Motion (DIM) and Data at Rest (DAR) encryption solutions based upon TLS 1.0 or higher, AES-256, and SHA-256 protocols/algorithms to the extent technically possible.

SSP ARTIFACT RECOMMENDATIONS: (CURRENT ARTIFACT DATE): CUI Guide, completed, separate document.

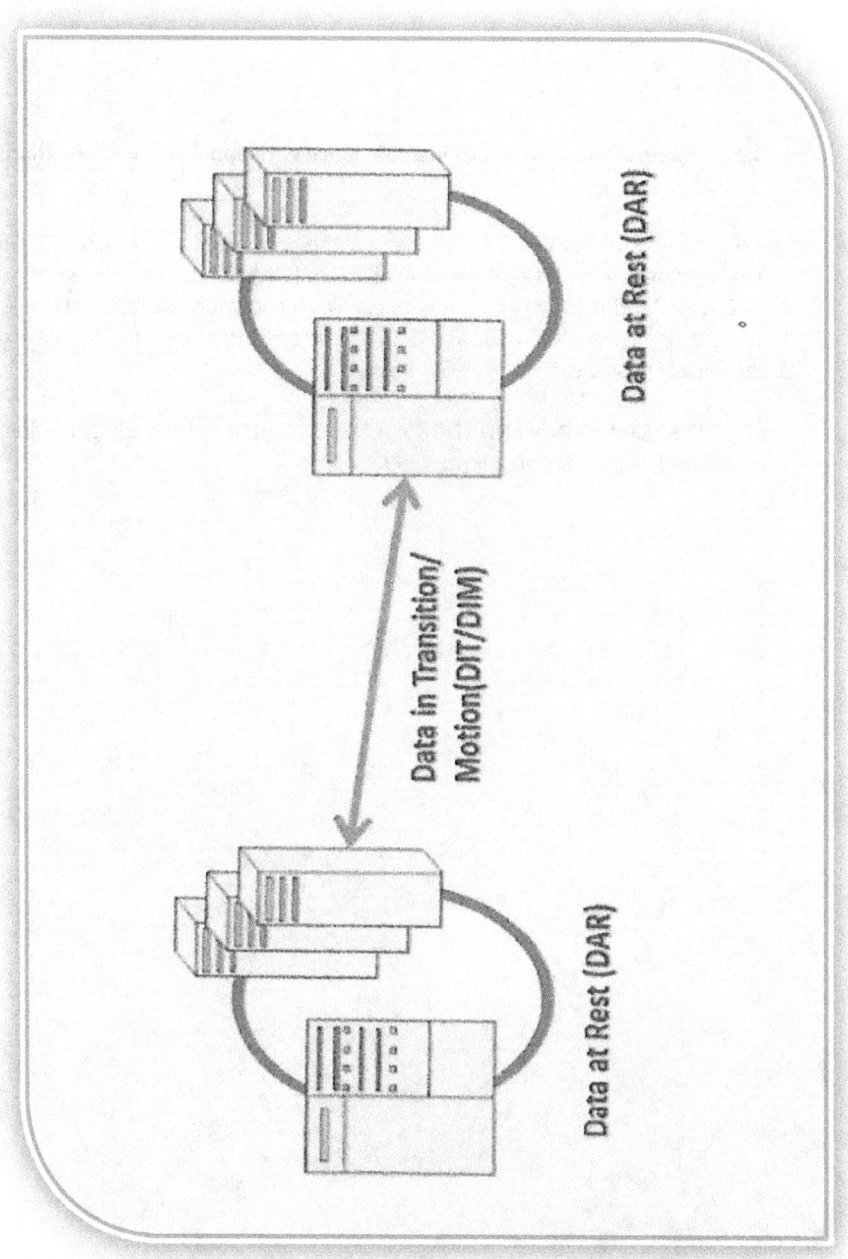

Data at Rest (DAR) versus Data in Transit/Motion (DIT/DIM) Conceptual Diagram

[CMMC AC.3.017]

3.1.4 Separate the duties of individuals to reduce the risk of malevolent activity without collusion.

👤 The principle of *separation of duties* will be met by privileged users to the greatest extent possible. Privileged access to root, administrative, and audit log data will be partitioned to avoid potential *insider threat* activities and accidental data, application, or system changes. This control will be met with an Administrator's Guide to be published (TBP).

The separation of duty policy is described and met by UR's *Separation of Duties for System Administration and Auditing* (See Annex T). All privileged users will be required to abide by this policy.

SSP ARTIFACT RECOMMENDATIONS: Annex T and subsequent System Administrator's Guide-TBP.

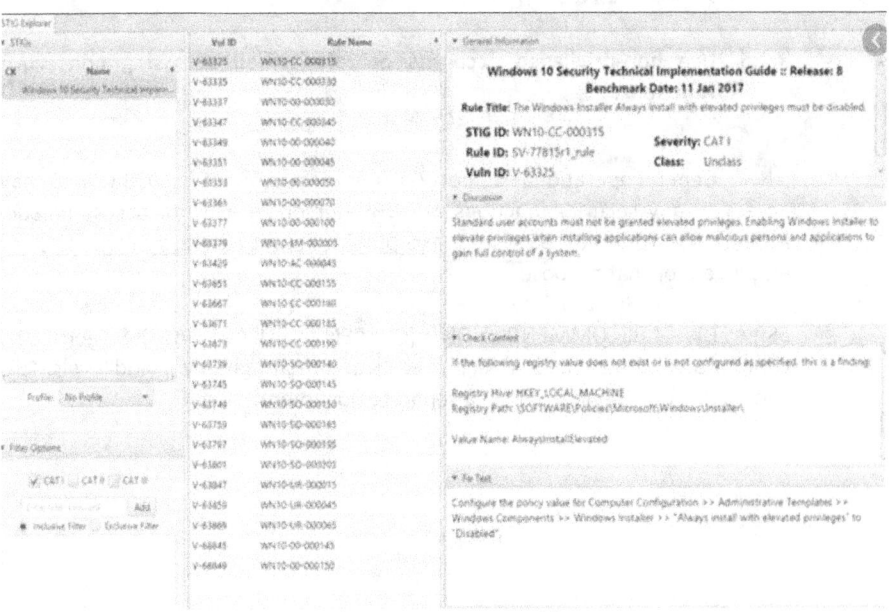

EXAMPLE ONLY ARTIFACT

[CMMC AC.2.007]

3.1.5 Employ the principle of least privilege, including for specific security functions and privileged accounts.

All users will meet the principle of least privilege. Only specified functions will be allowed based upon the duties and functions of the individual. Privileged access to root, administrative, and audit log data will be partitioned to avoid potential insider threat activities and accidental system changes. This control will further be addressed in the *System Administrator's Guide* (SAG) published (TBP).

SSP ARTIFACT RECOMMENDATIONS: (CURRENT ARTIFACT DATE): Screen capture of all current and privileged users and their rights type and levels. This should include the final SAG as a separate document.

[CMMC AC.2.008]

3.1.6 Use non-privileged accounts or roles when accessing nonsecurity functions.

General operational support Call Center personnel for DBS will not have access to any security functions. All DBS personnel will not access personal information from the DBS system <u>except with appropriate attribution solutions</u> employed for that purpose.

SSP ARTIFACT RECOMMENDATIONS: (CURRENT ARTIFACT DATE): Screen capture of all current and privileged users and their rights type and levels. This should include the final SAG as a separate document.

[CMMC AC.3.018]

3.1.7 Prevent non-privileged users from executing privileged functions and audit the execution of such functions.

Non-privileged users/basic users will not execute any privileged functions, including audit data or logs, at any time.

SSP ARTIFACT RECOMMENDATIONS: (CURRENT ARTIFACT DATE): Screen capture of all current and privileged users and their rights type and levels. This should include the final SAG as a separate document.

[CMMC AC.2.009]

3.1.8 Limit unsuccessful logon attempts.

Logons are limited to **3** failed logons (STIG-based)[3], and the DBS system will enforce it. Logon credential recovery will be accomplished only by designated privileged onsite administrators supporting the DEFENSE BUSINESS SOLUTION system.

SSP ARTIFACT RECOMMENDATIONS: (CURRENT ARTIFACT DATE): Screenshot of policy setting for numbers of failed logons provided from SysAdmin/NWA.

---

[3] The Security Technical Implementation Guides (STIGs) are the configuration standards for DOD IA and IA-enabled devices/systems. The STIGs contain technical guidance to "lock down" information systems/software that might otherwise be vulnerable to a malicious computer attack. (see STIG site: https://public.cyber.mil/stigs/).

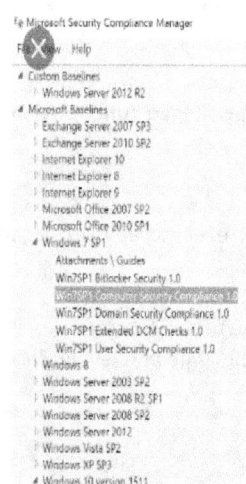

WINDOWS EXAMPLE ONLY ARTIFACT

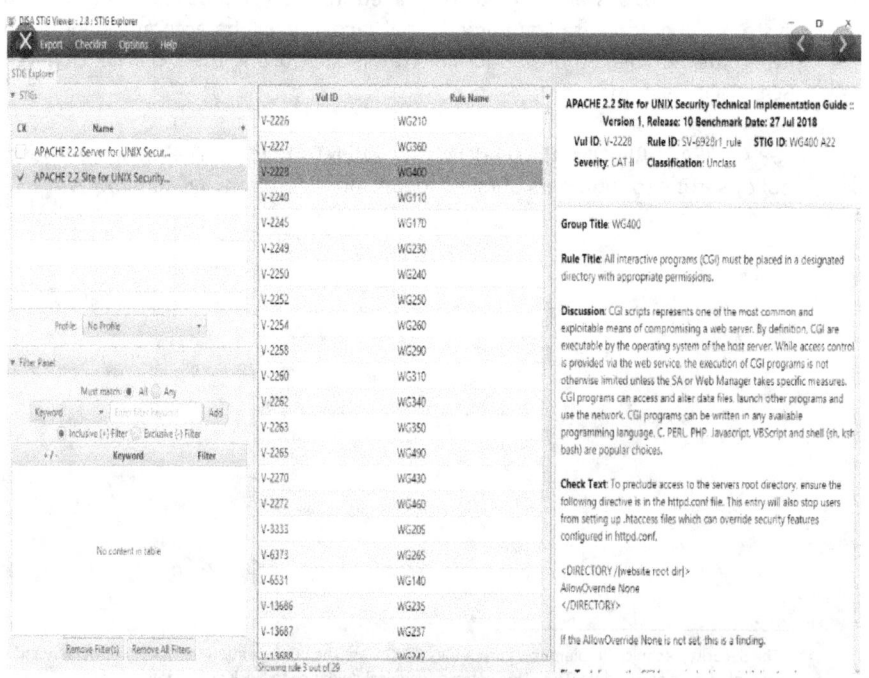

EXAMPLE STIG VIEWER ONLY

[CMMC AC.2.005]

3.1.9 Provide privacy and security notices consistent with applicable CUI rules.

DBS personnel will be required to read, understand, and accept the customer's Security Technical Implementation Guidance (STIG) privacy and security banner upon each logon. All privacy and security notifications will be implemented by logon system banners IAW *CUI Guide, January 20XX*.

SSP ARTIFACT RECOMMENDATIONS: (CURRENT ARTIFACT DATE): Logon screen capture. Access to CUI Guide for assessors.

[CMMC AC.2.010]

3.1.10 Use session lock with pattern-hiding displays to prevent access and viewing of data after period of inactivity.

Session locks will occur after 15 minutes of inactivity (STIG-based). The screen will change to the standard logon page. Users will be required to resubmit their security credentials for access.

SSP ARTIFACT RECOMMENDATIONS: (CURRENT ARTIFACT DATE): Screenshot of policy setting for session lockout time provided from SysAdmin/NWA.

[CMMC AC.3.019]

3.1.11 Terminate (automatically) a user session after a defined condition.

Upon logoff, all operational DBS personnel sessions will be terminated. Additionally, sessions will be automatically terminated after 15 minutes of inactivity (STIG-based). Users will be required to resubmit their security credentials for access.

SSP ARTIFACT RECOMMENDATIONS: (CURRENT ARTIFACT DATE): Screenshot of policy setting for session terminations.

[CMMC AC.2.013]

3.1.12 Monitor and control remote access sessions.

 Remote operational access sessions are not authorized.

Maintenance sessions will always use TLS 1.0 or higher security protocols./ Remote maintenance access sessions are restricted to designated privileged users that have been cleared and require access. The monitoring of this access will be via application access logs and reviewed at a minimum weekly by selected privileged users. (See Annex D—Remote Access Procedure for current control details).

SSP ARTIFACT RECOMMENDATIONS: (CURRENT ARTIFACT DATE): Screen shot of remote sessions, the system architecture showing remote connectivity, and/or the system's Cybersecurity Policy (CSP).

[CMMC AC.3.014]

3.1.13 Employ cryptographic mechanisms to protect the confidentiality of remote access sessions.

Remote operational access sessions are not authorized. Remote access will use TLS 1.0 or higher protocol to access DBS remotely for maintenance purposes. The monitoring of this access will be via application access logs and reviewed at a minimum weekly by designated personnel. (See Annex D—Remote Access Procedure for current control details).

AES-256 and SHA-256 are currently not used with the current DBS implementation.

Cryptographic mechanisms will meet or exceed UR's *Acceptable Encryption Policy*.

SSP ARTIFACT RECOMMENDATIONS: (CURRENT ARTIFACT DATE): Screen shot showing the system's CONFIDENTIALITY levels to include AES, TLS, and SSL security. This can also be shown in the network diagram as part of the connectivity between individuals and hardware components of the system. NOTE: Also, HASHING DOES NOT provide security. It provides INTEGRITY from the CIA Triad perspective—a common mistake!

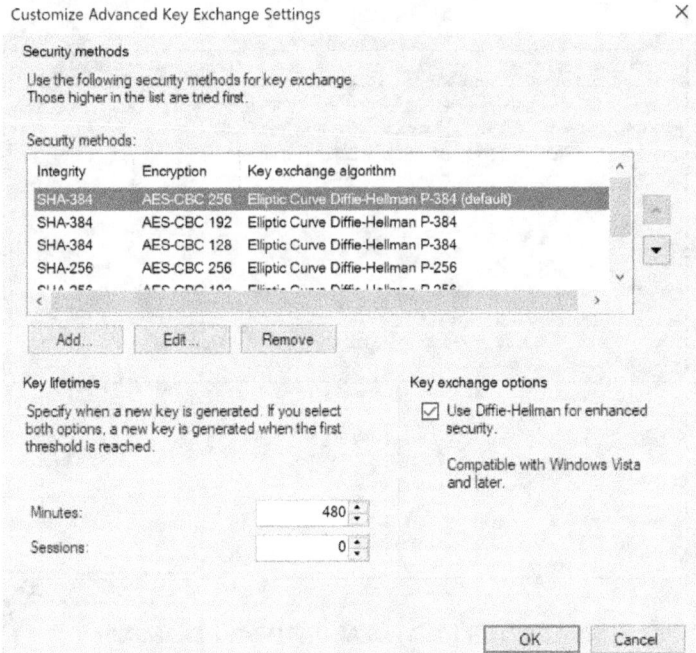

CRYPTO-KEY TYPES AND STORAGE EXAMPLE

[CMMC AC.2.015]

3.1.14 Route remote access via managed access control points.

Only access points from Reading, KY, and Huntsville, AL are currently whitelisted for this purpose and restricted to the designated Internet Protocol (IP) addresses only./ Remote maintenance access will employ whitelisting to meet this control. (See Annex D—*Remote Access Procedure* for current control details).

SSP ARTIFACT RECOMMENDATIONS: (CURRENT ARTIFACT DATE): Demonstrate this control in the network diagram.

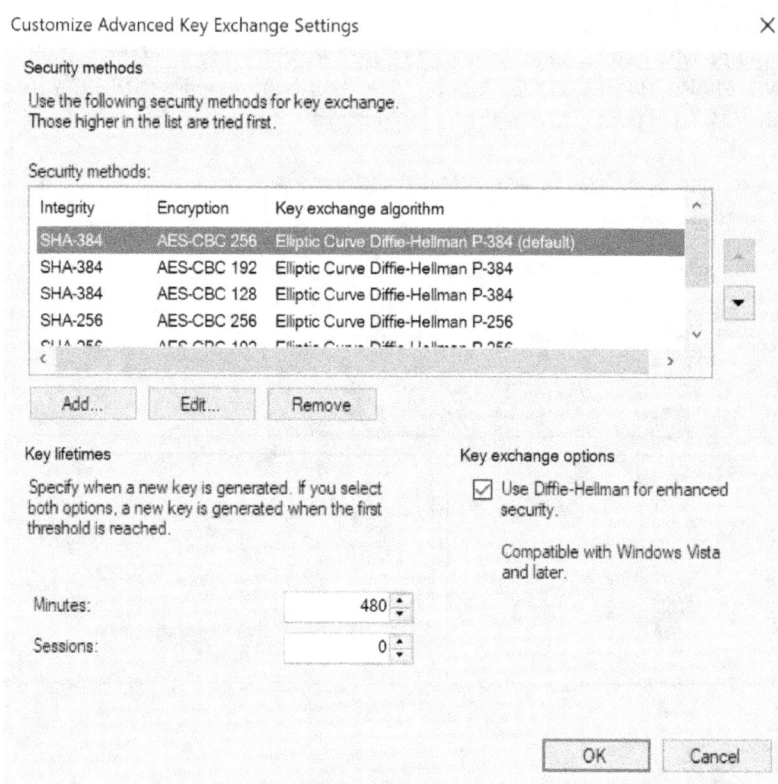

CRYPTO-KEY TYPES AND STORAGE EXAMPLE

[CMMC AC.3.021]

3.1.15 Authorize remote execution of privileged commands and remote access to security-relevant information.

Remote maintenance access will use whitelisting to meet this control. Only access points from Reading, KY, and Huntsville, AL, will access this system configuration. There will be no remote operational access./ Remote working access sessions are not authorized. (See Annex D—Remote Access Procedure for current control details).

SSP ARTIFACT RECOMMENDATIONS: (CURRENT ARTIFACT DATE): Screen capture of all current and privileged users and their rights type and levels. This should include the final SAG as a separate document. Also, have a Remote access procedure guide for assessors.

[CMMC AC.2.011]

3.1.16 Authorize wireless access prior to allowing such connections.

👤 The DBS system will not employ any wireless connections or connectivity. (See Annex E—Wireless Policy).

SSP ARTIFACT RECOMMENDATIONS: (CURRENT ARTIFACT DATE): Provide network topology showing the presence or lack of presence of wireless components.

[CMMC AC.3.012]

3.1.17 Protect wireless access using authentication and encryption.

⚙ No wireless will be used as part of the DBS system. (See Annex E—Wireless Policy).

SSP ARTIFACT RECOMMENDATIONS: (CURRENT ARTIFACT DATE): Provide network topology showing the presence or lack of presence of wireless components. Place test extract here from wireless guide showing encryption standards used to include 802.11xx.

[CMMC AC.3.020]

3.1.18 Control connection of mobile devices.

👤 ⚙ The DBS system will not be deployed to any mobile devices or systems.

SSP ARTIFACT RECOMMENDATIONS: (CURRENT ARTIFACT DATE): Provide network topology including or excluding mobile devices as external connections to the system.

[CMMC AC.3.022]

3.1.19 Encrypt CUI on mobile devices and mobile computing platforms.

⚙ There will be no mobile implementation of the DBS system.

SSP ARTIFACT RECOMMENDATIONS: (CURRENT ARTIFACT DATE): Show mobile device screen capture of encryption type and level, if used.

[CMMC AC.1.003]

3.1.20 Verify and control/limit connections to and use of external systems.

⚙ DBS is a self-contained system with secure connectivity pathways to the Internet through a commercial Cox Internet Service Provider (ISP) connection. These connections are continuously monitored using the ISP's commercial security solutions, including firewalls, and the DBS resident Windows' *Essential Security against Evolving Threat Events* (ESET) End-point Security solution (see below). ESET capabilities include real-time anti-virus, anti-spyware, anti-spam, anti-malware detection, and prevention devices (SOURCE: https://www.eset.com/us/business/endpoint-security/windows/).

		ESET Endpoint Security
Antivirus and Antispyware	ⓘ	✓
Virtualization Support	ⓘ	✓
Anti-Phishing	ⓘ	✓
Web Control	ⓘ	✓
Two-Way Firewall	ⓘ	✓
Botnet Protection	ⓘ	✓
Antispam	ⓘ	✓
Remote Management	ⓘ	✓

Business endpoint security for Windows

SSP ARTIFACT RECOMMENDATIONS: (CURRENT ARTIFACT DATE): Screen capture of system's audit logs showing external versus internal connections to the system, if used.

[CMMC AC.2.006]

3.1.21 Limit use of organizational portable storage devices on external systems.

Portable storage devices are not authorized. The use of Universal Serial Bus (USB), thumb, or flash drives is forbidden. Portable storage devices will be used and authorized into operational areas by the designated FSO and IAW, both the UR and ClownCar LLC SPPs.

Portable storage devices will be limited to only operational or forensic activities authorized by the customer and directed by the Prime Program Manager (PM).

SSP ARTIFACT RECOMMENDATIONS: (CURRENT ARTIFACT DATE): Show CSP specific to the use of portable storage devices to include USBs. Also, have the SysAdmin/NWA provide a screen capture showing end-point device settings for *registry settings* specific to storage devices.

[CMMC AC.1.004]

3.1.22 Control CUI posted or processed on publicly accessible systems.

CUI at no time will be posted to publicly accessible systems. (See Annex G—Publicly Accessible Information Policy).

SSP ARTIFACT RECOMMENDATIONS: (CURRENT ARTIFACT DATE): A PAI policy is sufficient.

Awareness and Training (AT)

[CMMC AT.2.056]

3.2.1 Ensure that managers, systems administrators, and users of organizational systems are made aware of the security risks associated with their activities and of the applicable policies, standards, and procedures related to the security of those systems.

SSP ARTIFACT RECOMMENDATIONS: (CURRENT ARTIFACT DATE): Show reports of the current status of all employees assigned to the system, their last completion of required training, and their next cycle to retake training, at least annually.

👤 All personnel assigned to DBS are made aware of security risks via required security training, education, and updates. Per the UR SPP:

Initial Security Briefings. All employees will receive an initial security briefing and sign a Nondisclosure Agreement (SF 312) before being granted access to classified material. The SF 312 is an agreement between the United States and a cleared individual.

Annual Security Briefings. Briefings will be provided to all employees to remind employees of their obligation to protect classified information and provide any updates to security requirements.

Debriefings. When a cleared employee no longer requires a security clearance or terminates employment with Unicorn Red, the employee will be debriefed by the FSO.

General Risks. All personnel is briefed on major vulnerabilities to the customer, company, the DBS system, and themselves, and they may include:

Espionage/Sabotage. All DBS personnel will report any information concerning existing or threatened espionage, sabotage, or subversive activities. The FSO will forward a report to the FBI and DSS.

Suspicious Contacts. Any individual, regardless of nationality, Suspicious contacts are efforts to obtain illegal or unauthorized access to classified information or compromise cleared employees. Personnel should report all suspicious contacts to the FSO. The FSO forwards all reports to the respective government agency for review and action.

Adverse Information. Adverse information is any information regarding a cleared employee or employee in the process for a clearance, which suggests that their ability to safeguard classified information may be impaired or that their access to classified information may not be in national security interest. Cleared personnel report adverse information regarding himself, herself, or another cleared individual to the FSO.

[CMMC AT.2.057]

3.2.2 **Ensure that organizational personnel are adequately trained to carry out their assigned information, security-related duties, and responsibilities.**

All personnel receive base security awareness training as required in control 3.2.1.

Those individuals designated as "information security-related duties and responsibilities" meet current customer cybersecurity training requirements IAW DOD 8570.01/8140.01 (current), *Cyber Workforce Management Program*.

SSP ARTIFACT RECOMMENDATIONS: (CURRENT ARTIFACT DATE): Especially for DOD contracts, ensure all cybersecurity professionals have the requisite security training. This should include there:
- Name
- Type of 8140 certificates they hold
- Dates of completion
- Certificate numbers
- Expiration dates

Numbers of Continuing Education Units (CEU) completed (this needs to be tracked by the company's training or security officer to ensure currency).

[CMMC AT.3.058]

3.2.3 **Provide security awareness training on recognizing and reporting potential indicators of insider threat.**

👤 DBS personnel accessing customer Information Technology (IT) communications' systems receive additional Insider Threat training and will re-certify annually.

SSP ARTIFACT RECOMMENDATIONS: (CURRENT ARTIFACT DATE): Show reports of the current status of all employees assigned to the system, specific to INSIDER THREAT training, their last completion of required training, and their next cycle to retake training, at least annually.

eLearning Courses

Internet-based, self-paced training courses

- Applying Assessment & Authorization (A&A) in the National Industrial Security Program (NISP) CS250.16 CompTIA
- Continuous Monitoring CS200.16 CompTIA
- CyberAwareness Challenge for DoD DS-IA106.06
- CyberAwareness Challenge for the Intelligence Community DS-IA110.06
- Cyberprotect DS-CP102.06 CompTIA
- Cybersecurity Awareness CS130.16
- Cybersecurity for Security Personnel CS160.16 CompTIA
- Introduction to DoD IDS Analysis DS-IA105.06 CompTIA
- Introduction to the NISP RMF A&A Process CS150.16 CompTIA
- Introduction to the Risk Management Framework (RMF) CS124.16
- Mission Assurance for Senior Leaders Course DS-IA115.16
- Phishing Awareness DS-IA103.06
- Portable Electronic Devices / Removable Storage Media DS-IA109.06
- Privileged User Cybersecurity Responsibilities DS-IA112.06
- Protected Distribution System CS140.16
- Risk Management Framework (RMF) Step 1: Categorization of the System CS102.16
- Risk Management Framework (RMF) Step 2: Selecting Security Controls CS103.16
- Risk Management Framework (RMF) Step 3: Implementing Security Controls CS104.16
- Risk Management Framework (RMF) Step 4: Assessing Security Controls CS105.16
- Risk Management Framework (RMF) Step 5: Authorizing Systems CS106.16
- Risk Management Framework (RMF) Step 6: Monitor Security Controls CS107.16
- Smartphones and Tablets DS-IA108.06
- Technical Implementation of A&A in the NISP CS300.06 CompTIA

Defense Security Services (DSS) eLearning Site for Cybersecurity Topics (no cost)
https://www.cdse.edu/catalog/cybersecurity.html

Audit and Accountability (AU)

The AU control is primarily about the ability of the system owner to monitor unauthorized access to the system through system logging functions of the Operating System and other network devices such as firewalls or other network security devices. A System Administrator (SysAdmin) or Network Administrator (NWA) is typically assigned to review log files, including authorized and unauthorized access to the network, applications, databases, financial systems, etc.

```
...sion Detection System

.**] [1:1407:9] SNMP trap udp (**)
[Classification: Attempted Information Leak] [Priority: 2]
03/06-8:14:09.082119 192.168.1.167:1052 -> 172.30.128.27:162
UDP TTL:118 TOS:0x0 ID:29101 IpLen:20 DgmLen:87

Personal Firewall

3/6/2006 8:14:07 AM,"Rule ""Block Windows File Sharing"" blocked (192.168.1.54,
netbios-ssn(139)).","Rule ""Block Windows File Sharing"" blocked (192.168.1.54,
netbios-ssn(139)). Inbound TCP connection. Local address,service is
(KENT(172.30.128.27),netbios-ssn(139)). Remote address,service is
(192.168.1.54,39922). Process name is ""System"."

3/3/2006 9:04:04 AM,Firewall configuration updated: 398 rules.,Firewall configuration
updated: 398 rules.

Antivirus Software, Log 1

3/4/2006 9:33:50 AM,Definition File Download,KENT,userk,Definition downloader
3/4/2006 9:33:09 AM,AntiVirus Startup,KENT,userk,System
3/3/2006 3:56:46 PM,AntiVirus Shutdown,KENT,userk,System

Antivirus Software, Log 2

240203071234,16,3,7,KENT,userk,,,,,,16777216,"Virus definitions are
current.",0,,0,,,,,0,,,,,,,,,SAVPROD,{ XXXXXXXX-XXXX-XXXX-XXXX-XXXXXXXXXXXX },2nd
User,(IP)-192.168.1.121,,GROUP,0:0:0:0:0:0,9.0.0.338,,,,,,,,,,,,,

Antispyware Software

DSO Exploit: Data source object exploit (Registry change, nothing done)  HKEY_USERS\S-
1-5-19\Software\Microsoft\Windows\CurrentVersion\Internet Settings\Zones\0\1004!=W=?
```

Audit log type examples. The logs above are good examples of system logs that should be reviewed regularly. UR is responsible for monitoring the network actively. Another term of such activity, called **Continuous Monitoring (ConMon),** is system and data protection measures.

[CMMC AU.2.042]

3.3.1 Create and retain system audit logs and records to the extent needed to enable the monitoring, analysis, investigation, and reporting of unlawful or unauthorized system activity.

AU DBS audit logs will include 1) system access and 2) application access logs. Logs shall be retained for 1-year. (https://www.archives.gov/about/records-schedule). Audit trail and log file records shall be managed following NIST-SP 800-92 (https://csrc.nist.gov/publications/search?keywords-lg=800-92&sortBy-lg=Number+DESC&viewMode-lg=brief&ipp-lg=ALL&status-lg=Final%2CDraft&series-lg=SP&topicsMatch-lg=ANY&controlsMatch-lg=ANY).

SSP ARTIFACT RECOMMENDATIONS: (CURRENT ARTIFACT DATE): At a minimum, this should include a sample system audit log shows:
- Date
- Time
- Userid
- Events
- Length of active connection
- Services used (ftp, http, smtp, ssh, etc.)

Date	Content
Thu Apr 23 2015 17:07:20 GMT-0700 (Pacific Da...	User secroot logged in from ipaddr 192.168.111.159
Thu Apr 23 2015 16:24:16 GMT-0700 (Pacific Da...	User secroot logged out from ipaddr 192.168.111.159
Thu Apr 23 2015 15:31:19 GMT-0700 (Pacific Da...	Changed following Settings :- GUI Session Timeout
Thu Apr 23 2015 15:31:09 GMT-0700 (Pacific Da...	User secroot logged in from ipaddr 192.168.111.159
Thu Apr 23 2015 15:02:02 GMT-0700 (Pacific Da...	Changed SMTP Auth Settings
Thu Apr 23 2015 15:01:58 GMT-0700 (Pacific Da...	Changed SMTP Auth Settings
Thu Apr 23 2015 15:01:31 GMT-0700 (Pacific Da...	Changed following Settings :- GUI Session Timeout
Thu Apr 23 2015 14:14:29 GMT-0700 (Pacific Da...	User secroot logged in from ipaddr 192.168.111.159
Thu Apr 23 2015 14:00:22 GMT-0700 (Pacific Da...	Full support login enabled on techpubs-kc2.hcs.int
Thu Apr 23 2015 09:44:43 GMT-0700 (Pacific Da...	User secroot logged out from ipaddr 192.168.111.153
Thu Apr 23 2015 09:14:32 GMT-0700 (Pacific Da...	User secroot logged in from ipaddr 192.168.111.153
Wed Apr 22 2015 15:55:44 GMT-0700 (Pacific D...	User secroot logged out from ipaddr 10.111.0.166
Wed Apr 22 2015 15:25:33 GMT-0700 (Pacific D...	Regenerated Admin Key
Wed Apr 22 2015 15:25:27 GMT-0700 (Pacific D...	Changed following Settings :- GUI Session Timeout

EXAMPLE ONLY ARTIFACT

[CMMC AU.2.041]

3.3.2 Ensure that the actions of individual system users can be uniquely traced to those users, so they can be held accountable for their actions.

The DBS application will ensure that the actions of individual system users can be uniquely traced to users for accountability purposes. This will be monitored by audit logs, as described in control 3.3.1.

SSP ARTIFACT RECOMMENDATIONS: (CURRENT ARTIFACT DATE): (See control 3.3.1).

[CMMC AU.3.045]

3.3.3 Review and update logged events.

The NWA or a designated representative of DBS privileged user personnel may be assigned as an alternate at the discretion of the PM. Privileged users will conduct a MANUAL weekly review of log changes and updates. This will include automated policy settings that will alert the NWA daily to out-of-band activities.

Updates include the addition of monitored endpoint devices as the architecture is updated.

SSP ARTIFACT RECOMMENDATIONS: (CURRENT ARTIFACT DATE): The SysAdmin or NWA will maintain a log, spreadsheet, or document to identify the dates and times of audit log reviews. The assigned ISSO/ISSM should, at a minimum, review this document for verification. This data should be readily available for assessor review, typically, in the system's CM files under "documentation." If an event is identified in the log, the System Owner, PM, etc., should notify the IRP.

[CMMC AU.3.046]

3.3.4 Alert in the event of an audit logging process failure.

The system will alert the NWA when any audit function process has failed. Policy settings will notify the audit logging process via email to the NWA for review. Furthermore, the NWA will notify the PM and ISSO of logging failures for longer than 15 minutes.

SSP ARTIFACT RECOMMENDATIONS: (CURRENT ARTIFACT DATE): Screen capture of policy settings.

[CMMC AU.3.051]

3.3.5 Correlate audit record review, analysis, and reporting processes for investigation and response to indications of unlawful, unauthorized, suspicious, or unusual activity.

The ISSO will notify the PM within 12 hours of recognition IAW the DBS Incident Response Plan (IRP)—Annex M. The NWA will notify the ISSO upon an event within 12 hours of recognition. (See DOD Precedence Categorization table below). The NWA and ISSO will conduct an initial review of the log findings and determine whether it is a categorized event.

SSP ARTIFACT RECOMMENDATIONS: (CURRENT ARTIFACT DATE): All current or past events and incidents should be available in the CM file under "documentation." If no current or past events or incidents, state here: NONE.

Precedence	Category	Description
0	0	Training and Exercises
1	1	Root Level Intrusion (Incident)
2	2	User Level Intrusion (Incident)
3	4	Denial of Service (Incident)
4	7	Malicious Logic (Incident)
5	3	Unsuccessful Activity Attempt (Event)
6	5	Non-Compliance Activity (Event)
7	6	Reconnaissance (Event)
8	8	Investigating (Event)
9	9	Explained Anomaly (Event)

DOD Precedence Categorization. Nine (9) is the lowest event where little is known, and IT personnel are attempting to determine whether this activity should be elevated to alert company leadership or to "close it out." One (1) is a severe attack. It identifies that the incident has gained "root" access. For example, this level of an incident is critical since an intruder has nearly unlimited access to the network and its data. (SOURCE: CYBER INCIDENT HANDLING PROGRAM, CJCSM 6510.01B, 18 December 2014, http://www.jcs.mil/Portals/36/Documents/Library/Manuals/m651001.pdf?ver=2016-02-05-175710-897)

[CMMC AU.3.052]

3.3.6 Provide audit record reduction and report generation to support on-demand analysis and reporting.

Audit record reduction is accomplished through the limited use of only those audit logs critical to daily DBS operations. They currently include:

1. Application Logs
2. System Logs
3. Anti-Virus/Anti-malware logs

SSP ARTIFACT RECOMMENDATIONS: (CURRENT ARTIFACT DATE): Audit reduction is afforded by the policy identifying only those audit logs critical to identifying insider and external threats. This should also be captured in a finalized SAG identifying this as a best practice choice.

[CMMC AU.2.043]

3.3.7 Provide a system capability that compares and synchronizes internal system clocks with an authoritative source to generate time stamps for audit records.

DBS uses the Network Time Protocol (NTP) on **NTP port 123** to provide US Naval Observatory timestamps as the standard for the network; this is used as the authoritative source. Log changes (timestamps) may indicate unauthorized access and manipulation of log files by potential hackers.

This is specifically used to identify log changes if timestamp synchronization is different from the external (Naval Observatory) and internal (endpoint/system) clock settings.

Additionally, Windows 2016 server processes can create audit logs. All authorized privileged users will only have read-only capabilities to conduct regular and ad hoc security audit log reviews.

SSP ARTIFACT RECOMMENDATIONS: (CURRENT ARTIFACT DATE): Provide screen capture of open ports to include (typically) port 123 (ntp).

[CMMC AU.3.049]

3.3.8 Protect audit information and audit logging tools from unauthorized access, modification, and deletion.

Only authorized and designated privileged users will conduct audit rereviews. Authorized privileged users will only have read-only capabilities to do regular and ad hoc security audit log reviews.

SSP ARTIFACT RECOMMENDATIONS: (CURRENT ARTIFACT DATE): Provide a screen capture of all users and their rights to include audit log read/write/delete privileges. This should be limited to only those designated to review records, including SysAdmin, NWA, ISSO, and ISSM, respectively.

[CMMC AU.3.50]

3.3.9 Limit management of audit logging functionality to a subset of privileged users.

Audit logging review is restricted to only those personnel with the skills and privileges to review logs. (See Annex I for more details and procedures).

SSP ARTIFACT RECOMMENDATIONS: (CURRENT ARTIFACT DATE): Same as control 3.3.8.

Configuration Management (CM)

The fundamental importance of Configuration Management is it is, in fact, the "opposite side of the same coin" called *cybersecurity*. CM is used to track and confirm changes to the DBS system's baseline. Changes could affect hardware, firmware, or software that alert IT professionals to potential unauthorized changes to the IT environment. CM is used to confirm and ensure programmatic controls prevent changes that have not been adequately tested or approved.

An effective CM process considers information security implications for the development and operation of information systems. CM requires establishing baselines for tracking, controlling, and managing a business's internal IT infrastructure specific to NIST 800-171. This will include the active management of changes to hardware, software, and documentation. (See the later discussion under the Risk Assessment and Security Assessment controls).

Active CM of information systems requires the integration of the management of secure configurations into the CM process. If good CM exists as a well-defined "change" process, the protection of the IT environment is more assured. This should be *considered as the second most crucial security control* after Access Control. Unicorn Red management and IT personnel have adequate knowledge and training to maintain this process since it is integral to good programmatic and cybersecurity practices.

Key CM considerations:

- The security impact of each change or modification to the system configuration shall be assessed against the security requirements and the accreditation conditions.

- Documenting all CM roles, responsibilities, and procedures, including the management of CM information and Assessment and Authorization (i.e., AA) certification.

- Ensuring the Information System (IS) is under the control of a Configuration Control Board (CCB)

- Ensuring software or hardware changes are made through an accurately charted CM process.

- Ensuring a testing process is in place to verify proposed configuration changes before implementation in the operational environment.

[CMMC CM.2.061]

3.4.1 Establish and maintain baseline configurations and inventories of organizational systems (including hardware, software, firmware, and documentation) throughout the respective system development life cycles.

UR will ensure that a current and comprehensive baseline inventory of software and hardware (to include manufacturer, type, model, physical location, and network topology or architecture) is in close coordination with the customer and other stakeholders. UR will lead the effort to maintain a Configuration Control Board (CCB) and accreditation documentation.

The CCB will conduct regular sessions quarterly and ad hoc based on customer direction or security urgency—as defined by a customer's Category 1 security vulnerability.

SSP ARTIFACT RECOMMENDATIONS: (CURRENT ARTIFACT DATE): The SSP will form the baseline of the system architecture. At a minimum, it includes hardware and software listings and network topologies. The assigned system engineer or architect should make any changes to these base documents within a specified period of time. After Full Operating Capability (FOC), changes should be by a more formal CCB with customer input and participation.

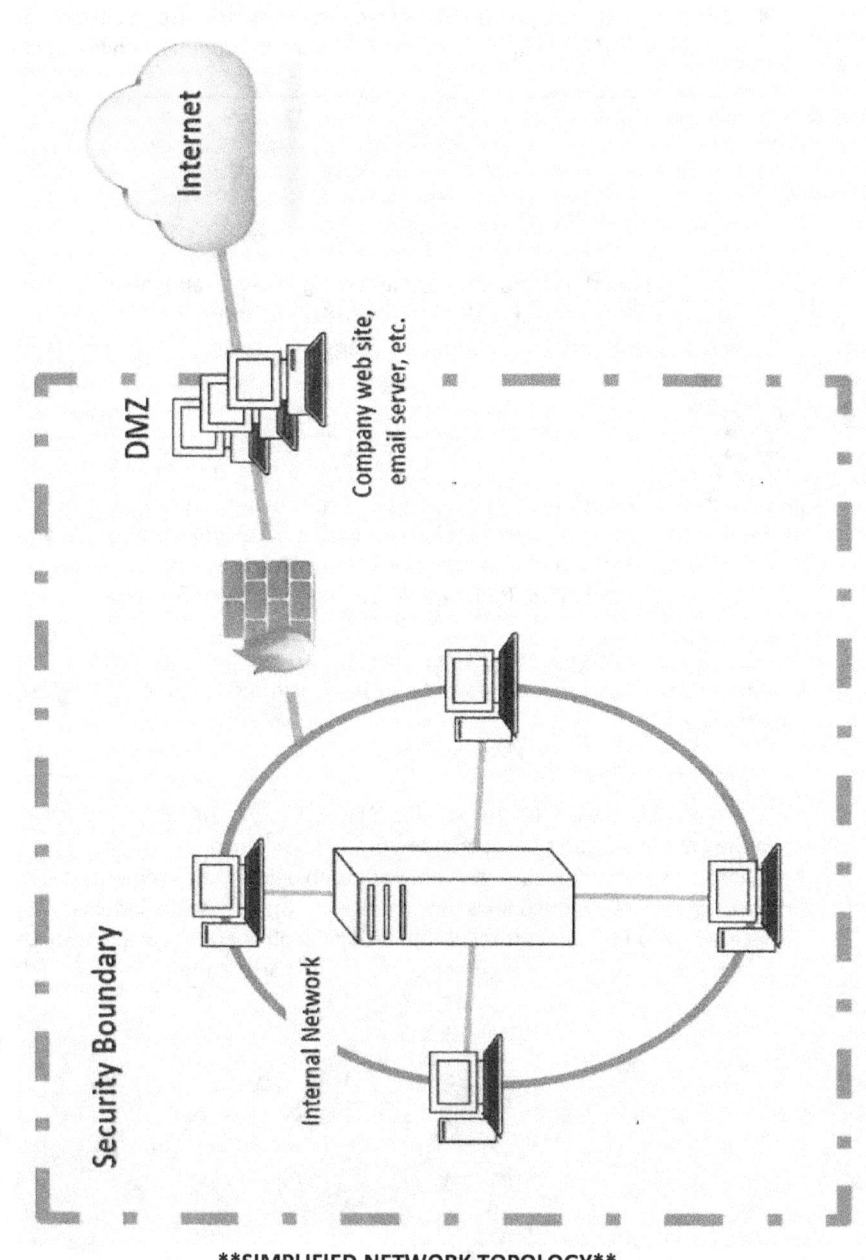

SIMPLIFIED NETWORK TOPOLOGY

[CMMC CM.2.064]

3.4.2 Establish and enforce security configuration settings for information technology products employed in organizational systems.

UR privileged users will support the CM process and its implantation following DODI 5000.02, Enclosure 12-5, NIST-SP 800-128, and STIGS for all hardware and software components (https://public.cyber.mil/stigs/).

This includes establishing levels of CM to maintain the accredited security posture following all implemented security controls. The CCB will generally include users, programmers, system engineers, system administrators, and cybersecurity personnel to provide varied expertise of system and system security lifecycle actions.

SSP ARTIFACT RECOMMENDATIONS: (CURRENT ARTIFACT DATE): This can be accomplished with a screen capture of the Operating System's STIG compliance. The SysAdmin or NWA should provide.

[CMMC CM.2.065]

3.4.3 Track, review, approve or disapprove, and log changes to organizational systems.

It will track, review, approve, disapprove, and document changes. Change management will occur through an established CCB convened quarterly upon the DBS system's full Operating Capability (FOC). Also, see control 3.4.2 and ANNEX J – Configuration Management Procedures.

SSP ARTIFACT RECOMMENDATIONS: (CURRENT ARTIFACT DATE): This should be demonstrated by the local data repository for all configuration changes. It should include reviewable locations such as local databases, Sharepoint sites, or CM-specific applications (e.g., Rationale Rose®).

[CMMC CM.2.066]

3.4.4 Analyze the security impact of changes prior to implementation.

CCB All changes following FOC will be approved by the designated CCB and customer to implement the solution based upon a Security Impact Assessment (SIA) conducted by assigned UR cybersecurity engineer or designated third-party representatives. The SIA will be started upon assignment by the DBS PM and will be begun within 1-week of notification. SIAs will typically require 30-days for analysis based upon the complexity of the change. Extensions will be coordinated between the PM and the customer as needed. (See control SA for more details).

SSP ARTIFACT RECOMMENDATIONS: (CURRENT ARTIFACT DATE): This should be demonstrated by changes to the baseline, typically after FOC. (See Annexes on formats). These should be documented reports from technical IT and cybersecurity professionals who have assessed whether the change, addition, or deletion of a component weakens the current cybersecurity posture. These reports should be included in the CM library to afford a historical view of the system's lifecycle.

[CMMC CM.3.067]

3.4.5 Define, document, approve, and enforce physical and logical access restrictions associated with changes to organizational systems.

CCB **POAM EXAMPLE** Specifics of this control will be addressed in future CCB Standard Operating Procedure (SOP)-TBP. A POAM will be written; an initial change management process will be completed based upon the customer's input and delivered within 90-days following these consultations.

SSP ARTIFACT RECOMMENDATIONS: (CURRENT ARTIFACT DATE): This will be defined by the system's CSP.

[CMMC CM.2.062]

3.4.6 Employ the principle of least functionality by configuring organizational systems to provide only essential capabilities.

⚙ The DBS system is configured based on the *principle of least functionality*. DBS is currently configured to provide only essential capabilities and functions required to implement the solution for the customer.

SSP ARTIFACT RECOMMENDATIONS: (CURRENT ARTIFACT DATE): This control can be demonstrated based on user rights as discussed under the AC control family.

[CMMC CM.3.068]

3.4.7 Restrict, disable, or prevent the use of nonessential programs, functions, ports, protocols, and services.

⚙ Only Ports, Protocols, and Services (PPS) required for DBS operations are activated by the assigned UR System/Network Administrator. All non-required PPSs will be deactivated.

All nonessential software programs and functionality installed is controlled by application whitelisting solutions.

There are currently 4 (four) active operational; all others are closed.

Currently, only ports 8080 (http), 443(https), 123(ntp), and 53(dns) are active.

SSP ARTIFACT RECOMMENDATIONS: (CURRENT ARTIFACT DATE): This control can be demonstrated based on user rights as discussed under the AC control family.

[CMMC CM.3.069]

3.4.8 Apply deny-by-exception (blacklisting) policy to prevent the use of unauthorized software or deny-all, permit-by-exception (whitelisting) policy to allow the execution of authorized software.

Application whitelisting is established to prevent unauthorized software deployment on the DBS system.

SSP ARTIFACT RECOMMENDATIONS: (CURRENT ARTIFACT DATE): Provide screen captures for whitelisted IP addresses (more common) and blacklisted IP addresses (less common) that identify firewall and other Intrusion Detection/Prevention devices.

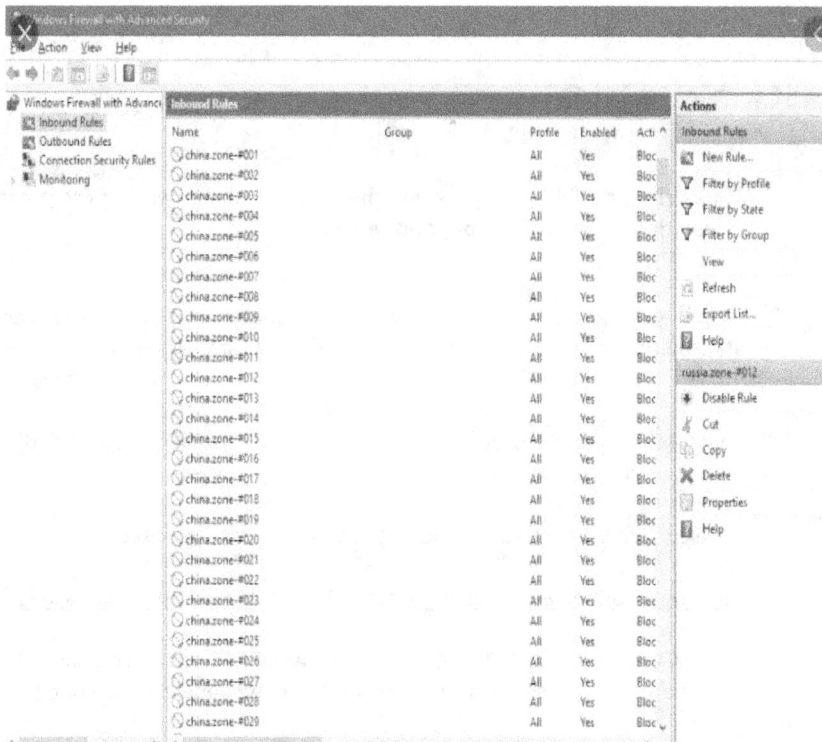

BLACKLIST ARTIFACT EXAMPLE

[CMMC CM.2.063]

3.4.9 Control and monitor user-installed software.

With approval from the customer, only authorized system administrators will install operational and administrative software tools and applications authorized under the CCB process. DBS personnel will at no time install personal software. Auditing activities will monitor for changes to the approved baseline DBS configuration (See AU controls).

All software installed is controlled by application whitelisting solutions. The DBS application will capture attempts via weekly audits of user activity reviews.

SSP ARTIFACT RECOMMENDATIONS: (CURRENT ARTIFACT DATE): Identify any software or managed service products (e.g., from Cloud Service Providers [CSP]) that prevents basic users from "system administrator" rights that would allow user-installed software. Also, we can use earlier screen captures to show user rights under the AC control family.

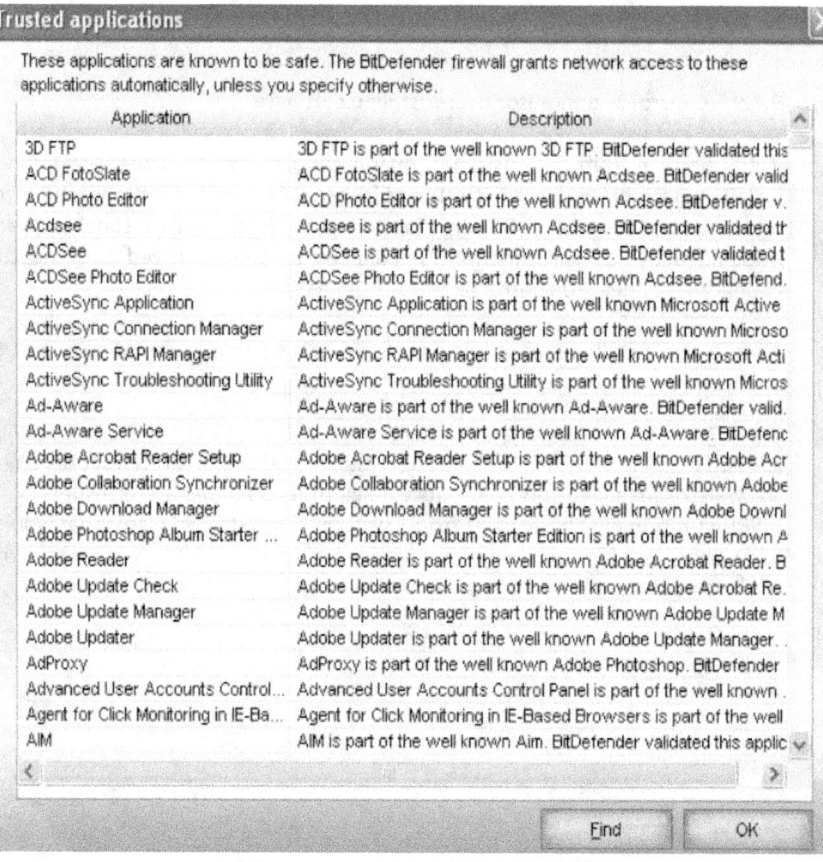

APPLICATION WHITELISTING ARTIFACT EXAMPLE

Identification and Authentication (IA)

Based on federal requirements and mandates, UR ensures that all offices within the agency meet the minimum-security needs defined in the Federal Information Processing Standards (FIPS) Publication 200, Minimum Security Requirements for Federal Information, and Information Systems. All information systems must meet the security requirements using the security controls defined in the NIST SP 800-171, Revision 1.

[CMMC IA.1.076]

3.5.1 Identify system users, processes acting on behalf of users, and devices. Authenticate (or verify) the identities of users, processes, or devices, as a prerequisite to allowing access to organizational systems.

This control will be met the DBS system as described under the AU control (above). The system will continuously audit, at a minimum, user identity, running applications and processes, and the device access in real-time. The NWA will review weekly and report discrepancies to the PM and ISSO within 12 hours of recognition.

SSP ARTIFACT RECOMMENDATIONS: (CURRENT ARTIFACT DATE): This can be accomplished by using a sample system access log as used under the AU control family artifacts.

[CMMC IA.1.077]

3.5.2 Authenticate (or verify) the identities of those users, processes, or devices as a prerequisite to allowing access to organizational information systems.

All users will authenticate based upon userid and password. Devices will show only those authorized components and devices approved for operation on the overall DBS architecture.

Multi-factor Authentication (MFA) is currently not deployed and will be included in future versions.

SSP ARTIFACT RECOMMENDATIONS: (CURRENT ARTIFACT DATE): Verification is accomplished typically by userid and password. Access logs should meet minimum standards. However, MFA is required under the DOD's governance process. This is considered more acceptable.

[CMMC IA.3.083]

3.5.3 Use multifactor authentication (MFA) for local and network access to privileged accounts and for network access to non-privileged accounts.

POAM EXAMPLE   To be resolved in future DBS versions. MFA is currently not deployed in the DBS system. A POAM will be written with an objective resolution within 90-days upon FOC approval.

SSP ARTIFACT RECOMMENDATIONS: (CURRENT ARTIFACT DATE): Use artifact for control 3.5.2.

[CMMC IA.3.084]

3.5.4 Employ replay-resistant authentication mechanisms for network access to privileged and non-privileged accounts.

DBS employs TLS 1.0 (or higher) to prevent replay attacks for both privileged and non-privileged accounts.

SSP ARTIFACT RECOMMENDATIONS: (CURRENT ARTIFACT DATE): Screen capture of SSL or TLS used within system communications will answer this control.

[CMMC IA.3.085]

3.5.5 Prevent reuse of identifiers for a defined period.

Individual, group, role, or device identifiers will not be reused until the 25th iteration (per STIG). The DBS system and Windows® Server 16 provide the technical solution for this control.

SSP ARTIFACT RECOMMENDATIONS: (CURRENT ARTIFACT DATE): Screen capture of current system access STIG settings.

[CMMC IA.3.086]

3.5.6 Disable identifiers after a defined period of inactivity.

The system will deactivate accounts and their associated identifiers at 30-days of nonactivity. Upon return to duty, the user will have to reinitialize their account with the local UR DBS NWA. The DBS system and Windows® Server 16 provide the technical solution for this control.

SSP ARTIFACT RECOMMENDATIONS: (CURRENT ARTIFACT DATE): Screen capture of inactivity policy setting showing the inactivity period and actions taken by the system.

[CMMC IA.2.078]

3.5.7 Enforce a minimum password complexity and change of characters when new passwords are created. Prohibit password reuse for a specified number of generations.

All users, including contractors and vendors with access to systems, are responsible for taking the appropriate steps to select and secure their passwords. Passwords are an essential aspect of our security. A weak password may result in unauthorized access or exploitation of resources.

All DBS personnel will abide by the *Unicorn Red Solutions Password Policy*. This DBS CSP policy enhances those requirements to include:

- All user-level and system-level passwords must be at least 14 characters with alphanumeric and symbols. At least two characters will be used from all three categories: alphabetical, numerical, and special character, respectively, IAW Windows Sever 16 STIG.
- Users must not use the same password for the account as other non-access (for example, personal email account, bank account, and so on).

- Passwords may not be reused for at 24 iterations of password changes IAW applicable STIG.

SSP ARTIFACT RECOMMENDATIONS: (CURRENT ARTIFACT DATE): Provide screenshots for all policy settings required by this control.

[CMMC IA.2.079]

3.5.8 Prohibit password reuse for a specified number of generations.

Passwords may not be reused for at 24 iterations of password changes IAW applicable STIG.

SSP ARTIFACT RECOMMENDATIONS: (CURRENT ARTIFACT DATE): Provide a screenshot for this policy setting.

[CMMC IA.2.080]

3.5.9 Allow temporary password use for system logons with an immediate change to a permanent password.

All temporary passwords issued for account initialization will be changed immediately and enforced by the DBS system.

SSP ARTIFACT RECOMMENDATIONS: (CURRENT ARTIFACT DATE): Provide a screenshot for this policy setting and temporary logon screen demonstrating this control fully.

[CMMC IA.2.081]

3.5.10 Store and transmit only cryptographically protected passwords. Obscure feedback of authentication information.

All cryptographic passwords and keys will be stored encrypted in the system. Passwords will be protected IAW UR's *Acceptable Encryption Policy*.

SSP ARTIFACT RECOMMENDATIONS: (CURRENT ARTIFACT DATE): Include in SAG, show crypto-storage location in network diagram (to include if using Cloud Service Provider).

[CMMC IA.2.082]

3.5.11 Obscure feedback of authentication information.

The DBS system currently obscures visible authentication information, such as passwords, and prevents shoulder surfing intrusions by unauthorized users.

SSP ARTIFACT RECOMMENDATIONS: (CURRENT ARTIFACT DATE): Use screen capture that shows password (authentication) obfuscation features such as asterisks, stars, bullets, (•), etc.

OBFUSCATION EXAMPLE ONLY

Incident Response (IR)

Incident Response Handling procedures aim to detect and identify unauthorized use, misuse, and abuse of computer assets by internal network users and external attackers. Incidents that require action include, but are not limited to, Malware, Unauthorized Access, Denial of Service, Electronic Spillage, and all other Computer Network Attack/Computer Network Event (CNA/CNE).

Unicorn Red shall detect, analyze, contain, eradicate, and recover from attacks, intrusions, service disruptions, and incidents that threaten operations security and report computer security incidents. Unicorn Red shall work closely with the customer to provide local monitoring when central monitoring is not feasible or to further the defense-in-depth and breadth strategies.

Incident handling and reporting shall be performed following NIST-SP 800-61, NIST-SP 800-83, and NIST-SP 800-86. An After-Action Report (AAR) shall be completed for incidents, and the Incident Handler shall make a corresponding entry in the Incident Handling Log.

[CMMC IR.2.092]

3.6.1 Establish an operational incident-handling capability for organizational systems that includes preparation, detection, analysis, containment, recovery, and user response activities.

IRP SSP ARTIFACT RECOMMENDATIONS: (CURRENT DATE OF ARTIFACT): See Annex N –Incident Response Plan (IRP) that addresses this control.

[CMMC IA.3.098]

3.6.2 Track, document, and report incidents to designated officials and/or authorities both internal and external to the organization.

IRP SSP ARTIFACT RECOMMENDATIONS: (CURRENT DATE OF ARTIFACT): See Annex N –Incident Response Plan (IRP) that addresses this control.

[CMMC IA.3.099]

3.6.3 Test the organizational incident response capability.

IRP   The IRP will be tested annually with an initiation date of the FOC declaration.

SSP ARTIFACT RECOMMENDATIONS: (CURRENT ARTIFACT DATE): First testing of the IRP should happen within 30 days of FOC. All subsequent IRP tests should occur annually and are directed by the System Owner (SO), supported by the SAs, NWAs, ISSOs, and ISSM. Documentation of annual tests should be placed in the CM repository upon review by the SO and approved by the customer.

Maintenance (MA)

[CMMC MA.2.111]

3.7.1 Perform maintenance on organizational systems.

Software code maintenance is accomplished by UR software developer to include creating and updating application code. Hardware maintenance is provided by the UR network and logistics personnel. They will provide or coordinate fixes, replacements, or third-party maintainers. Furthermore, all software and hardware warranty services are administered by UR IT Operations. The UR Program Manager has overall responsibility for ensuring maintenance activities are timely, prompt, and complete.

SSP ARTIFACT RECOMMENDATIONS: (CURRENT ARTIFACT DATE): Create or use existing organizational secure maintenance procedure guide. Typically, the purchasing or logistic division should produce; however, IT operational staff may also have based on the size and scope of the company or agency size and complexity.

[CMMC MA.2.112]

3.7.2 Provide controls on the tools, techniques, mechanisms, and personnel used to conduct system maintenance.

All tools and mechanisms will be subject to the DBS CCB process. These tools and mechanisms will be scanned, inspected, and certified by UR IT Operations, the ISSO, and PM (in order), certifying the security of all UR tools, techniques, mechanisms, and personnel before affording access to the DBS system.

SSP ARTIFACT RECOMMENDATIONS: (DATE OF CURRENT ARTIFACT): Tools, techniques, and mechanisms should be addressed through an active Security Impact Assessment[4] (SIA), as described earlier. All SIA reports will be

---

[4] See Annex regarding example SIA formats.

maintained in the CM database. Personnel controls are handled by the PS control family and associated policies.

[CMMC MA.3.115]

3.7.3 Ensure equipment removed for off-site maintenance is sanitized of any CUI. Check media containing diagnostic and test programs for malicious code before the media are used in organizational systems.

SSP ARTIFACT RECOMMENDATIONS: (DATE OF CURRENT ARTIFACT): Media sanitization for CUI will be IAW Annex O.

[CMMC MA.3.116]

3.7.4 Check media containing diagnostic and test programs for malicious code.

All media diagnostic tools will be scanned by ESET to ensure that malicious code/software is not resident of the media before introduction into the DBS security boundary. The NWA will work with software maintenance efforts to provide physical media is scanned if required.

SSP ARTIFACT RECOMMENDATIONS: (DATE OF CURRENT ARTIFACT): Identify any applications, e.g., ESET®, that provide real-time scanning for malware and viruses. Remote computers should scan external media with the requisite malicious code capabilities. Designated personnel should, at a minimum, maintain a monthly log of all external media intended or attached to the system over the previous month.

EXAMPLE ESET® SCREEN CAPTURE ONLY

[CMMC MA.2.113]

3.7.5 Require multifactor authentication (MFA) to establish nonlocal maintenance sessions via external network connections and terminate such connections when nonlocal maintenance is complete.

POAM EXAMPLE   Nonlocal maintenance sessions will be established using TLS 1.0 secure protocols; however, MFA is currently technically not feasible. MFA will be added within 90-days of the approved DBS FOC date. (A POAM will be developed; See DBS POAM document).

SSP ARTIFACT RECOMMENDATIONS: (DATE OF CURRENT ARTIFACT): Identify the MFA solution used for remote/nonlocal maintenance activities. Also, include this solution in network topology diagrams.

[CMMC MA.2.114]

3.7.6 Supervise the maintenance activities of maintenance personnel without required access authorization.

These individuals will always be under escort when working on the DBS system./ / All third-party maintenance personnel will be vetted based upon UR personnel security policy. This policy will abide by ClownCar LLC's duly approved Facility Security requirements (SPP).

SSP ARTIFACT RECOMMENDATIONS: (DATE OF CURRENT ARTIFACT): Provide physical security policy and maintain physical or virtual logs of all maintenance personnel who do not regularly provide support and have not been vetted by PS controls; however, personnel are required to provide onsite maintenance as required.

Media Protection (MP)

Most MP physical and virtual control protections will be IAW Unicorn Red Solutions, Controlled Unclassified Information (CUI)/Controlled (or Critical) Defense Information Marking Guide for the DBS System [The CUI Guide]. The CUI Guide will be maintained under configuration management controls for documents and stored in the Unicorn Red Sharepoint repository.

> **Special Topic: DOD USB Policy**
>
> A UNIVERSAL SERIAL BUS (USB) OR THUMB DRIVE WHILE PROVIDING GREAT FLEXIBILITY TO MOVE DATA TO AND FROM SYSTEM DATA STORES, THEY ARE ALSO MAJOR MEANS TO INJECT MALICIOUS SOFTWARE SUCH AS VIRUSES AND RANSOMWARE INTO A COMPANY'S SECURITY BOUNDARY. DOD PROHIBITS USB USE IN DOD ENVIRONMENTS. IT'S CRITICAL TO ADDRESS THE PROPER CARE AND USE OF THESE IN A COMPANY'S IT INFRASTRUCTURE AND ASSOCIATED PROCEDURE GUIDE.

The MP control handles the challenges of managing and protecting the computer media storing CUI. This would include the governments' concerns about removable hard drives and especially the ability for a threat to employ the use of a Universal Serial Bus (USB) "thumb drive."

While most computer users are aware of the convenience of the thumb drive to help store, transfer, and maintain data, it is also a well-known threat vector where criminals and foreign threats can introduce dangerous malware and viruses into unsuspecting users' computers; the DOD forbids their use except under particular and controlled instances.

MP assures the proper destruction and sanitization of old storage devices has occurred. In many instances, federal agencies have not implemented an effective sanitization process, and the public has released the inadvertent disclosure of national security data. Cases include salvage companies discovering hard drives and disposed of computers containing CUI and, in many instances, national security classified information, has occurred.

The media sanitization process requires high-grade industry or government-approved applications that entirely and effectively destroy all target drive data. Other procedures may include physical shredding of the drive or destruction methods that further prevent the reconstruction of any virtual data by unauthorized personnel.

[CMMC MP.2.119]

3.8.1 Protect (i.e., physically control and securely store) system media containing CUI, both paper and digital.

All personnel will protect CUI paper and digital materials IAW *The CUI Guide*.

SSP ARTIFACT RECOMMENDATIONS: (DATE OF CURRENT ARTIFACT): See CUI security and storage guides.

[CMMC MP.2.120]

3.8.2 Limit access to CUI on system media to authorized users.

Only personnel assigned to or in direct support to the DBS system will have access to CUI materials received, stored, or generated in support of the customer's operational mission.

SSP ARTIFACT RECOMMENDATIONS: (DATE OF CURRENT ARTIFACT): Virtual access to CUI is controlled through the AC control family, and the PS family controls physical access.

[CMMC MP.1.118]

3.8.3 Sanitize or destroy system media containing CUI before disposal or release for reuse.

Media sanitization for CUI will be IAW Annex O. Furthermore, sanitization and destruction of CUI media will be IAW *The CUI Guide*.

SSP ARTIFACT RECOMMENDATIONS: (DATE OF CURRENT ARTIFACT): Maintain sanitization and destruction log.

EXAMPLE ONLY

[CMMC MP.3.122]

3.8.4 Mark media with necessary CUI markings and distribution limitations.

All markings and distribution will be per the existing customer's Security Classification Guide (SCG) and *The CUI Guide*. The CUI Guide provides current direction specific to this control created by the National Archives Repository Administration (NARA), the Executive Agent for the national CUI program.

SSP ARTIFACT RECOMMENDATIONS: (DATE OF CURRENT ARTIFACT): Provide CUI Guide and provide samples of current markings used within the system's physical locations and how virtual data is marked (screen shot).

[CMMC MP.3.124]

3.8.5 Control access to media containing CUI and maintain accountability for media during transport outside of controlled areas.

This control is about "transport outside of controlled areas." This is a matter of only authorized individuals approved by position, training, and security verification. In the case of courier requirements of CUI media or documents will be provided either courier card or orders that an authorized FSO representative signs.

UR may hire an outside contract service that transports both physical and computer media containing CUI if required. These individuals will abide by the ClownCar LLC SPP and UR personnel security standards.

SSP ARTIFACT RECOMMENDATIONS: (DATE OF CURRENT ARTIFACT): When CUI data needs to be transported, it should be marked appropriately and packaged per the CUI Guide. Refer to CUI Guide pages.

[CMMC MP.3.125]

3.8.6 Implement cryptographic mechanisms to protect the confidentiality of CUI stored on digital media during transport unless otherwise protected by alternative physical safeguards.

 This is a Data at Rest (DAR) issue. All data will be encrypted IAW UR's encryption standards (See Annex C). The ZIS infrastructure and services will secure application and database stores.

SSP ARTIFACT RECOMMENDATIONS: (DATE OF CURRENT ARTIFACT): Identify the application used to encrypt DAR. Provide encryption type and any current licensing (lifetime, limited, etc.)

[CMMC MP.2.121]

3.8.7 Control the use of removable media on information system components.

All DBS personnel are prohibited from using any removable media.

SSP ARTIFACT RECOMMENDATIONS: (DATE OF CURRENT ARTIFACT): Refer to CSP.

[CMMC MP.3.123]

3.8.8 Prohibit the use of portable storage devices when such devices have no identifiable owner.

All DBS personnel are prohibited from using any portable storage device when such devices have no identifiable owner. Furthermore, staff will report these devices to on-duty call center managers immediately for action.

SSP ARTIFACT RECOMMENDATIONS: (DATE OF CURRENT ARTIFACT): Refer to CSP.

[CMMC RE.2.138]

3.8.9 Protect the confidentiality of backup CUI at storage locations.

Both local site and ZIS (cloud) stored data will be encrypted as Data at Rest (DAR). Local data is encrypted IAW UR encryption policy standards. Confidentiality of all local backups will be IAW UR's *Acceptable Encryption Policy. (See Annex S)*. DAR at ZIS location will be IAW, the existing contract/Service Level Agreement between UR and ZIS.

SSP ARTIFACT RECOMMENDATIONS: (DATE OF CURRENT ARTIFACT): Identify current application solution. Conduct backup tests monthly to ensure they are being performed. Document and log monthly backup tests and maintain them in the system's CM repository.

Personnel Security (PS)

[CMMC PS.2.127]

3.9.1 Screen individuals prior to authorizing access to organizational systems containing CUI.

All personnel will have a minimum of SECRET before accessing the DBS system with an objective clearance of TOP SECRET./ All UR Solutions employees assigned to the DBS system are processed for a personnel security clearance (when a determination has been made that access is necessary for performance on a classified contract that includes the potential access, creation, and use of CUI materials in the performance of their duties. The number of employees processed for a clearance will be limited to the minimum necessary for operational efficiency. IAW, the Unicorn Red Standard Practices and Procedures (SPP), will handle and protect classified information [The SPP].

The FSO will ensure that before initiating the e-QIP action, the applicant is provided a copy of NISPOM paragraph 2-202. This ensures the employee knows that the SF-86 is subject to review by the FSO only to determine that the information is adequate and complete. Still, it will be used for no other purpose and protected under the Privacy Act of 1974. Unicorn Red initiates the clearance process for employees. The government will determine whether an individual can access classified information, include non-national security information, and include CUI or CUI and grant the personnel clearance.

Reinvestigations. Individuals holding security clearances are subject to a periodic reinvestigation (PR) at a minimum of every six years for Top Secret, ten years for Secret, and 15 years for Confidential. The Unicorn Red FSO is responsible for reviewing all access records to ensure employees are submitted for PRs as required and provides no break in access to DBS.

SSP ARTIFACT RECOMMENDATIONS: (DATE OF CURRENT ARTIFACT): According to company policy, conduct background checks for criminal and financial issues of candidates before accessing the system. A national security clearance is required, ensure a final adjudication is provided to the company and its designated FSO.

[CMMC PS.2.128]

3.9.2 **Ensure that organizational systems containing CUI are protected during and after personnel actions such as terminations and transfers.**

All DBS personnel records who resign, transfer, or are terminated are stored in IAW NARA and Human Resource (HR) laws and policy. These records are encrypted, retained, and destroyed per federal labor law requirements. Per NIST 800-171 control, 3.13.15, all records are stored encrypted at a minimum of AES -256-bit security standards.

SSP ARTIFACT RECOMMENDATIONS: (DATE OF CURRENT ARTIFACT): The ISSO and NWA/SysAdmin will verify monthly departures and deactivation of departed personnel. The ISSO should log this review.

Physical Protection (PP)

Physical security is the responsibility of ClownCar LLC, and sub-contractor to the customer, in close coordination with members of UR's security representatives. A little-known fact is that the guiding principle for any *true* cybersecurity professional is to protect the life and safety of the people supported. This control is also about safeguarding damage to corporate assets, facilities, or equipment; this includes any loss or destruction of the material computer equipment secured by the PP security control. These controls address physical security, including guards, alarm systems, cameras, etc., that help protect sensitive company data specific to DBS implementation.

Protecting vital CUI while seemingly expansive under this control allows for reasonable flexibility. ***Most PP controls are <u>inherited</u> control via ClownCar LLC's Standard Practices and Procedures (SPP).***

[CMMC PE.1.131]

3.10.1 Limit physical access to organizational systems, equipment, and the respective operating environments to authorized individuals.

All Unicorn Red personnel will sign the most current version of ClownCar LLC's SPP./ All DBS personnel will be briefed on physical access and the protection of systems, equipment, and respective operating environments by authorized personnel. Disciplinary action will be referred to as Unicorn Red for movement via the prime contractor's Program Manager of Record.

SSP ARTIFACT RECOMMENDATIONS: (DATE OF CURRENT ARTIFACT): Identify current local and corporate-wide physical security policies that include the designated system's protections.

[CMMC PE.2.135]

3.10.2 Protect and monitor the physical facility and support infrastructure for organizational systems.

All Unicorn Red personnel will sign the most current version of ClownCar LLC's SPP. All DBS personnel will be briefed on the physical facility and support infrastructure protections. Disciplinary action will be referred to as Unicorn Red for action via the prime contractor's Program Manager of Record.

SSP ARTIFACT RECOMMENDATIONS: (DATE OF CURRENT ARTIFACT): Same as 3.10.1 applies.

[CMMC PE.1.132]

3.10.3 Escort visitors and monitor visitor activity.

Visitors are required to be signed into the DBS operational rooms and areas. All incoming classified visits must be approved in advance of the visit by the local FSO. The FSO will verify each visitor's security status before allowing access. Identification of the person must be made before the disclosure of classified information to a visitor.

The local FSO is responsible for determining that the requesting contractor has been granted an appropriate clearance based upon an existing contractual relationship involving classified information.

The responsibility for determining need-to-know in connection with a classified visit rests with the PROGRAM MANAGER in coordination with the customer designated COR.

All DBS personnel will be briefed on the escorting of visitors. All Unicorn Red personnel will sign the most current version of ClownCar LLC's SPP specific to escort requirements and duties. Disciplinary action will be referred to as Unicorn Red for action via the prime contractor's Program Manager of Record.

SSP ARTIFACT RECOMMENDATIONS: (DATE OF CURRENT ARTIFACT): Maintain escort log for all visitors not part of the direct operational or support staff.

YEAR	VISITOR REGISTER LOG			ORGANIZATION
MONTH	VISITOR IDENTIFICATION			SIGNATURE OF ESCORT
DAY	NAME (Last, First, Middle Initial)	GRADE	ORGANIZATION OR FIRM	

EXAMPLE ONLY

[CMMC PE.1.133]

3.10.4 Maintain audit logs of physical access.

Visitors are required to be signed in to all DBS operational rooms and areas. The on-duty call center manager will maintain a log to identify and log visitors to the UR spaces.

SSP ARTIFACT RECOMMENDATIONS: (DATE OF CURRENT ARTIFACT): Same as 3.10.3 applicable.

[CMMC PE.1.134]

3.10.5 Control and manage physical access devices.

All-access badges, passwords, and PINS will be managed by the ClownCar LLC on-site local FSO. The FSO will issue all requisite security briefings and badges IAW facility security requirements.

SSP ARTIFACT RECOMMENDATIONS: (DATE OF CURRENT ARTIFACT): Provide the current local security procedure guides and policies to assessors.

[CMMC PE.3.136]

3.10.6 Enforce safeguarding measures for CUI at alternate work sites.

The alternate site will be located at the Unicorn Red Headquarters, Herndon, VA. All security safeguard measures for CUI apply to all Unicorn Red personnel at the alternate site and non-DBS staff. Physical and virtual security measures will be under the site's local security policies and procedures.

SSP ARTIFACT RECOMMENDATIONS: (DATE OF CURRENT ARTIFACT): Provide to assessors the current local security procedure guides and policies to include alternate sites *specifically described*.

Risk Assessment (RA)

The RA control relies on a continual process to determine whether hardware, software, or architecture changes create a significant positive or negative **security-relevant** effect against specific controls. This is typically initiated by using a **Change Request** (CR) that may result in a Security Risk Assessment (SRA) or a more general Security Impact Assessment (SIA). If an upgrade to, for example, the Windows 10 ® Secure Host Baseline Operating System software improves the network's security posture, a Risk Assessment (RA) is needed, and associated **risk analysis** should be performed by authorized technical cybersecurity personnel. Working with its IT staff, management should determine thresholds when a formal RA activity needs to occur. This could take the form of a technical report that management accepts from its IT staff for approval or disapproval of the change.

The RA process affords a significant amount of flexibility during the system's life and should be used when other-than, for example, a new application or **security patches** are applied. Security patches updates are typically integrated into Operating Systems and applications. IT personnel should also regularly manually check for standard functional patches and security patch updates from the software companies' websites.

"Negative" security-relevant effects on the corporate IT infrastructure include, for example, a major re-architecture event or a move to a Cloud Service Provider. While these events may not seem "negative," NIST standards require a complete reassessment. In other words, plan accordingly if the company will embark on a significant overhaul of its IT system. Under these circumstances, there will be a need to consider the current Authority to Operate (ATO) impacts. These types of events typically necessitate that the NIST 800-171 process is redone; prior work in terms of policies and procedures can be reused to receive an updated ATO.

The differences between a Security Risk Assessment (SRA), a Security Impact Assessment (SIA), and Security Assessment (SA) control.

- *An SRA is specific to assessing a systems' security controls and recommendations to correct or mitigate those failed or failing controls. The SRA is part of the organization's corporate governance and risk management processes.*

- *An SIA is an overall assessment of changes or modifications as part of a formal change management/configuration control process.*

- *The SA control is about a process that re-assesses the state of all security controls and whether changes have occurred requiring additional mitigations due to new risks or threats to the system.*

[CMMC RM.2.141]

3.11.1 **Periodically assess the risk to organizational operations (including mission, functions, image, or reputation), organizational assets, and individuals resulting from the operation of organizational systems and the associated processing, storage, or transmission of CUI.**

CCB   CYBER   The RA control and actions are outlined in Annex P.

UR completed a preliminary RA (physical and virtual) that occurred in 20XX—See Annex X. A subsequent RA will occur during the developmental phase of DBS in 2020. Unicorn Red RA review procedures will occur annually as of the formal declaration of an ATO.

ANNEX R will be used to select the 1/3 controls as part of active continuous monitoring activity.

Unicorn Red will reassess 1/3 of the security controls upon approval of Authority to Operate (ATO) by the customer's designated Authorizing Official (AO).

The following controls will be assessed as follows:

> Year 1: Controls 3.1.1 through 3.4.9
> Year 2: Controls 3.5.1 through 3.9.2
> Year 3: Controls 3.10.1 through 3.14.7

SSP ARTIFACT RECOMMENDATIONS: (DATE OF CURRENT ARTIFACT): Broadly, the ISSO will update the Risk Assessment Report (RAR). This is a comprehensive document looking at annual changes to the system impacting security. The RAR also looks at Insider Threats, Advanced Persistent Threats, and rogue hackers that targeted the company or system. Furthermore, the ISSO or designated personnel conduct a 1/3 review of security controls annually. The ISSO will document and advise the SO and customer upon completion of any findings requiring their attention.

[CMMC RM.2.142]

3.11.2 Scan for vulnerabilities in organizational systems and applications periodically and when new vulnerabilities affecting those systems and applications are identified.

ESET provides a real-time scan of the system for any vulnerabilities. The NWA will verify updates to ESET patching daily, and he will authorize updates within 4 hours of the daily check.

SSP ARTIFACT RECOMMENDATIONS: (DATE OF CURRENT ARTIFACT): Provide copies of recent scans with a real-time scanning solution. This can include anti-virus and anti-malware solutions where this is done manually, including audit logs that track suspicious activities.

[CMMC RM.2.143]

3.11.3 Remediate vulnerabilities in accordance with risk assessments.

All identified vulnerabilities will be forwarded to the CM CCB process, and upon approval, will be implemented by Unicorn Red from immediate to 90-days based upon the classification of the identified vulnerability. (See UR's *Risk Assessment Procedures* for further details).

All legitimate vulnerabilities were discovered from scans and penetration testing following an organizational assessment of risk. POAMs are developed for the appropriate system or program for identified deficiencies as follows:

(1) Critical Vulnerabilities (Category 1) – mitigate or remediate within two calendar days. If more than two days are required, create a POAM.

(2) High Vulnerabilities (Category 2) – mitigate or remediate within 30 calendar days. If more than 30 days are required, create a POAM.

(3) Moderate Vulnerabilities (Category 3) – mitigate or remediate within 60 calendar days. If more than 60 days are required, create a POAM.

(4) Low Vulnerabilities (Category 4) –Correct within 90 calendar days. If more than 90 days are needed, create a POAM.

SSP ARTIFACT RECOMMENDATIONS: (DATE OF CURRENT ARTIFACT): As part of the Change Management process (CCB):

1. Track the vulnerability/POAM
2. Identify its vulnerability level (CAT 1-4)
3. Identify when it was corrected or mitigated.

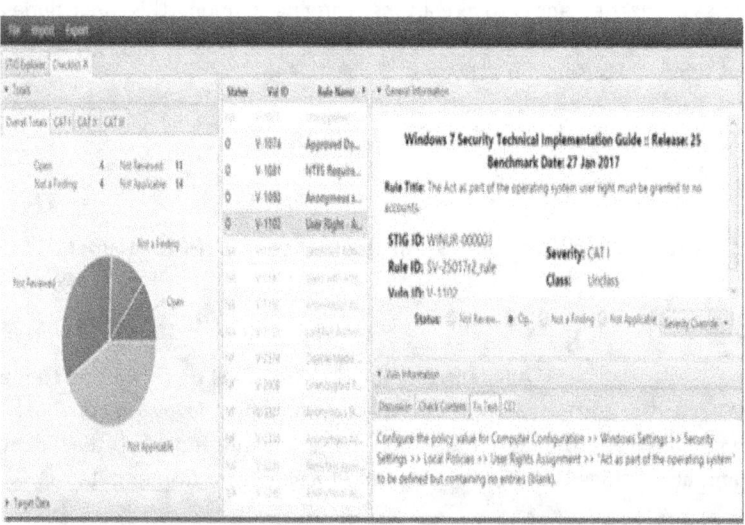

EXAMPLE ONLY ARTIFACT

Security Assessment (SA)

The SA control is about a process that re-assesses the state of all security controls and whether changes have occurred requiring additional mitigations of new risks or threats. The standard is 1/3rd of the controls are to be re-assessed annually. This control would require designated IT personnel to conduct a SA event[5] of approximately 36-37 controls per year. This should be captured in what is called a **ConMon Plan**. (See Annex Q –Continuous Monitoring).

Continuous Monitoring is a vital component of the NIST 800 series cybersecurity protection framework. It is defined as "…maintaining ongoing awareness of information security, vulnerabilities, and threats to support organizational risk management decisions." (SOURCE: NIST Special Publication 800-137, *Information Security Continuous Monitoring (ISCM) for Federal Information Systems and Organizations*, http://nvlpubs.nist.gov/nistpubs/Legacy/SP/nistspecialpublication800-137.pdf).

[CMMC CA.2.158]

3.12.1 Periodically assess the security controls in organizational systems to determine if the controls are effective in their application.

ANNEX R will be used to select 1/3 of security controls as part of active continuous monitoring activity.

Unicorn Red's ISSO, ISSE, or designated cybersecurity professional will reassess 1/3 of the security controls upon approval of Authority to Operate by the customer's designated Authorizing Official (AO).

The following controls will be assessed as follows:

> Year 1: Controls 3.1.1 through 3.4.9
> Year 2: Controls 3.5.1 through 3.9.2
> Year 3: Controls 3.10.1 through 3.14.7

---

[5] A "SA Event" is typically accomplished annually and is different than a SIA as discussed under the RA control.

SSP ARTIFACT RECOMMENDATIONS: (DATE OF CURRENT ARTIFACT): This can be explicitly answered by control 3.11.1 and based on the 1/3 annual review of controls.

[CMMC CA.2.159]

3.12.2 Develop and implement plans of action designed to correct deficiencies and reduce or eliminate vulnerabilities in organizational systems.

Plans of action will be created if the deficiency cannot be resolved within 1-week of approval by the CCB approval. Faults will be addressed IAW the DBS Configuration Management process. (See Annex J).

SSP ARTIFACT RECOMMENDATIONS: (DATE OF CURRENT ARTIFACT): Create POAMs to categorize, describe, and track system vulnerabilities. POAMs will be part of the overall CCB process.

POAM EXAMPLE ONLY ARTIFACT (SPECIFIC)

CONTROLLED UNCLASSIFIED INFORMATION/CRITICAL DEFENSE INFORMATION (DOD ONLY)--[WHEN FILLED IN]

NIST 800-171 Agile Plan of Action & Milestones®

SYSTEM NAME:

System Information:

System Name	
Company/Organization	
Sponsoring Service/Agency	

POAM Contact Information:

POC Name/Title	
POC Phone	
POC Email	

POAM History:

Date of this POAM	
Date of Last Update	
Date of Original POAM	

Security Costs (optional):

Security Costs [TOTAL]:	
Personnel	
Equipment	

MORE Compliant Controls to meet lab

(1) Status (G, Y, R)	(2) NIST 800-171 Control Family	(3) NIST 800-171 Identifier	(4) Scan Identifier	(5) Weakness or Deficiency	(6) Weakness or Deficiency	(7) POC	(8) Resources Required	(9) Overall Completion Date	(10A) Milestone Activity-1	(10A) Milestone Completion Date-1	(10B) Milestone Activity-2	(10B) Milestone Completion Date-2	(10C) Milestone Activity-3	(10C) Milestone Completion Date-3	**ADD ADDITIONAL COLUMNS for MILESTONE ACTIVITY & COMPLETION DATE AS NEEDED** (11) Changes to Milestone	(12) Risk Level (High/Moderate /Low/High)	(13) Estimated Sec. Cost	(14) Comments
G	3.1.8		System Administrat attempts	No limits on unsuccessful logon	Susan James	None	1-Jun-18	Set policy setting to forced lockout of users failing 3 logon	1-Jun-18						Low		$0	(Policy setting update required by authorized privileged user
Y	3.2.3	ACAS	Elbow Breed Patch missing	No assigned insider threat security officer	Alice Cooper	Additional budget for one full-time security person	5-Jun-18	Job announcement out on	5-Apr-18	Begin interviews	5-May-18	Sabot/begin new insider threat	5-Jun-18		Mod	$180,000	Hiring action approved by President 10 Jun
R		CVE-1234	Patch computer activated	Elbow Breed Patch missing	John Smith	Patch computer activated	20-Apr-18	Test patch in lab/test environment ABC123	15-Apr-18	Deploy Patch to 200 servers globally	20-Apr-18			None	Mod	$0	Testing patch with roll back standard IT procedures
R	3.5.3		System Administrat authentication for local and or network access	Not using multifactor	Bob Dole	Equipment, servers, IA consultant, tokens for all employees	20-Oct-18	Conduct research on solutions	15-Jun-18	Recommend to Sr. leadership	4-Jul-18	Begin/complete install of all equipment	20-Oct-18		High	$205,000	May require POAM extension if all PPT components not in place by 20 Oct 2019

Active POAMs | Completed POAMs

POAM EXAMPLE ONLY ARTIFACT (GENERAL TRACKER)

[CMMC CA.3.161]

3.12.3 Monitor security controls on an ongoing basis to ensure the continued effectiveness of the controls.

One-third (1/3) of security controls will be reviewed and assessed by designated Unicorn Red cybersecurity personnel. The assessment findings will be reported to the customer and CCB within 30-days after completion of that assessment. See Annex Q –*Continuous Monitoring of Security Controls* that identifies the tri-annual review of specified controls.

ANNEX R will be used to select the 1/3 controls as part of active continuous monitoring activity.

Unicorn Red's ISSO, ISSE, or designated cybersecurity professional will reassess 1/3 of the security controls upon approval of Authority to Operate by the customer's designated Authorizing Official (AO).

The following controls will be assessed as follows:

> Year 1: Controls 3.1.1 through 3.4.9
> Year 2: Controls 3.5.1 through 3.9.2
> Year 3: Controls 3.10.1 through 3.14.7

SSP ARTIFACT RECOMMENDATIONS: (DATE OF CURRENT ARTIFACT): Same as 3.12.1.

[CMMC CA.2.157]

3.12.4 Develop, document, and periodically update system security plans that describe system boundaries, system environments of operation, how security requirements are implemented, and the relationships with or connections to other systems.

The DBS SSP will be updated when a significant configuration change is implemented to the baseline. The designated Configuration manager will edit all architecture documents and notify the assigned ISSO to correct the current SSP. SSP updates will be accomplished within two weeks of notification and approved by the System Owner/Program Manager. Furthermore, significant changes will be communicated to the customer within 72-hours upon update.

SSP ARTIFACT RECOMMENDATIONS: (DATE OF CURRENT ARTIFACT): This SSP will be reviewed annually; it serves as its artifact for assessment.

System and Communications Protection (SC)

[CMMC SC.1.175]

3.13.1 Monitor, control, and protect communications (i.e., information transmitted or received by organizational systems) at the external boundaries and key internal boundaries of organizational systems.

This control will be met by auditing that checks and implemented, in general, by human and technical oversight via the AU control set. Checks will occur weekly. This control will also be technically met by, for example, "smart" firewalls solutions to include Cisco 5500-5600. Planning efforts will consist of constant consideration of future technologies meant to enhance the cybersecurity posture of the DBS system.

SSP ARTIFACT RECOMMENDATIONS: (DATE OF CURRENT ARTIFACT): This should include a screenshot of any applications monitoring external traffic, especially traffic from any Internet connection.

[CMMC SC.3.180]

3.13.2 Employ architectural designs, software development techniques, and systems engineering principles that promote effective information security within organizational systems.

DBS employs Defense in Depth as the basis of all security measures. It begins with security and awareness training of all UR directly or indirectly supporting DBS. Access control measures and associated auditing ensure Identity Management and accountability of only those personnel who need to access the DBS system. Active technical measures include smart firewall solutions that protect the application, database, and services through whitelisting as one of many steps to ensure the system's security. Cloud-based solutions such as ESET and associated ZIS services provide real-time technical protection of the DBS security boundary. Finally, the philosophy is also of Continuous Monitoring of the IT environment. UR uses both manual and automated capabilities of the system to protect critical data from compromise.

UR is committed to the absolute security, privacy, and protection of CUI data IAW customer requirements and direction.

DBS also employs SNORT for Intrusion Detection/Prevention Systems (IDS/IPS).

SSP ARTIFACT RECOMMENDATIONS: (DATE OF CURRENT ARTIFACT): The "best artifact" is a description of how the organization applies Defense in Depth (DID) principles. This control will be supported by architecture diagrams showing the security devices (e.g., firewalls, IDS, IPS, etc.). This can also include security scans of the raw code by static and dynamic code review applications that identify and categorize vulnerabilities.

```
         The
        Threat
          ↓
       Firewall
      Anti-virus
  Active Patching Process
     Access Control
       Encryption
  Continuous Monitoring
        Backups
        Training
          CUI
```

The Principle of Defense in Depth

Snort-Intrusion Detected Report

Log Time	Intrusion Classification	Intrusion Type	Source IP Address	Source Port Number
05:29:50 AM	Potentially Bad Traffic	(http_inspect) NON-RFC DEFINED CHAR	192.168.60.21	62644
04:22:14 AM	Unknown Traffic	(http_inspect) NO CONTENT-LENGTH OR TRANSFER-ENCODING IN HTTP RESPONSE	192.168.60.7	88
12:29:50 AM	Potentially Bad Traffic	(http_inspect) NON-RFC DEFINED CHAR	192.168.60.21	412
08:37:26 PM	Unknown Traffic	(http_inspect) NO CONTENT-LENGTH OR TRANSFER-ENCODING IN HTTP RESPONSE	192.168.60.35	736
04:45:02 PM	Unknown Traffic	(http_inspect) NON-RFC DEFINED CHAR	192.168.60.49	1060
12:52:38 PM	Unknown Traffic	(http_inspect) NO CONTENT-LENGTH OR TRANSFER-ENCODING IN HTTP RESPONSE	192.168.60.63	1384
09:00:14 AM	Potentially Bad Traffic	(http_inspect) NON-RFC DEFINED CHAR	192.168.60.77	1708
05:07:50 AM	Unknown Traffic	(http_inspect) NO CONTENT-LENGTH OR TRANSFER-ENCODING IN HTTP RESPONSE	192.168.60.91	2032
01:15:26 AM	Potentially Bad Traffic	(http_inspect) NON-RFC DEFINED CHAR	192.168.60.105	2356
09:23:02 PM	Unknown Traffic	(http_inspect) NO CONTENT-LENGTH OR TRANSFER-ENCODING IN HTTP RESPONSE	192.168.60.119	2680
05:30:38 PM	Unknown Traffic	(http_inspect) NON-RFC DEFINED CHAR	192.168.60.133	3004
01:38:14 PM	Unknown Traffic	(http_inspect) NO CONTENT-LENGTH	192.168.60.147	3328

SNORT INTRUSION DETECTION EXAMPLE

[CMMC SC.3.181]

3.13.3 Separate user functionality from system management functionality. Prevent unauthorized and unintended information transfer via shared system resources.

These protections begin with disallowing privileged users from using their basic user credentials to access user services (e.g., email and Internet access). Separation of access is a basic network security principle intended to hamper insider and external threats; this principle is closely aligned with Control 3.1.4 and its discussion of the **separation of duties.**

The ability to oversee especially privileged user activity will be anonymously inspected by the ISSO monthly. Any discrepancies will be reported to the PM within 24 hours of recognizing questionable activities by a designated privileged user.

SSP ARTIFACT RECOMMENDATIONS: (DATE OF CURRENT ARTIFACT): 1) Copy of initial screenshot of user and privileged users rights. "Prevent unauthorized and unintended information transfer via shared system resources" is typical of peer-to-peer enabled services on the network. Have SysAdmin/NWA create a screen capture showing peer-to-peer services are disabled.

[CMMC SC.3.182]

3.13.4 Prevent unauthorized and unintended transfer via shared system resources.

Peer-to-peer networking is not authorized. Data will be created and stored in a secure ZIS environment. Designated privileged users with responsibilities only authorize transfers to effect transfers in the conduct of normal DBS operations.

Additionally, regular audit activity by designated IT personnel will be reviewed to ensure compliance with this control; this would include unauthorized connections to include peer-to-peer networking.

SSP ARTIFACT RECOMMENDATIONS: (DATE OF CURRENT ARTIFACT): Disable Server Message Block (SMB) to prevent file sharing (see artifact below as an example).

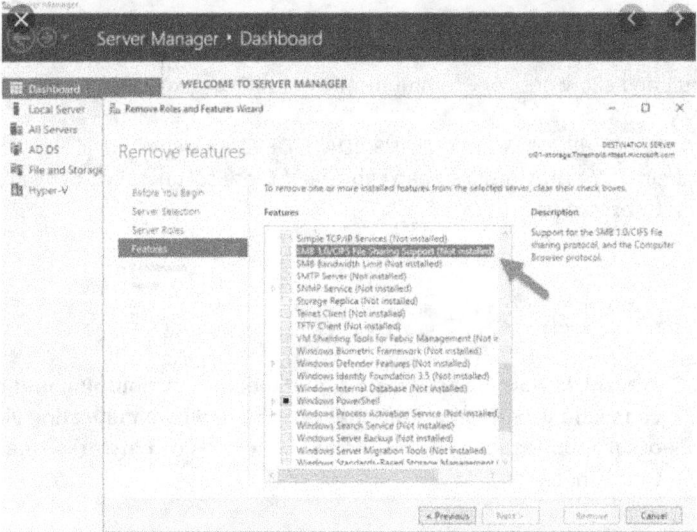

SMB EXAMPLE ONLY

[CMMC SC.1.176]

3.13.5 Implement subnetworks for publicly accessible system components that are physically or logically separated from internal networks.

 This control is NA. (See Annex G—Publicly Accessible Information Policy)

SSP ARTIFACT RECOMMENDATIONS: (DATE OF CURRENT ARTIFACT): This should be shown in the overall network topology; it should show access to the Internet if not a "closed system[6]."

[CMMC SC.3.183]

3.13.6 Deny network communications traffic by default and allow network communications traffic by exception (i.e., deny all, permit by exception).

---

[6] A closed system is considered "closed" if it does not connect anywhere to the Internet; these are not typical.

⚙ Whitelisting is used to control or deny network communications traffic by default and allow network communications traffic by exception.

SSP ARTIFACT RECOMMENDATIONS: (DATE OF CURRENT ARTIFACT): SysAdmin/NWA provides a screen capture of these settings, i.e., deny all | permit by exception.

[CMMC SC.3.184]

3.13.7 Prevent remote devices from simultaneously establishing non-remote connections with organizational systems and communicating via some other connection to resources in external networks (i.e., split tunneling).

⚙ No remote connections are authorized for operational use. (See Annex D—Remote Access Procedure for current control details).

SSP ARTIFACT RECOMMENDATIONS: (DATE OF CURRENT ARTIFACT): Show TLS 1.0 (or similar) enabled as a policy setting.

[CMMC SC.3.185]

3.13.8 Implement cryptographic mechanisms to prevent unauthorized disclosure of CUI during transmission unless otherwise protected by alternative physical safeguards.

⚙ The following cryptographic mechanisms will be used to prevent unauthorized CUI disclosure during transmission, including 1) HTTPS (port 443) and 2) TLS 1.0 or higher. These standards are both at the current AES-256 level.

SSP ARTIFACT RECOMMENDATIONS: (DATE OF CURRENT ARTIFACT): Screen capture of crypto encryption levels (see prior control artifacts). Refer to PS control and all local security procedures in force to provide physical safeguards of equipment and facilities.

[CMMC SC.3.186]

3.13.9 Terminate network connections associated with communications sessions at the end of the sessions or after a defined period of inactivity.

⚙ All operational and maintenance activities will be terminated after 15-minutes of inactivity (STIG-based).

SSP ARTIFACT RECOMMENDATIONS: (DATE OF CURRENT ARTIFACT): See prior control specific to the 15-minute termination.

[CMMC SC.3.187]

3.13.10 Establish and manage cryptographic keys for cryptography employed in organizational systems.

⚙ Cryptographic keys are managed IAW, the current ZIS contract/SLA that maintains and secure key stores.

SSP ARTIFACT RECOMMENDATIONS: (DATE OF CURRENT ARTIFACT): Identify where cryptographic keys are stored locally, or in the case of Cloud Service providers, develop a Service Level Agreement (SLA) specific to this control.

[CMMC SC.3.177]

3.13.11 Employ FIPS-validated cryptography when used to protect the confidentiality of CUI.

⚙ All cryptography is implemented and verified against FIPS 140-2. Official NIST site to confirm FIPS 140-2 cryptographic compliance: https://csrc.nist.gov/projects/cryptographic-module-validation-program/validated-modules/search

SSP ARTIFACT RECOMMENDATIONS: (DATE OF CURRENT ARTIFACT): Provide hardware and software listings demonstrating the following as a minimum, as part of the SSP:
1. Hardware or Software name
2. Version
3. Initial date of FIPS 140-2 compliance review
4. Subsequent (at least annually) the dates of follow-on FIPS 140-2 review

[CMMC SC.2.178]

3.13.12 Prohibit remote activation of collaborative computing devices and provide indication of devices in use to users present at the device.

 All DBS personnel are prohibited from remote operational use and activation of any collaborative computing devices.

(See Annex D—Remote Access Procedure for current control details).

SSP ARTIFACT RECOMMENDATIONS: (DATE OF CURRENT ARTIFACT): Provide a screenshot of collaborative hardware devices on the network, including phones, conference call devices, etc. Also, show that all collaborative software capabilities, such as chat, SMS, Skype®, etc., are application blacklisted.

[CMMC SC.3.188]

3.13.13 Control and monitor the use of mobile code.

No mobile code is used as part of the DBS system or architecture.

SSP ARTIFACT RECOMMENDATIONS: (DATE OF CURRENT ARTIFACT): Any use of mobile devices should be identified in the network topology diagrams. Provide a screen capture of policy settings that monitor "end-point" activities, if used.

[CMMC SC.3.189]

3.13.14 Control and monitor the use of Voice over Internet Protocol (VoIP) technologies.

The DBS system will not allow for any VOIP communications at any time. Current requirements preclude its need or use.

SSP ARTIFACT RECOMMENDATIONS: (DATE OF CURRENT ARTIFACT):): Any use of VOIP should be identified in the network topology diagrams. Provide a screen capture of policy settings that monitor "end-point" activities, if used. Also, include a screen capture of disabled VOIP ports to include TCP/UDP 5060 (unencrypted) or TCP 5061 (encrypted).

[CMMC SC.3.190]

3.13.15 Protect the authenticity of communications sessions.

All communication sessions will employ TLS 1.0 or higher to provide connection authenticity and confidentiality.

SSP ARTIFACT RECOMMENDATIONS: (DATE OF CURRENT ARTIFACT): Provide a screenshot of TLS used for application-to-application connections and any hashing supporting asymmetric user communications (logons) [See diagram below].

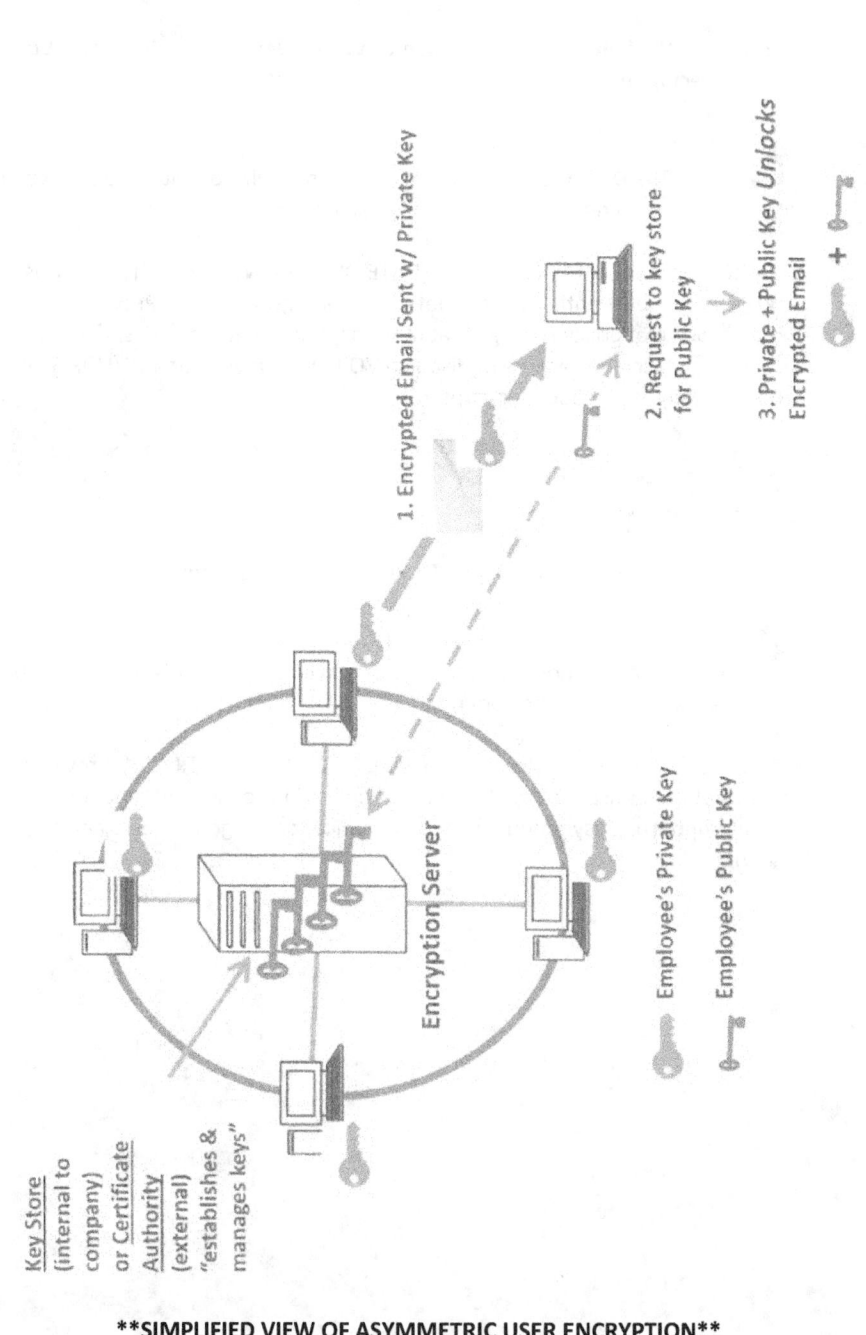

SIMPLIFIED VIEW OF ASYMMETRIC USER ENCRYPTION

[CMMC.SC.3.191]

3.13.16 **Protect the confidentiality of CUI at rest.**

⚙ All DAR will be encrypted. Data will be ensured meeting confidentiality standards IAW UR's *Acceptable Encryption Policy*.

SSP ARTIFACT RECOMMENDATIONS: (DATE OF CURRENT ARTIFACT): Identify an application that encrypts DAR, for example, BitLocker®, affords a general solution.

System and Information Integrity (SI)

[CMMC SI.1.210]

3.14.1 Identify, report, and correct system flaws in a timely manner.

All DBS personnel may submit Change Requests to their managers for submission to the CCB. Flaws will be corrected based on security impacts and risks to the system.

SSP ARTIFACT RECOMMENDATIONS: (DATE OF CURRENT ARTIFACT): Provide CCB procedure guides and policies. Create a Change Request (CR) form (hardcopy or virtual) to identify requested modifications by the customer, engineers, etc., to the system's baseline configuration. CRs will ALSO include an SRA or SIA as appropriate.

Change Request			
Project:		Date:	
Change Requestor:		Change No:	
Change Category (Check all that apply):			
☐ Schedule	☐ Cost	☐ Scope	☐ Requirements/Deliverables
☐ Testing/Quality	☐ Resources		
Does this Change Affect (Check all that apply):			
☐ Corrective Action	☐ Preventative Action	☐ Defect Repair	☐ Updates
☐ Other			
Describe the Change Being Requested:			
Describe the Reason for the Change:			
Describe all Alternatives Considered:			
Describe any Technical Changes Required to Implement this Change:			
Describe Risks to be Considered for this Change:			
Estimate Resources and Costs Needed to Implement this Change:			
Describe the Implications to Quality:			
Disposition:			
☐ Approve	☐ Reject	☐ Defer	
Justification of Approval, Rejection, or Deferral:			

Change Board Approval:		
Name	Signature	Date

EXAMPLE CHANGE REQUEST FORM

[CMMC SI.1.211]

3.14.2 Provide protection from malicious code at designated locations within organizational systems.

⚙ Malicious code detection relies upon Microsoft's ESET endpoint detection and prevention.

SSP ARTIFACT RECOMMENDATIONS: (DATE OF CURRENT ARTIFACT): Include a screen capture of active malicious code detection and prevention applications.

[CMMC SI.2.214]

3.14.3 Monitor system security alerts and advisories and take action in response.

⚙ ESET provides security alerts to DBS personnel. The NWA will provide daily notifications of on-duty DBS managers of any identified malicious code or application activity.

SSP ARTIFACT RECOMMENDATIONS: (DATE OF CURRENT ARTIFACT): Identify and create logs for events or incidents discovered during the system's lifecycle. This should be maintained in the CCB repository. (Refer to IR control family for more details).

[CMMC SI.1.212]

3.14.4 Update malicious code protection mechanisms when new releases are available.

⚙ 🗂 CCB The NWA will ensure and allow ESET malicious code detection software and patches daily. Checks for patches will not occur during weekends or major federal holidays and will be accomplished the next business day to ensure the security posture of DBS.

SSP ARTIFACT RECOMMENDATIONS: (DATE OF CURRENT ARTIFACT): Provide a screen capture of malicious code updates that are active. This should be set to "request permission to update." The SysAdmin or NWA will verify weekly or more often as required.

[CMMC SI.1.213]

3.14.5 Perform periodic scans of organizational systems and real-time scans of files from external sources as files are downloaded, opened, or executed.

CCB CYBER ESET performs automatic real-time scans of all files from external sources as files are downloaded, opened, or executed.

SSP ARTIFACT RECOMMENDATIONS: (DATE OF CURRENT ARTIFACT): Provide a screenshot of how to scan periods occur. The preferred selection should be **real-time.**

[CMMC SI.2.216]

3.14.6 Monitor organizational systems, including inbound and outbound communications traffic, to detect attacks and indicators of potential attacks.

ESET performs detection of all inbound and outbound communications traffic of potential attacks.

SSP ARTIFACT RECOMMENDATIONS: (DATE OF CURRENT ARTIFACT): Provide a screenshot of inbound/outbound monitoring of all connections to the system. The preferred selection should be **real-time.**

[CMMC SI.2.217]

3.14.7 Identify unauthorized use of organizational systems.

Manual audit reviews, as described above in the AU control, are designed to detect unauthorized use. The NWA is the primary privileged user conducting weekly inspections of all audited events.

SSP ARTIFACT RECOMMENDATIONS: (DATE OF CURRENT ARTIFACT): Refer to audit log captures as found under the AU control family. SysAdmin or NWA should maintain a review log and have the ISSO, ISSM, or System Owner verify at least weekly.

ANNEXES

ANNEX A – Acceptable Use Policy (AUP)

Overview

UNICORN RED's intentions for publishing an Acceptable Use Policy (AUP) are not to impose restrictions contrary to Unicorn Red's established culture of openness, trust, and integrity. UNICORN RED is committed to protecting Unicorn Red's employees, partners, and the company from illegal or damaging actions by individuals, either knowingly or unknowingly.

Internet/Intranet/Extranet-related systems, including but not limited to computer equipment, software, operating systems, storage media, network accounts providing electronic mail, WWW browsing, and FTP, are the property of Unicorn Red. These systems are to be used for business purposes to serve the company's interests and our clients and customers during normal operations. Please review Human Resources policies for further details.

Adequate security is a team effort involving every Unicorn Red employee and affiliate who deals with information or information systems. It is the responsibility of every computer user to know these guidelines and to conduct their activities accordingly.

Purpose

The purpose of this policy is to outline the acceptable use of computer equipment at Unicorn Red. These rules are in place to protect the employee and Unicorn Red. Inappropriate use exposes Unicorn Red to risks, including virus attacks, compromise of network systems and services, and legal issues.

Scope

This policy applies to the use of information, electronic and computing devices, and network resources to conduct Unicorn Red business or interact with internal networks and business systems, whether owned or leased by Unicorn Red, the employee, or a third party. All employees, contractors, consultants, temporary, and other workers at Unicorn Red and its subsidiaries are responsible for exercising good judgment regarding appropriate use of information, electronic devices, and network resources per Unicorn Red policies and standards, and local laws and regulation.

This policy applies to employees, contractors, consultants, temporaries, and other workers at Unicorn Red, including all personnel affiliated with third parties. This policy applies to all equipment that is owned or leased by Unicorn Red.

Policy

General Use and Ownership

Unicorn Red proprietary information stored on electronic and computing devices, whether owned or leased by Unicorn Red, the employee, or a third party, remains the sole property of Unicorn Red. You must ensure through legal or technical means that proprietary information is protected under the Data Protection Standard.

You have a responsibility to promptly report the theft, loss, or unauthorized disclosure of Unicorn Red proprietary information.

You may access, use, or share Unicorn Red proprietary information only to the extent it is authorized and necessary to fulfill your assigned job duties.

Employees are responsible for exercising good judgment regarding the reasonableness of personal use. Individual departments are responsible for creating guidelines concerning personal use of Internet/Intranet/Extranet systems. In the absence of such policies, employees should be guided by departmental policies on personal use, and if there is any uncertainty, employees should consult their supervisor or manager.

For security and network maintenance purposes, authorized individuals within Unicorn Red may monitor equipment, systems, and network traffic at any time, per Unicorn Red Audit Policy.

Unicorn Red reserves the right to audit networks and systems periodically to ensure compliance with this policy.

Security and Proprietary Information
All mobile and computing devices that connect to the internal network must comply with the Minimum Access Policy.

System-level and user-level passwords must comply with the Password Policy. Providing access to another individual, either deliberately or through failure to secure its access, is prohibited.

All computing devices must be secured with a password-protected screensaver with the automatic activation feature of 15 minutes or less. You must lock the screen or log off when the device is unattended.

Postings by employees from a Unicorn Red email address to newsgroups should contain a disclaimer stating that the opinions expressed are strictly their own and not necessarily those of Unicorn Red unless posting is during business duties.

Employees must use extreme caution when opening e-mail attachments received from unknown senders, which may contain malware.

Unacceptable Use
The following activities are, in general, prohibited. Employees may be exempted from these restrictions during their legitimate job responsibilities (e.g., systems administration staff may need to disable the network access if that host disrupts production services).

Under no circumstances is an employee of Unicorn Red authorized to engage in any illegal activity under local, state, federal, or international law while utilizing Unicorn Red-owned resources.

The lists below are by no means exhaustive but attempt to provide a framework for activities that fall into the category of unacceptable use.

System and Network Activities

The following activities are strictly prohibited, with no exceptions:

1. Violations of the rights of any person or company protected by copyright, trade secret, patent or other intellectual property, or similar laws or regulations, including, but not limited to, the installation or distribution of "pirated" or other software products that are not appropriately licensed for use by Unicorn Red.

2. Unauthorized copying of copyrighted material includes digitization and distribution of photographs from magazines, books, or other copyrighted sources, copyrighted music, and the installation of any copyrighted software for which Unicorn Red or the end-user does not have an active license is strictly prohibited.

3. Accessing data, a server, or an account for any purpose other than conducting Unicorn Red business is prohibited even if you have authorized access.

4. Exporting software, technical information, encryption software or technology, in violation of international or regional export control laws is illegal. The appropriate management should be consulted before the export of any material that is in question.

5. Introduction of malicious programs into the network or server (e.g., viruses, worms, Trojan horses, e-mail bombs, etc.).

6. Revealing your account password to others or allowing the use of your account by others. This includes family and other household members when work is being done at home.

7. Using a Unicorn Red computing asset to actively engage in procuring or transmitting material violates sexual harassment or hostile workplace laws in the user's local jurisdiction.

8. Making fraudulent offers of products, items, or services originating from any Unicorn Red account.

9. Making statements about warranty, expressly or implied, unless it is a part of regular job duties.

10. Effecting security breaches or disruptions of network communication. Security breaches include, but are not limited to, accessing data of which the employee is not an intended recipient or logging into a server or account that the employee is not expressly authorized to access unless these duties are within the scope of regular duties. For purposes of this section, "disruption" includes, but is not limited to, network sniffing, pinged floods, packet spoofing, denial of service, and forged routing information for malicious purposes.

11. Port scanning or security scanning is expressly prohibited unless prior notification to UNICORN RED is made.

12. Executing any form of network monitoring, which will intercept data not intended for the employee's host, unless this activity is a part of the employee's regular job/duty.

13. Circumventing user authentication or security of any host, network, or account.

14. Introducing honeypots, honeynets, or similar technology on the Unicorn Red network.

15. Interfering with or denying service to any user other than the employee's host (for example, denial of service attack).

16. Using any program/script/command, or sending messages of any kind, with the intent to interfere with, or disable, a user's terminal session, via any means, locally or via the Internet/Intranet/Extranet.

17. Providing information about, or lists of, Unicorn Red employees to parties outside Unicorn Red.

Email and Communication Activities

When using company resources to access and use the Internet, users must realize they represent the company. Whenever employees state an affiliation to the company, they must also clearly indicate that "the opinions expressed are my own and not necessarily those of the company." Questions may be addressed to UNICORN RED.

1. Sending unsolicited email messages, including sending "junk mail" or other advertising material to individuals who did not specifically request such content (email spam).

2. Any form of harassment via email, telephone, or paging, whether through language, frequency, or size of messages.

3. Unauthorized use, or forging, of email header information.

4. Solicitation of email for any other email address, other than that of the poster's account, with the intent to harass or to collect replies.

5. Creating or forwarding "chain letters," "Ponzi," or other "pyramid" schemes of any type.

6. Use of unsolicited email originating from within Unicorn Red's networks of other Internet/Intranet/Extranet service providers on behalf of, or to advertise, any service hosted by Unicorn Red or connected via Unicorn Red's network.

7. Posting the same or similar non-business-related messages to large numbers of Usenet newsgroups (newsgroup spam).

Blogging and Social Media

1. Whether using Unicorn Red's property and systems or personal computer systems, Blogging by employees is also subject to the terms and restrictions outlined in this Policy. Limited and occasional use of Unicorn Red's systems to engage in blogging is acceptable if it is done professionally and responsibly, does not otherwise violate Unicorn Red's policy, and is not detrimental to its best interests does not interfere with an employee's regular work duties. Blogging from Unicorn Red's systems is also subject to monitoring.

2. Unicorn Red's Confidential Information policy also applies to blogging. As such, Employees are prohibited from revealing any Unicorn Red confidential or proprietary information, trade secrets, or any other material covered by Unicorn Red's Confidential Information policy when engaged in blogging.

3. Employees shall not engage in any blogging that may harm or tarnish the image, reputation, and/or goodwill of Unicorn Red or any of its employees. Employees are also prohibited from making discriminatory, disparaging, defamatory, or harassing comments when blogging or otherwise engaging in any conduct prohibited by Unicorn Red's Non-Discrimination and Anti-Harassment policy.

4. Employees may also not attribute personal statements, opinions, or beliefs to Unicorn Red when blogging. If an employee expresses their views or opinions in blogs, they may not expressly or implicitly represent themselves as an employee or representative of Unicorn Red. Employees assume all risks associated with blogging.

5. Apart from following all laws about the handling and disclosure of copyrighted or export-controlled materials, Unicorn Red's trademarks, logos, and any other Unicorn Red intellectual property may also not be used in connection with any blogging activity

Policy Compliance

Compliance Measurement
The UNICORN RED teams will verify compliance to this policy through various methods, including but not limited to periodic walk-throughs, video monitoring, business tool reports, internal and external audits, and feedback to the policy owners.

Exception
The UNICORN RED team must approve any exception to the policy in advance.

Non-Compliance
An employee found to have violated this policy may be subject to disciplinary action, up to and including termination of employment.

ANNEX B – System Administrator (SysAdmin) Guide [3.1.4] -- RESERVED[7]

(To be published separately)

---

[7] RESERVED alerts the assessor that the document is either incomplete or partially completed. If the document answers a control, but is not completed, a POAM should also be generated with an expected completion date.

ANNEX C – Controlled Unclassified Information (CUI)/Critical Defense Information (CUI) Marking, Handling & Storage Guide [3.1.9]

(Published separately)

ANNEX D – Remote Access Procedures [3.1.12]

Remote access is currently unauthorized for both operational and maintenance employment. This procedure is formulated for future needs and considerations of the DBS system.

Unicorn Red shall control remote access to the DBS information system per references NIST-SP 800-46 and NIST-SP 800-114.

All remote connections will be identified, authenticated, and logged. All remote access to information systems and networks shall be mediated through a managed access control point, such as a remote access server in a Demilitarized Zone (DMZ). Remote access shall use encryption to protect the confidentiality of the session.

Authentication and confidentiality requirements for remote access sessions will be implemented using National Security Agency (NSA)-approved COMSEC and keying material for classified systems and the National Institute of Standards and Technology (NIST)-approved COMSEC and DoD Public Key Infrastructure (PKI) certificates for unclassified systems. The use of PKI certificates, protected by a hardware token, such as the CAC, and accessed through the associated, approved reader and middleware, is the primary method for remote client-side authentication.

All computers used for remote access must have approved antivirus and firewall protection that includes automated updates. The most current definitions and updates for these applications must be loaded before establishing remote access sessions. For antivirus definitions, scanning shall be performed monthly following INFOCON requirements and CTO 09-08. Update settings shall be set to automatic and verified weekly.

Unicorn Red Remote Access Policy

1. Overview
Remote access to our corporate network is essential to maintain our Organization's productivity. Still, in many cases, this remote access originates from networks that may already be compromised or are at a significantly lower security posture than our corporate network. While these remote networks are beyond the control of the Unicorn Red policy, we must mitigate these external risks to the best of our ability.

2. Purpose
The purpose of this policy is to define rules and requirements for connecting to Unicorn Red networks from any host. These rules and requirements are designed to minimize the potential exposure to Unicorn Red from damages, which may result from unauthorized use of Unicorn Red resources. Damages include the loss of sensitive or company confidential data, intellectual property, damage to public image, damage to critical Unicorn Red internal systems, and fines or other financial liabilities incurred as a result of those losses.

3. Scope

This policy applies to all Unicorn Red employees, contractors, vendors, and agents with a Unicorn Red-owned or personally-owned computer or workstation used to connect to the Unicorn Red network. This policy applies to remote access connections used to work on behalf of Unicorn Red, including reading or sending email and viewing intranet web resources. This policy covers all technical implementations of remote access used to connect to Unicorn Red networks.

4. Policy

It is the responsibility of Unicorn Red employees, contractors, vendors, and agents with remote access privileges to Unicorn Red's corporate network to ensure that their remote access connection is given the same consideration as the user's on-site connection Unicorn Red.

Universal access to the Internet for recreational use through the Unicorn Red networks is strictly limited to Unicorn Red employees, contractors, vendors, and agents (hereafter referred to as "Authorized Users"). When accessing the Unicorn Red network from a personal computer, Authorized Users are responsible for preventing access to any Unicorn Red computer resources or data by non-Authorized Users. The performance of illegal activities through the Unicorn Red network by any user (Authorized or otherwise) is prohibited. The Authorized User bears responsibility for the consequences of misuse of the Authorized User's access. For further information and definitions, see "Acceptable Use Policy."

Authorized Users will not use Unicorn Red networks to access the Internet for outside business interests.

4.1 Requirements

4.1.1 Secure remote access must be strictly controlled with encryption (i.e., Virtual Private Networks (VPNs)) and strong passphrases. For further information, see the "Acceptable Encryption Policy" and "Password Policy."
4.1.2 Authorized Users shall protect their login and password, even from family members.
4.1.3 While using a Unicorn Red-owned computer to connect to the Unicorn Red corporate network remotely, Authorized Users shall ensure the remote host is not linked to any other system at the same time, except for personal systems that are under their complete control or the complete control of an Authorized User or Third Party.
4.1.4 Use of external resources to conduct Unicorn Red business must be approved in advance by UNICORN RED and the appropriate Operating Group Manager.
4.1.5 All hosts connected to Unicorn Red internal networks via remote access technologies must use the most up-to-date anti-virus software; this includes personal computers. The third-party connection must comply with requirements, as stated in the "Third Party Agreement."
4.1.6 Personal equipment used to connect to the Unicorn Red networks must meet the needs of Unicorn Red-owned equipment for remote access, as stated in the "Hardware and Software Configuration Standards for Remote Access to Unicorn Red Networks."

5. Policy Compliance

5.1 Compliance Measurement

The UNICORN RED teams will verify compliance to this policy through various methods, including but not limited to periodic walk-throughs, video monitoring, business tool reports, internal and external audits, and feedback to the policy owners.

5.2 Exception
The UNICORN RED team must approve any exception to the policy in advance.

5.3 Non-Compliance
An employee found to have violated this policy may be subject to disciplinary action, up to and including termination of employment.

6. Related Standards, Policies, and Processes
• Acceptable Encryption Policy

• Acceptable Use Policy

• Password Policy

• Third Party Agreement

• Hardware and Software Configuration Standards for Remote Access to Unicorn Red Networks

ANNEX E – Wireless Policy [3.1.16]

The DBS System will not employ wireless at any time.

Wireless Networking and Security Standards

Summary

These standards address the need for an organized approach in deploying wireless technologies on the Unicorn Red enterprise network. Adherence to these standards will allow Unicorn Red departments and Labs to use wireless networks without compromising the integrity of the Unicorn Red network. The compatibility will result in better user experiences and lower support requirements.

Standard Practice

This section summarizes an appropriate model for wireless networks and wireless access points connecting to the UNICORN RED enterprise network. Additional capabilities can be added by users and by Information Technology Operations (UNICORN RED) as the central Authentication and Authorization system permits.

Access points configured to support the following standards are acceptable for use on the UNICORN RED campus network following the posted procedure for notifying UNICORN RED of access point installation.

General:

1. Ownership

    1. Wireless LAN implementations are responsible for the units that control the space they operate unless an alternative responsible party is documented with UNICORN RED.
    2. Units are expected to know what is occurring in that space and to take steps to make sure that all wireless implementations active in their area follow the standards defined here.
    3. Every wireless LAN installation within UNICORN RED must be authorized by the unit's leadership in which it is occurring. While they may choose to delegate details to technical staff, the department chair or another responsible person should know what activities are happening and take responsibility for verifying that a security plan exists and that proper coordination is happening with other units close enough that interference might occur.

2. Due diligence

    1. Anyone installing wireless LAN equipment must check the registration database before installation for conflicting station identifiers (SSID) and not install any new equipment that might reasonably be expected to interfere with existing equipment without first discussing their plans with contacts the existing equipment.

2. A Radio Frequency Site Survey must accompany any installation over three (3) wireless access points by a department in proximity to each other.

3. Service Set Identifiers (SSID) must be set to not conflict with reserved Unicorn Red names and will not cause confusion with neighboring wireless networks.

3. All wireless access points must be securely mounted so that they are inaccessible to unauthorized personnel.

4. All wireless access points must be registered with UNICORN RED.

Interference Management:

1. Conflicting or overlapping set service identifiers (SSID) can confuse and could inadvertently allow data leakage. UNICORN RED reserves the following SSID names for Campus-wide initiatives:

    1. Unicorn Red -HotSpot
    2. Unicorn Red guest
    3. Unicorn Red net
    4. Unicorn Red VPN
    5. Unicorn Red WPA

2. Wireless access points utilize shared public radio spectrums and can interfere with the operation of communications and computational devices

    1. Wireless access point owners are responsible for ensuring non-interference with the proper functioning of the Unicorn Red wired and wireless networks.
    2. Wireless communication networks must be consistent with Federal and State laws and regulations

Security and Information Protection:

1. Every wireless LAN implementation within Unicorn Red must be done per a security plan. This plan must address at least the following issues:

    1. Restricting access to the network so that only authorized people can use it
    2. Preventing unauthorized users from being able to see confidential data appearing on the network, notably Unicorn Red passwords

2. If unauthorized wireless access points are detected, the Security Incident Response program will include a wireless security response procedure.

3. Vendor default settings such as encryption keys, SNMP passwords, pre-shared keys (PSK), and passphrases for wireless access points must be changed based on the Unicorn Red password standards.

4. Wireless access point owners and managers are responsible for updating software, hardware, and firmware of devices to ensure that vulnerabilities are addressed.

5. Encryption and Data Protection:

1. WPA2/AES-CCMP, as defined by 802.11i, is strongly recommended for departments that deal with highly sensitive information such as patient and HR/staff information. WPA2/AES-CCMP provides a higher degree of encryption protection for sensitive data being transmitted wirelessly.
2. WPA and WPA2 (RSN), as defined by 802.11i, are the standard protocols for UNICORN RED wireless security.

6. Wireless network security awareness should be part of the existing end-user security education program.

Operational/Functional Impact

Wireless access points are radio transmitters and receivers. As such, they do not respect walls, buildings, or even campus boundaries. They can be subject to interference from other access points or other communications devices, just as one radio station can cause interference. Therefore, the use of wireless LAN is, by default, a community matter. Users will have to work collaboratively with others to install wireless technology, and registration of access points to minimize interference and maximize security is essential.

Technical Impact

To support the implementation of these guidelines, UNICORN RED will:

1. Create web-based configuration instructions for a limited preselected list of vendor access points.
2. Assist units with the configuration of a limited preselected list of vendor access points.
3. Assist departments in developing wireless plans if desired.
4. Recommend consultancies and value-added resellers to assist in RF Site Surveys or design a wireless network solution.

Considerations and Rationale

The goal of this document is to provide wireless LAN security using open standards. The practice of proper deployment of security standards has become a focus on risk mitigation in wireless networking. This document will be reviewed by UNICORN RED annually.

Compliance Issues

VPN use for Unicorn Red intranet access is permitted. For business reasons non-compliance with this standard, please contact UNICORN RED for an exception request and handling. Non-compliant access points without authorized exceptions to this standard will be disconnected from the Unicorn Red enterprise network. Access points causing impact to the Unicorn Red campus wired or wireless networks may be removed if attempts to remediate are unsuccessful.

For those exceptional wireless connectivity arrangements, UNICORN RED can assist in the risk analysis, configuration and provide information for upgrading switches and routers connecting to these wireless access points.

Security Issues

Implementation and enforcement of these wireless security standards will increase the overall security of Unicorn Red networks and systems.

Definition of Terms

Access point: The term access point includes special-purpose hardware and general-purpose computers configured to act as base stations or transceivers for wireless LANs. For pure peer-to-peer applications (where it may not be clear which system is the base station), one unit should be registered so that the channel, SSID, and other information are in the database.

The Institute of Electrical and Electronics Engineers or IEEE is responsible for setting industry-wide data communications standards, including wireless LAN standards.

Radio Frequency (RF) Site Survey: This procedure identifies the optimal locations for access points to maximize coverage and minimize interference. Typically, this is done with specialized equipment operated by trained personnel.

Secure Mounting: Mounting access points in a physically secure manner introduces physical security in addition to network security. Access points are far less likely to be stolen or removed without authorization. Also, unauthorized configuration changes to the access points are less likely to occur. Secure mounting is easy to implement and provides a baseline of security and interoperability.

SSID: The SSID (Service Set Identifier) is a wireless data communication packets token identifying an 802.11 (wireless) network. It identifies the name of a wireless network. All wireless devices on a WLAN must employ the same SSID to communicate with each other. Wireless access points can be configured to broadcast their SSID or not to broadcast their SSID.

VPN: An approach to providing authentication and secure data communications. VPN (Virtual Private Network) technology creates an encrypted networking layer on another network, including a wireless network. VPN technology provides a practical and secure means of accessing computers on the UNICORN RED network. A user's computer must run VPN client software to use VPN technology. VPN client software is available for nearly all computers and operating systems, including laptops.

WAP: Wireless access point. Also sometimes referred to as the wireless base station.

WEP: Wireless encryption protocol. WEP is an approved standard for encrypting data in a wireless network and is intended to protect privacy. The user must specify an encryption key or password, and the same key must be used by all parties wishing to communicate. WEP keys can be either 40-bits or 128-bits in length; 128-bit keys provide more robust encryption. WEP does not provide an authentication mechanism; that is, it does not control who can use your network. (The same can be said of any end-to-end encryption protocol since anyone who knows the encryption key can decrypt encrypted data.)

WPA: The Wi-Fi Protected Access (WPA and WPA2) protocol implements most of **the IEEE 802.11i standard, specifying security mechanisms for wireless networks. It replaced the original standard's short Authentication and privacy clause with a detailed** *Security* **clause, deprecating the broken WEP.**

Further, the Temporal Key Integrity Protocol (TKIP) for more robust encryption key protection was brought into WPA.

802.1x: 802.1X is an IEEE standard for providing authentication, controlling user traffic, and dynamically varying encryption keys for wired and wireless Ethernet networks. In wireless LAN applications, the Authenticator is the wireless access point. 802.1X is particularly well suited for wireless LAN applications because it requires very little processing power on the part of the Authenticator.

802.11i: 802.11i is an amendment to IEEE 802.11, replacing insecure components and updating standards to match newer technology.

ANNEX F – Portable Storage Devices [3.1.21] -- RESERVED

ANNEX G – Publicly Accessible Information [3.1.22] –RESERVED

ANNEX H – Awareness and Training [3.2.1 – 3.2.3]

Additional DBS Training Courses: (TBP)

ANNEX I – Audit Policy and Procedure [3.3.1-3.3.9] --RESERVED

ANNEX J – Configuration Management Procedure [3.4.1-3.4.9]

CONFIGURATION MANAGEMENT PLAN
DEFENSE BUSINESS SOLUTION System

UNICORN RED SOLUTIONS

[DATE]

Introduction

The purpose of the Configuration Management Plan (CMP) is to describe how Configuration Management (CM) will be conducted throughout the DEFENSE BUSINESS SOLUTION system project lifecycle. The CMP includes documenting how CM is managed, roles and responsibilities, how Configuration Item (CI) changes are made, and communicating all aspects of CM to project stakeholders. The DBS Project will utilize procured and dedicated network infrastructure and add capabilities to improve monitoring changes to network tools and devices. To effectively manage the DBS system, a coordinated CMP is needed. This plan will establish CM roles and responsibilities and describe how the DBS team will track, implement, and communicate CIs and changes throughout the project lifecycle.

Roles and Responsibilities

The following roles and responsibilities pertaining to the CM Plan for Unicorn Red's DBS system.

Configuration Control Board (CCB)

The CCB is comprised of the customer/Project Sponsor, Prime Program Manager (PPM), Unicorn Red (UR) PM, Configuration Manager/ISSO, and the Lead Engineer for the Cis under consideration. The CCB is responsible for the following:
- Reviews and approves/rejects configuration change requests.
- Ensures all approved changes are added to the Configuration Management Database (CMDB).
- Seek clarification on any CIs as required.

Project/Customer Sponsor

The customer or a designated representative will assist in the following CMP activities to provide oversight and direction to change management efforts:
- Chairing all CCB meetings
- Providing approval for any issues requiring additional scope, time, or cost

Prime and UR Program Managers

The Program Managers are responsible for:
- Overall responsibility for CM activities related to the DBS project.
- Identification of CIs.
- All communication of CM activities to project stakeholders (in coordination with each other).
- Participation in CCB meetings.
- Re-baselining, if necessary, any items affected by CM changes.

Configuration Manager/UR Information Systems Security Officer (ISSO)

The Configuration Manager will be appointed by the Program Management Office (PMO). The Configuration Manager is responsible for:
- Overall management of the CMDB.
- Identification of CIs.
- Providing configuration standards and templates to the project team.
- Providing any required configuration training.
- Conducting or assigning a Unicorn Red ISSE to conduct Security Impact Assessment (SIA).

Lead Engineers (software, hardware)
All identified CIs will be assigned to a Lead Engineer. The assigned Lead Engineer is responsible for:
- Designating a focus group to develop the Change Request (CR).
- Ensure all change CRs comply with organizational templates and standards before the CCB.
- Identification of CIs.

IT Engineers & Architects
Each CI will be assigned to an Integrated Product Team (IPT) consisting of engineers and architects with the requisite and knowledge and experience with the DBS system implementation. Each member of the IPT will provide input to the change request before submitting the change request to the lead engineer for review and presentation at the CCB. This will include conflicts with existing configurations and security changes that reduce the security posture of DBS.

Configuration Control (CC)

A key component to CM is having a well-defined and followed the process for both document and data management. CC is the process of systematically controlling and managing all steps of configuration throughout the project lifecycle. To effectively handle project CM, Unicorn Red will use a method that ensures only necessary configuration changes are made. The DBS system will use a standardized CC process throughout the project lifecycle to ensure all CIs are handled consistently. Any approved changes are fully vetted regarding the impact and communicated to stakeholders.

Additionally, configuration change decisions must be made to understand *the operational and security impacts of a change to the overall system*.

As the project team identifies CIs, the Configuration Manager/ISSO will assign a CI name, and the CI will be entered the CMDB in an "initiate" status. The CI will then be designated to an IPT. Each member of a CIs focus group will have the ability to access the CI through the CMDB, make changes and edits, and enter the CI into the CMDB with a description of the change/edit annotated in the CMDB log.

It is imperative that for any software changes, testing is conducted by the IPT to validate any changes. The Lead DBS Engineer will manage the IPTs and ensure that testing has been completed, a test report is produced, and all changes/edits are correctly saved into the CMDB. The Lead Engineer is also responsible for assigning new version numbers and CMDB status for any changes made by their assigned focus group.

A CI will have a relationship with one or more other CIs within a project. The Lead DBS Engineer, CM/ISSO, and Program Manager will fully understand these relationships. The Lead DBS Engineer and CM/ISSO will then be responsible for illustrating these relationships and co-dependencies to the customer, PPM, and the CMDB to ensure a complete understanding of each CI and how they relate.

Any configuration changes identified by the project team or stakeholders must be captured in a Configuration Change Request (CCR) and submitted to the CCB. The CCB will review, analyze, and approve/deny the request based on the proposed change's impact, scope, time, and cost. If the change is approved, the project requirements will be re-baselined (if necessary), and all changes will be communicated to the project team and stakeholders by the Program Manager.

Denied CCRs may be re-submitted with additional or new information for re-consideration by the CCB.

GRAPHIC OF CM PROCESS HERE

Configuration Management Database (CMDB)

The CMDB contains the configuration information for assets and information about the assets such as physical location, ownership, and its relationship to other configurable items (CIs). The CMDB will be the centralized repository for all configuration information for the DBS project. The CMDB provides a common platform for the project team to edit, change, revise, and review CIs and ensure all documents and data are updated with the latest revision and release formats.

Access to the CMDB will be granted and governed by standard permissions. Two types of CMDB access will be given for the DBS project:

1) **Full read and write access** will be issued to the CM/ISSO, Program Managers, Lead DBS Engineer, and select engineers and architects. These individuals will be authorized to access the CMDB to make changes, edit documents and data, review and approve versions and CI statuses.

2) **Read-only access** will be granted to the Project Sponsor and all other stakeholders. This access will allow these individuals to view all CIs and CI data. They will not be authorized to make any changes to the CMDB. If these individuals identify the need for a change or edit, they will notify the CM/ISSO, reviewing the notification and providing feedback.

The CMDB will ensure that members of the project team are always working from the latest versions of software, hardware, architecture, data, and documentation. It is vital to maintain the history of these assets throughout the project lifecycle. As these assets are changed and updated, the Lead Engineers/architects of the CI's assigned IPT will be responsible for updating the status of the CI and providing new revision numbering. This numbering will be done following UR's standard revision control numbering process, wherein higher version numbers indicate more recent versioning.

Configuration Status Accounting

Accounting for the configuration status involves collecting, processing, and reporting the configuration data for all CIs at any given time. This also includes management stored configuration information held in the CMDB. This may consist of approved configuration documents, software, data, and their current version numbers; build reports; status of any submitted changes; or discrepancies identified through configuration audits.

It is essential for the DBS Project. The Project Sponsor/customer can review configuration status at any given time. The UR Program Managers will also submit weekly reports to include configuration status monthly to the PPM. Reports will consist of the following information as part of the configuration status section:

1) Change requests
   a. Aging - How long have change requests been open?
   b. Distribution – Number of change requests submitted by the owner/group?
   c. Trending – What area(s) are approved changes occurring?

2) Version Control
   a. Software
   b. Hardware
   c. Architecture (network topology)
   d. Data
   e. Documentation (user guides, training manuals, etc.)

3) Build Reporting
   a. Files
   b. CI relationships
   c. Incorporated Changes

4) Audits
   a. Physical Configuration
   b. Functional Configuration

Before any new software releases, the CM/ISSO will work with each Lead IPT Engineer to ensure all CIs are updated with the latest release versions.

Configuration Audits

Audits are an essential part of project and configuration management. The purpose of an audit is to ensure that established processes are being followed as intended and to provide an opportunity to correct any deviations from these processes. Configuration audits will be an ongoing part of the DBS project lifecycle. The purpose of the configuration audit is to ensure all team members are following the established procedures and processes for configuration management. Project audits for the DBS Project will occur before any major software release or at the Program Manager or customer's discretion if they determine the need for one.

The CM will perform all DBS configuration audits. The CM works closely with Lead Engineers throughout the project to ensure that all configuration processes and procedures are followed. As part of the configuration audit, the CM will perform the following tasks:

1) Establish an audit environment in the CMDB.
2) The CM will copy all the latest software, data, and document versions into the audit environment.
3) The CM will ensure all versions are correctly numbered and that version control has been appropriately performed.
4) The CM will analyze historical versions and timestamps of all software, data, and documents to ensure all changes/edits were recorded correctly and captured.
5) The CM will copy the latest software versions and conduct software testing to ensure requirements are being met.
6) The CM will ensure all required artifacts are present and current in the CMDB.

7) The CM will ensure all approved CCRs have been incorporated into the project and are recorded in the CMDB.

Once the audit has been performed, the CM will compile their audit findings. For each outcome, the CM must work with the Program Manager/Team to identify the corrective action(s) necessary to resolve the discrepancy and assign responsibility for each corrective action.

Upon completing the project audit and findings, the CM will note all discrepancies and compile a report to the Customer, Prime Program Manager, and Unicorn Red PM.

CUSTOMER ACCEPTANCE

PENDING APPROVAL

Approved by the Project Sponsor:

_____   Date:
_____

<Customer Sponsor>
<Customer Sponsor Title>

ANNEX K – Multi-factor Authentication (MFA) Implementation [3.5.2] – RESERVED

ANNEX L – Password Policy [3.5.5, 3.5.7]

1. Overview
Passwords are an essential aspect of our security. A weak password may result in unauthorized access or exploitation of resources. All users, including contractors and vendors with access to systems, are responsible for taking the appropriate steps, as outlined below, to select and secure their passwords.

2. Purpose
The purpose of this policy is to establish a standard for the creation of strong passwords, the protection of those passwords, and the frequency of change.

3. Scope
The scope of this policy includes all personnel who have or are responsible for an account (or any form of access that supports or requires a password) on any systems that reside at any Unicorn Red facility, have access to the network, or stores any non-public information.

4. Policy

4.1   Password Creation

4.1.1 All user-level and system-level passwords must conform to the Password Construction Guidelines.
4.1.2 Users must not use the same password for the account as other non-access (personal email account, bank account, and so on).
4.1.3 User accounts that have system-level privileges granted through group memberships or programs such as Sudo must have a unique password from all other accounts held by that user to access system-level privileges.

4.2   Password Change

4.2.1 All system-level passwords (for example, root, enable, NT admin, application administration accounts, and so on) must be changed on at least an annual basis.
4.2.2 Password cracking or guessing may be performed periodic or random by the UNICORN RED team or its delegates. If a password is guessed or cracked during these scans, the user must change it to follow the Password Construction Guidelines.

4.3   Password Protection

4.3.1 Passwords must not be shared with anyone. All passwords are to be treated as sensitive information. Corporate Information Security recognizes that legacy application does not support proxy systems in place. Please refer to the technical reference for additional details.

4.3.2 Passwords must not be inserted into email messages or other forms of electronic communication (except for a system-generated email during a user's initial account setup).

4.3.3 The password must not be revealed over the phone to anyone.

4.3.4 Do not show a password on any questionnaires or security forms.

4.3.5 Do not hint at the format of a password (for example, "my family name")

4.3.6 Do not share passwords with anyone, including administrative assistants, secretaries, managers, co-workers while on vacation, and family members.

4.3.7 Do not write passwords down and store them anywhere in your office. Without encryption, do not store passwords in files on a computer system or mobile devices (phone or tablet).

4.3.8 Do not use the "Remember Password" feature of applications or web browsers.

4.3.9 Any user suspecting that their password may have been compromised must report the incident to UNICORN RED and change all passwords as soon as practical.

4.4   Application Development

4.4.1 Applications must support the authentication of individual users, not groups.

4.4.2 Applications must not store passwords in clear text or any easily reversible form.

4.4.3 Applications must provide some role management, such that one user can't take over the functions of another without having to know the other's password.

5. Policy Compliance

5.1   Compliance Measurement
The UNICORN RED teams will verify compliance to this policy through various methods, including but not limited to periodic walk-throughs, video monitoring, business tool reports, internal and external audits, and feedback to the policy owners.

5.2   Exception
The UNICORN RED team must approve any exception to the policy in advance.

5.3   Non-Compliance
An employee found to have violated this policy may be subject to disciplinary action, up to and including termination of employment.

ANNEX M – Incident Response Plan (IRP) [3.6.1-3.6.3]

DEFENSE BUSINESS SOLUTION System Incident Response Plan (IRP)

[DATE]

1. Specific References
   a. National Institute of Standards and Technology (NIST) Special Publication 800-61 Revision 2, *Computer Security Incident Handling Guide*, August 2012.

   b. National Institute of Standards and Technology (NIST) Special Publication 800-83 Rev 1, *Guide to Malware Incident Prevention and Handling for Desktops and Laptops*, July 2013.

   c. National Institute of Standards and Technology (NIST) Special Publication 800-86, *Guide to Integrating Forensic Techniques into Incident Response*, August 2006.

2. Introduction
This appendix addresses the Computer Incident Response and Handling Plan for the DEFENSE BUSINESS SOLUTION PROGRAM. This IRP should show those incident response issues as it applies to the DBS system and serve as a guide to help members identify incidents and then take the appropriate corrective measures when such incidents occur.

2.1 Background

   a. Unicorn Red Solutions has implemented a defense-in-depth strategy to ensure the availability, integrity, authentication, confidentiality, and non-repudiation of its information and information systems. This strategy is based on the concept that attacks forced to penetrate multiple protection layers are less likely to succeed. In addition to this layered approach, protection mechanisms are distributed among various locations, and each component of defense within the system provides an appropriate level of robustness. The objective of this strategy is risk management.

   b. An incident is an assessed occurrence having actual or potential adverse effects on an information system. This includes, but is not limited to, attempted entry, unauthorized entry, malicious code execution, or an information attack on an information system as indicated by categories.

3. Purpose
The purpose of this Incident Response Plan is to:
   a. Help personnel quickly and efficiently recover from security incidents. These guidelines reflect "lessons learned" from experience in responding to several security incidents over the past year. Following the procedures in these guidelines will adequately provide proven response measures.
   b. Minimize the loss or theft of information or disruption of critical computing services when incidents occur.

c. Guide the proper way to respond systematically to a security breach. Following the procedures in this document will increase the likelihood that personnel will carry out all necessary steps to handle an incident correctly.
d. Guide on protecting Information System (IS). As desirable as placing extremely high levels of defenses (e.g., special access controls) on all computing resources is impossible due to cost and other practical constraints. Being able to detect and recover from incidents quickly can, in many respects, be considered a protection strategy to supplement system and network protection measures.
e. Guide on using resources efficiently. Having both technical and managerial personnel respond to an incident requires a substantial amount of resources. These resources could be devoted to another mission if an incident were to be short-lived. Therefore, ending the incident as quickly as possible is a high priority so that resources can once again be expended on "normal" operations.

4. Scope
The guidelines contained herein contain necessary information about responding to incidents intended to be used independently of hardware platforms or operating systems. As such, this guide includes neither technically detailed information nor an *exhaustive* set of incident response procedures. This guide is intended to provide a quick, practical source of guidance on incident response.

5. Definitions
a. **Incident:** The term "incident" refers to an adverse event in an IS or network or the threat of the occurrence of such an event. Examples of incidents include unauthorized use of another user's account, unauthorized use of system privileges, and execution of malicious code that destroys data. Other adverse events include floods, fires, electrical outages, and excessive heat that cause system crashes. However, adverse events such as natural disasters and power-related disruptions are not within the scope of this guide. For this guide, therefore, the term "incident" refers to an adverse event that is related to the technical aspects of INFOSEC.

b. **Event:** An "event" is *any* observable occurrence in a system or network. Examples of events include the system boot sequence, a system crash, and packet flooding within a network. Events sometimes indicate that an incident is occurring. Events caused by human error (e.g., unintentionally deleting a critical directory and all files contained therein) are the most costly and disruptive.

c. **Types of Incidents:** The term "incident" encompasses the following general categories of adverse events:

1. **Malicious code attacks.** Malicious code attacks include attacks by programs such as viruses, Trojan horse programs, worms, and scripts used by crackers/hackers to gain privileges, capture passwords, or modify audit logs to exclude unauthorized activity. Malicious code is particularly troublesome in that it is typically written to masquerade as benign code and thus is often challenging to detect. Self-replicating malicious code such as viruses and worms can furthermore replicate rapidly, thereby making containment a challenging problem.

2. **Unauthorized access.** Unauthorized access encompasses a range of incidents from improperly logging into a user's account (e.g., when a hacker logs in to a legitimate

user's account) to unauthorized access to files and directories stored on a system or storage media by obtaining superuser privileges. Unauthorized access could also entail network data by planting an illegal "sniffer" program or device to capture all packets traversing the network at a point.

3. **Unauthorized utilization of services.** It is not necessary to access another user's account to perpetrate a system or network attack. An intruder can access information, plant Trojan horse programs, and so forth by misusing available services. Examples include using the Network File System (NFS) to mount the file system of a remote server machine, the VMS file access listener to transfer files without authorization, or inter-domain access mechanisms in Windows NT to access data and directories in another organization's domain.

4. **Disruption of service.** Users rely on services provided by network and computing services. Perpetrators and malicious code can disrupt these services in many ways, including erasing a critical program, "mail spamming" (flooding a user account with electronic mail), and altering system functionality by installing a Trojan horse program.

5. **Electronic Spillage.** Electronic Spillage (sometimes referred to as a compromise or unauthorized disclosure) is defined as "Information of a higher classification that is intentionally or inadvertently placed on machines or networks of a lower classification or less restrictive policy" (E.G., SCI Spillage onto TS, TS Spillage onto SECRET, SECRET onto UNCLAS, etc.).

6. **Misuse.** Misuse occurs when someone uses a computing system other than official purposes, such as when a legitimate user uses a government computer to store personal tax records.

7. **Espionage.** Espionage is stealing information to subvert the interests of a corporation or government. Many cases of unauthorized access to U. S. military systems during Operation Desert Storm and Operation Desert Shield were manifestations of espionage activity against the U.S. Government.

8. **Hoaxes.** Hoaxes occur when false information about incidents or vulnerabilities is spread. In early 1995, for example, several users with Internet access distributed information about a virus called the Good Times Virus, even though the virus did not exist.

6. Organizational Roles

Unicorn Red Solutions

a. **Security Organization.** The Program Manager and the Director are responsible for compliance with and implementing the Unicorn Red Solutions Information and Personnel Security Program.

b. **Security Personnel Duties and Responsibilities.**

a. **Facility Security Officer (FSO):**
All security matters shall be referred to as the FSO.-The FSO is responsible to the Director for the management of the Security Program. The following pertains to the various responsibilities of the FSO and the Alternate FSO.

-Serve as the principal advisor on all security program issues. Responsible to the Director for the management of the security program.

-Maintain applicable security directives, regulations, manuals, and guidelines to discharge duties adequately.

-Develop and maintain written security instructions.

-Ensure personnel who perform security duties are advised of changes in policies and procedures and aid in problem-solving.

-Provide classification management assistance when needed.

-Ensure classified material is appropriately accounted for, controlled, safeguarded, packaged, transmitted, and destroyed following governing directives and the need to know the rule is applied before disseminating material.

-Ensure continuous coordination with the Information System Security Manager (ISSM) and Information System Security Officer (ISSO) on all matters concerning information system (IS) security to ensure full compliance with applicable security directives.

b. **Assistant Facility Security Officer (AFSO).**

-Develop local instructions and procedures to support the protection of classified material and the Information Security Program.

-Conduct new employee basic security training within five days of individual reporting to duty.

-Conduct annual basic security training to assigned personnel.

-Process, maintain and issue badges.

-Coordinate with the ISSM on issues relating to IS security or reporting requirements.

-Provide support as warranted for security violations/incidents.

-Respond to alarms during duty hours as warranted.

-Ensure liaison with other security offices is conducted to obtain security education material. Ensure material or information is disseminated.

-Ensure personnel who perform security duties are kept abreast of changes in policies and procedures and aid in problem-solving.

c. **Information System Security Manager (ISSM):** The ISSM, designated in writing by the Program Manager duties include:

-Develop and maintain a formal IS Security Program.

-Implement and enforce IS security policies.

-Review/update all accreditation documentation and endorses those found to be acceptable.

-Oversee performance of all Information System Security Officers (ISSOs) to ensure they follow established information security policies and procedures.

-Ensure ISSOs receive the necessary technical and security training to carry out their duties.

-Ensure the development of system certification documentation by reviewing and endorsing such documentation and recommending action.

-Ensure approved procedures are in place for clearing, purging, declassifying, and releasing system memory, media, and output.
-Coordinate IS security inspections, tests, and reviews.
-Develop procedures for responding to system security incidents and for investigating and reporting
-Ensure proper protection or corrective measures are taken when an incident or vulnerability has been discovered within a system.

d. **Information System Security Officer (ISSO):** ISSOs are designated for each information system, and network ISSO duties include:

-Ensure systems are operational, maintained, and disposed of following internal security policies and practices outlined in the security plan.
-Ensure that all users have the requisite security clearance eligibility, authorization, and need-to-know, and are aware of their security responsibilities before granting access to the IS.
-Report all security-related incidents to the ISSM.
-Initiate, with the approval of the ISSM, protective or corrective measures when a security incident or vulnerability is discovered.
- Ensure that system recovery processes are monitored to ensure that security features and procedures are properly restored.
-Ensure all IS security-related documentation is current and accessible to duly authorized individuals.

Procedures for Responding to Incidents
The processes and procedures detailed in the Computer Security Incident Handling Guide, Guide to Malware Incident Prevention and Handling for Desktops and Laptops, and Guide to Integrating Forensic Techniques into Incident Response should be utilized for incident response activities. An Incident Handling Checklist and After-Action Report (AAR) are completed for each incident. Entry into the Incident log with information from the AAR is completed for each incident. The Incident log is a section in the IA Activity log binder located in the ISSM's office.

Stages of Responding to Incidents
There are at least five identifiable stages of response to an INFOSEC incident. They include preparation, identification, containment, eradication, and recovery. Knowing about each step facilitates responding more methodically (and thus efficiently) and helps users understand the process of responding better to deal with unexpected incidents.

Preparation
One of the most critical facets of responding to incidents is meeting *before* an incident occurs. Without adequate preparation, it is exceptionally likely that response efforts to an incident will be disorganized and that there will be considerable confusion among personnel. Practice accordingly limits the potential for damage by ensuring response actions are known and coordinated. Measures to be taken include:

- Establish and employ standard backup and recovery procedures. Regularly backing up systems and data helps ensure operational continuity. This practice also enables personnel to check the integrity of systems and data---to verify whether unauthorized changes have occurred by comparing files to the corresponding backups. Because recovery is often a complex process, establishing and following recovery procedures is also a critical part of the preparation process. Standardizing these procedures makes it

easier for *anyone* to perform them; during an emergency, someone not assigned to a system or network may be called on to complete recovery procedures.
- Provide training to personnel. A workshop on responding to incidents can be one of the most valuable ways to help staff at an organization learn how to handle incidents. Staff should also be required to participate in periodic mock incidents in which written incident response procedures are followed for simulated incidents.
- Obtain potentially helpful tools in advance. As explained in more detail, technical devices are often essential in successfully responding to an incident. Examples include virus detection and eradication tools, restoring mainframes and workstations, and incident detection tools. Order tools you project to be critical to incident handling efforts *now* because the procurement process can be time-consuming.
- Inform users whom they should contact. Have stickers made that display the telephone number of the organization's INFOSEC group that can assist in a malicious code incident? Ensure that a label is displayed visibly on every computer. Users report incidents more often and with minor delays when they know whom to call.

Identification
Identification involves determining whether an incident has occurred and if one has the nature of the incident. Identification begins typically after someone has noticed an anomaly in a system or network. Determining whether that anomaly is symptomatic of an incident is often tricky because apparent evidence of security incidents often turns out to indicate something less--- errors in system configuration or an application program, hardware failures, and, most commonly, user errors. Typical indications of security incidents include any or all the following:
- A system alarm or similar indication from an intrusion detection tool.
- Suspicious entries in system or network accounting (e.g., a UNIX user obtains root access without going through the typical sequence necessary to obtain this access).
- Accounting discrepancies (e.g., someone notices an 18-minute gap in the accounting log in which no entries whatsoever appear).
- Unsuccessful logon attempts.
- Unexplained, new user accounts.
- Unexplained new files or unfamiliar file names.
- Unexplained modifications to file lengths or dates, especially in system executable files.
- Unexplained attempts to write to system files or changes in system files.
- Unexplained modification or deletion of data.
- Denial of service or inability of one or more users to login to an account.
- System crashes.
- Poor system performance.
- Unauthorized operation of a program or sniffer device to capture network traffic.
- "Doorknob rattling" (e.g., using attack scanners, remote requests for information about systems or users, or social engineering attempts).
- Unusual usage time (remember, more security incidents occur during non-working hours than any other time).
- As indicated last time of usage of a user account does not correspond to the actual last time of use for that user.

- Unusual usage patterns (e.g., programs are being compiled in the account of a user who does not know how to program).

As soon as an incident is identified, notify the ISSM/ISSO so the process of containment can be initiated.

Containment
The first critical decision to be made during the containment stage is what to do with essential information or computing services. Work within the security staff to determine whether sensitive information should be left on the server or removed. Suppose the determination is made to take the data off, and the recovery process will take a great deal of time. In that case, it may be best to move critical computing services to another system on another network with considerably less chance of interruption.

The next decision concerns the operational status of the compromised system itself. Should this system be shut down entirely, disconnected from the network, or allowed to continue running in its normal operational status so that any activity on the system can be monitored? The answer depends on the type and magnitude of the incident. It is almost certainly best to quickly eradicate any viruses in a single virus incident without shutting the infected system down. If there is a reasonable chance that a perpetrator can be identified by letting a system continue to run as normal, risking some damage, disruption, or compromise of data may be advisable. Again, work within the security staff to reach a decision. Continue to follow proper reporting procedures during this phase of activity by keeping others informed of the status of efforts performed.

Eradication
Eradicating an incident entails removing the cause of the incident. In a virus incident, eradication requires removing the virus from all systems and media (e.g., disks), usually by virus eradication software. In the case of a network intrusion, eradication is more ambiguous. Network intrusions are best eradicated by bringing the perpetrators into legal custody and convicting them in a court of law. From a statistical viewpoint, however, the likelihood of obtaining a conviction is minimal. The network intruder(s) may instead terminate efforts to gain unauthorized access or temporarily discontinue an attack, then attack the same system several months later.

Recovery
Recovery means restoring a system to its regular mission status. In the case of relatively simple incidents (such as attempted but unsuccessful intrusions into systems), recovery requires only assurance that the incident did not in any way affect system software or data stored on the network. Recovery may require a complete restore operation from backups in complex incidents, such as malicious code planted by insiders. In this case, it is essential first to determine the integrity of the backup itself. Once the restore has been performed, it is also crucial to verify that the restore operation was successful and that the system is back to its normal condition.

Types of Attacks

Malicious Code Attacks
The following procedures will facilitate efforts to deal with malicious code incidents.
1. **Virus incidents:** A PC virus is a program that can make a copy of it and spread from PC to PC, usually without knowing it. Some viruses deliberately destroy documents or data files, and others can put messages on a screen or otherwise create a nuisance and interrupt the work environment. Viruses may be present in files, particularly software

(executable files) and Word files (documents and templates). They may also be present in the hidden system areas of disks (the partition sector of hard disks and the boot sector of floppy and hard disks). A virus may be present on disks that contain no files. Viruses are user-initiated and would pose virtually no threat if every user always followed sound procedures. All PC users should take precautions to detect viruses and prevent the spreading of viruses. A quick anti-virus strategy for all PCs might be: Provide users with training concerning how viruses work and the procedures that limit the spread of viruses.

- Prevention - Adopt good virus awareness habits for PC use.
- Beware of an E-mail message with a binary file attachment.
- Detection - Viruses can typically be detected using current antiviral software.
- Install a memory-resident virus checker to detect suspicious program activity.
- Cure – Immediately after a virus is detected, it should be eliminated.

If a user suspects that a virus may have infected a machine, a Virus scan should be run on the suspect machine. If a virus is detected, leave the computer on[8] and call technical support. Leave a quarantine sign on the computer screen to warn others not to use the computer. Do not attempt to eradicate the virus and restore the system without the assistance of a qualified technical support specialist. Be sure additionally that the virus is eradicated from all backup disks. Failure to clean backup drives is the primary cause of re-infections.

5. **Macro Viruses:** Macro viruses are a type of virus that uses an application's macro programming language to distribute themselves. Unlike previous viruses, macro viruses do not infect programs; but infect documents. The three (3) macro viruses that are the most widely recognized are the Word Prank Macro, the Concept virus, the DMV virus, and the Nuclear virus. The most dangerous viruses are passed through Word and Excel macros.

6. **Worms:** Worms are self-replicating codes that are self-contained (i.e., capable of operating without modifying any software). Worms are best noticed by looking at system processes. If an unfamiliar process (usually with an unusual name) is running and is consuming a large proportion of a system's processing capacity, a worm may have attacked the system. Worms also sometimes write unusual messages to users' displays to indicate their presence. Messages from unknown users that request users to copy E-mail messages to a file may also propagate worms. Worms generally propagate themselves over networks. As such, worms can spread quickly, so the system administrator or technical support specialist should be informed immediately if a worm is noticed.

7. **Trojan Horses:** Trojan horse programs are hidden programs, often with a mis-advertised purpose. Most malicious codes are a Trojan horse program in one way or another. A virus that disguises its presence then executes later is technically a Trojan horse program to some degree since the virus is hidden for part of its life cycle. Trojan horse programs are

---

1. Studies indicate that user's do far more damage to systems infected with viruses than the viruses themselves do. Leaving your computer on and calling technical support minimizes the threat of damage to your system. If the virus has "triggered," i.e., indicated its presence through some overt action such as writing a message on the screen, it will most likely have already destroyed files if it was programmed to do so. Turning your computer off at this point will, therefore, probably do no good anyway.

often designed to trick users into copying and executing them.

8. **Cracking utilities:** Cracking utilities are programs planted in systems by attackers for various purposes such as elevating privileges, obtaining passwords, disguising the attacker's presence, and so forth.

Cracker/Hacker Attacks

Crackers and hackers are unauthorized users who attempt to obtain unauthorized access to remote systems. Modem dial-in is another favorite way to crack systems. The nature of these attacks has, however, changed substantially over the last few years. Several years ago, crackers sat at a terminal entering commands, waiting to see what would happen, then came more commands. Today, however, most cracking attacks are automated and take only a few seconds. This makes identifying and responding to the intrusion more difficult. A study showed that less than one percent of the system administrators noticed the intrusions and reported it when a particular team penetrated their systems.

Protecting against a cracker/hacker attack is generally not an easy task. The best measures to adopt include always using a good (difficult-to-guess) password and setting file access permissions conservatively (e.g., so that the "world" cannot write to the home directory). System administrators should install password filters to prevent users from adopting easy-to-guess passwords and tools that check file integrity. A device becoming increasingly necessary because there are so many sniffer attacks is a one-time password tool. This tool provides a list of passwords, each of which is to be used with a login. This prevents any password from being used successfully more than once; if a perpetrator captures a password over the network as someone logs on remotely, that password will not work when the perpetrator enters it.

Crackers now generally use "cracking utilities" when they obtain or attempt to get unauthorized remote access to systems. Cracking utilities usually are different from conventional malicious code attacks in that most cracking services do not disrupt systems or destroy code[9]. Cracking utilities are typical "a means to an end"---obtaining access as a system administrator, modifying audit logs, etc. A checksum or crypto-checksum tool helps spot changes in files and is, therefore, valuable in detecting cracking utilities. Compute a checksum or crypto-checksum to use these tools simultaneously and then compare the results to the results obtained. If there is a difference and no readily available explanation, the integrity of the examined file may have been compromised. Remember, though, that saboteurs can modify a program to which they have access, so store the checksum/crypto-checksum programs offline and securely (e.g., on a write-locked disk stored in a safe) unless they are running.

Indications that a hacker has compromised a system include most of the symptoms of incidents listed earlier. There may be changes to directories and files, a displayed last time of login that was not the actual time of the previous login, finding that someone else is logged into an individual's account from another terminal, and inability to login to an account (often because someone has changed the password).

If these or other suspicious signs are noticed, the system administrator should be notified immediately. Be sure to avoid using E-mail because many crackers can read other individual's

---

[2]. In conventional malicious code attacks, removing the malicious code eradicates the incident. In a cracker/hacker attack, however, removing cracking utilities does not terminate the incident. Getting the cracker to cease the unauthorized activity is the conclusive step in terminating such an incident.

E-mail routinely. If a cracker is caught in the act of obtaining unauthorized access, the best course of action is to determine how much danger the attack poses promptly. If the attacker has received superuser access, is deleting or changing user files, or has access to a machine that supports critical Naval operations or contains sensitive data, the attack poses a severe threat. In this case, it is best to lock the cracker out of this system (by killing the processes the cracker has created). On the other hand, the cracker did not obtain superuser access and did not appear to damage or disrupt a system. In that case, it is often best to let the cracker continue to have access while authorities receive information necessary to catch and possibly prosecute the perpetrator.

A critical stage in cracker/hacker attacks is eradication. Because crackers frequently use cracking utilities, it is essential to ensure no cracking scripts remain on the system once the cracker's attack has ceased. Leaving some cracking utilities can allow the attacker easy re-entry and possibly superuser access if the hacker attacks the compromised system again sometime later. Be sure also to restore any file permissions and configuration settings that the cracker may have changed.

Another critical component of responding to cracker/hacker attacks is handling evidence that is gathered. System log printouts, copies of malicious code discovered in systems, backup tapes, and entries recorded in logbooks may conceivably be used as evidence against perpetrators.

Resolving cracker/hacker attacks is generally not easy. Not only are these attacks challenging to detect, but they also tend to be very short-lived, making them difficult to monitor and trace.

User-Detected Technical Vulnerabilities
Users have discovered most of the currently known technical vulnerabilities in applications and operating systems. These vulnerabilities are often identified as users attempt to run a program or change configurations. If a technical vulnerability is discovered that can be used to subvert system or network security, immediately document that vulnerability. Record the following:
- What is vulnerability?
- How vulnerability can defeat security mechanisms.
- How to exploit the vulnerability (including special conditions under which the vulnerability occurs).

After documenting the vulnerability, someone else in the organization should verify that the vulnerability exists. Then move the information up the reporting chain, as shown in the reporting chain diagram below.

Legal Procedures
This guide is not intended to provide detailed legal guidance. However, legal precedent dictates to avoid compromising the ability to prosecute perpetrators of computer crime that the following procedures should be adhered to.

Warning Banners
Every system should display a warning banner visible to all users who attempt to login to the system based on, FOR EXAMPLE, the DOD Memorandum "Policy on Use of Department of Defense (DOD) Information Systems Standard Consent Banner and User Agreement," dated 9 May 2008. The legally approved warning banner to be used is as follows:

"You are accessing a U.S. Government (USG) Information System (IS) that is provided for USG-authorized use only. By using this IS (which includes any device attached to this IS), you consent to the following conditions:

-The USG routinely intercepts and monitors communications on this IS for purposes including, but not limited to, penetration testing, COMSEC monitoring, network operations and defense, personnel misconduct (PM), law enforcement (LE), and counterintelligence (CI) investigations.

-At any time, the USG may inspect and seize data stored on this IS.
-Communications using, or data stored on, this IS being not private, are subject to routine monitoring, interception, and search, and may be disclosed or used for any USG authorized purpose.

-This IS including security measures (e.g., authentication and access controls) to protect
USG interests--not for your benefit or privacy.

-Notwithstanding the above, using this IS does not constitute consent to PM, LE, or CI investigative searching or monitoring of the content of privileged communications or work products related to personal representation or services by attorneys, psychotherapists, or clergy and their assistants. Such communications and work products are private and confidential. See User Agreement for details."

Audit Data
Another similar legal issue concerning monitoring systems and networks is the concerns around privacy. Reading audit logs is not considered an invasion of privacy. HOWEVER, the U.S. Department of Justice advises that capturing packets transmitted over networks, then reading those packets verbatim constitutes a possible violation of the Electronic Privacy Act. Therefore, one should not use sniffer devices and sniffer programs to monitor the content of messages transmitted over networks, nor should one use an intrusion detection tool that does the same. Using monitoring tools that determine what type of packet was sent, its source and destination, etc., is not problematic from a legal standpoint.

Evidence
Anything related in any way to an incident or possible incident is potentially a piece of evidence. As such, notes, audit logs and backups, copies of malicious code, and so forth are critical. Soon after (e.g., daily), new information is recorded in the logbook, take to the ISSM. The ISSM should copy each new page of the logbook, store the copy in a locked container, and provide a signed and dated receipt. Audit logs and other physical entities should be handled similarly. If these procedures are not followed, trial attorneys for the defense may argue that the evidence was fabricated successfully.

Reporting Procedures
Personnel is required to report incidents involving the loss or compromise or potential loss or compromise as soon as the incident becomes known. Unicorn Red personnel shall report all incidents to the prime contractor's PM.

Personnel will report computer network attacks to include incidents of computer virus attacks.

Individual Responsibility. It is personally incumbent upon all personnel to ensure no loss or compromise of sensitive data to include CUI, CUI, FCI, PII, PHI, etc., material occurs. All employees are obligated to report any known or suspected incident upon discovery. Those found guilty of the violation will be held fully accountable and may face both administrative and legal action depending on the severity of the incident.

Incident Handling Checklist

SOURCE: **Adapted from NIST SP 800-61, R2, August 2012**

		Action	Completed
		Detection and Analysis	
1.		Determine whether an incident has occurred	
	1.1	Analyze the precursors and indicators	
	1.2	Look for correlating information	
	1.3	Perform research (e.g., search engines, knowledge base)	
	1.4	As soon as the handler believes an incident has occurred, begin documenting the investigation and gathering evidence	
2.		Prioritize handling the incident based on the relevant factors (functional impact, information impact, recoverability effort, etc.)	
3.		Report the incident to the appropriate internal personnel and external organizations	
		Containment, Eradication, and Recovery	
4.		Acquire, preserve, secure, and document evidence	
5.		Contain the incident	
6.		Eradicate the incident	
	6.1	Identify and mitigate all vulnerabilities that were exploited	
	6.2	Remove malware, inappropriate materials, and other components	
	6.3	If more affected hosts are discovered (e.g., new malware infections), repeat the Detection and Analysis steps (1.1, 1.2) to identify all other affected hosts, then contain (5) and eradicate (6) the incident for them	
7.		Recover from the incident	
	7.1	Return affected systems to an operationally ready state	
	7.2	Confirm that the affected systems are functioning normally	
	7.3	If necessary, implement additional monitoring to look for future related activity	
		Post-Incident Activity	
8.		Create a follow-up report	
9.		Hold a lessons learned meeting (mandatory for major incidents, optional otherwise)	

After Action Report

Adapted from NIST SP 800-61, R2, August 2012

Contact Information for the Incident Handler
Name
Organizational unit
Email address
Phone number
Location
Incident number
Incident Category

Incident Response Checklist

AI #	ACTION ITEM	Person who performed action
	1.0 Detection and Analysis	
1.1	Prioritize the handling of the incident based on its business impact	
1.2	Identify which resources have been affected and forecast which resources will be affected	
1.3	Estimate the current and potential technical effect of the incident	
1.4	Find the appropriate cell(s) in the prioritization matrix, based on the technical effect and affected resources	
1.5	Report the incident to the appropriate internal personnel and external organizations	
	2.0 Containment, Eradication, and Recovery	
2.1	Contain the incident	
2.2	Identify infected systems	
2.3	Disconnect infected systems from the network	
2.4	Mitigate vulnerabilities that were exploited by the malicious code	
2.5	If necessary, block the transmission mechanisms for the malicious code	
2.6	Eradicate the incident	
2.7	Disinfect, quarantine, delete and replace infected files	
2.8	Mitigate the exploited vulnerabilities for other hosts within the organization	
2.9	Recover from the incident	
2.10	Confirm that the affected systems are functioning normally	
2.11	If necessary, implement additional monitoring to look for future related activity	
	3.0 Post-Incident Activity	
3.1	Create a follow-up report	
3.2	Hold a lessons-learned meeting	

Incident Details

Date/time (including time zone) when the incident was discovered.

Estimated date/time (including time zone) when the incident started.

Type of incident (e.g., denial of service, malicious code, unauthorized access, inappropriate usage).

The physical location of the incident (e.g., city, state).

Source/cause of the incident (if known), including hostnames and IP.

Description of the incident (e.g., how it was detected, what occurred).

Operating system, version, and patch.

Antivirus software installed, enabled, and current (yes/no).

Description of affected resources.

Mitigating factors.

Estimated technical impact of the incident (e.g., data deleted, the system crashed, application unavailable).

Response actions performed (e.g., shut off host, disconnected host from a network).

Other organizations contacted (e.g., software vendors).

If any PII was compromised during the incident, what type of PII.

Incident Handler Data Fields

Status of the incident:

Summary of the Incident:

Incident Handling Actions:

Incident Handler Comments:

Cause of the Incident:

Business Impact of the Incident:

Federal Agency Incident Categories

http://www.us-cert.gov/government-users/reporting-requirements.html

Category	Name	Description	Reporting Timeframe
CAT 0	Exercise/Network Defense Testing	This category is used during state, federal, national, international exercises and approved activity testing of internal/external network defenses or responses.	Not Applicable; this category is for each agency's internal use during exercises.
CAT 1	Unauthorized Access	In this category, an individual gains logical or physical access without permission to a federal agency network, system, application, data, or other resources	Within one (1) hour of discovery/detection.
CAT 2	Denial of Service (DoS)	An attack that *successfully* prevents or impairs the normal authorized functionality of networks, systems, or applications by exhausting resources. This activity includes being the victim or participating in the DoS.	Within two (2) hours of discovery/detection, if the successful attack is still ongoing and the agency cannot successfully mitigate the activity.
CAT 3	Malicious Code	*Successful* installation of malicious software (e.g., virus, worm, Trojan horse, or other code-based malicious entity) infects an operating system or application. Agencies are NOT required to report malicious logic that has been *successfully quarantined* by antivirus (AV) software.	Daily Note: Within one (1) hour of discovery/detection, if widespread across the agency.
CAT 4	Improper Usage	A person violates acceptable computing use policies.	Weekly
CAT 5	Scans/Probes/Attempted Access	This category includes any activity that seeks to access or identify a federal	Monthly Note: If the

		agency computer, open ports, protocols, service, or any combination for later exploit. This activity does not directly result in a compromise or denial of service.	system is classified, report within one (1) hour of discovery.
CAT 6	Investigation	*The reporting entity deemed unconfirmed incidents that are potentially malicious or anomalous activity to warrant further review.*	Not Applicable; this category is for each agency to categorize a potential incident currently being investigated.

Incident Response Testing and Exercises:

a. The testing and exercising of this plan will occur **annually**. Testing will respond to current threats and vulnerabilities, as seen in the operational environment, e.g., the introduction of malicious software, insider threat activities, etc.
b. The documentation of the results of testing will abide by this plan.
c. The effectiveness of incident response capabilities will be following this plan and a component of the After-Action activities.

Incident Response Refresher Training: This will occur in the direction of the Information Systems Security Manager (ISSM), typically, before testing and exercising this plan.

ANNEX N – Maintenance Procedures [3.7.1-3.7.5] – RESERVED

ANNEX O – Media Sanitization Procedures [3.8.3]

1.0 Purpose

The purpose of this policy is to outline the proper disposal/sanitization/destruction of CUI media (physical or electronic) for Unicorn Red Solutions. These rules are in place to protect sensitive information, employees, and Unicorn Red. Inappropriate disposal of information may put Unicorn Red Solutions at risk. All destruction will be IAW NARA rules and regulations regarding CUI destruction and sanitization measures.

2.0 Scope

This policy applies to all Unicorn Red employees, contractors, temporary staff, and other workers accessing Unicorn Red systems or data, sensitive information, and media. This policy applies to all equipment that processes, stores, or transmits Unicorn Red and sensitive owned or leased data.

3.0 Policy

When no longer usable, hard drives, diskettes, tape cartridges, CDs, ribbons, hard copies, printouts, and other similar items used to process, store or transmit CUI and classified and sensitive data shall be appropriately disposed of following measures established by Unicorn Red.

Physical media (printouts and other physical media) shall be disposed of by one of the following methods:

1) Shredded using Super_Fine_Cut issued cross-cut shredders.

2) Placed in locked shredding bins for Super_Fine_Cut to come on-site and cross-cut shred, witnessed by [agency name] personnel throughout the entire process.

3) Incineration using Super_Fine_Cut incinerators or witnessed by Super_Fine_Cut personnel onsite at an agency or contractor incineration site, if conducted by non-authorized staff.

4) Electronic media (hard-drives, tape cartridge, CDs, printer ribbons, flash drives, printer, and copier hard-drives, etc.) shall be disposed of by one of Unicorn Red methods:

    a. Overwriting (at least three times) - an effective method of clearing data from magnetic media. As the name implies, overwriting uses a program to write (1s, 0s, or a combination of both) onto the location of the media where the file to be sanitized is located.

    b. Degaussing - a method to magnetically erase data from magnetic media. Two types of degaussing exist strong magnets and electric degausses. Standard magnets (e.g., those used to hang a picture on a wall) are weak and cannot effectively degauss magnetic media.

    c. Destruction – a method of destroying magnetic media. As the name implies, the destruction of magnetic media is to physically dismantle by crushing, disassembling, etc., ensuring that the platters have been physically destroyed so that no data can be pulled.

IT systems that have been used to process, store, or transmit CUI or sensitive and classified information shall not be released from Unicorn Red's control until the equipment has been sanitized and all stored data has been cleared using one of the above methods.

4.0 Penalties

Any employee found to have violated this policy may be subject to disciplinary action, up to and including termination.

ANNEX P – Risk Assessment Procedure [3.11.1- 3.11.3]

Risk Assessments of the overall DBS system will occur annually upon the anniversary of the Full Operating Capability (FOC) declaration or as directed by the customer. The RA will result in an RA Report (RAR) due within 30-days of completion of the assessment. The results of that RAR will be reported to the CCB and customer during regular sessions of the CCB at a time proscribed.

Ad hoc RA may occur at the discretion of the CCB and customer to assess the overall impacts of Change Requests (CR). The assessors' findings deemed "security-relevant" will adhere *to the Risk Assessment Decision Process* (next page).

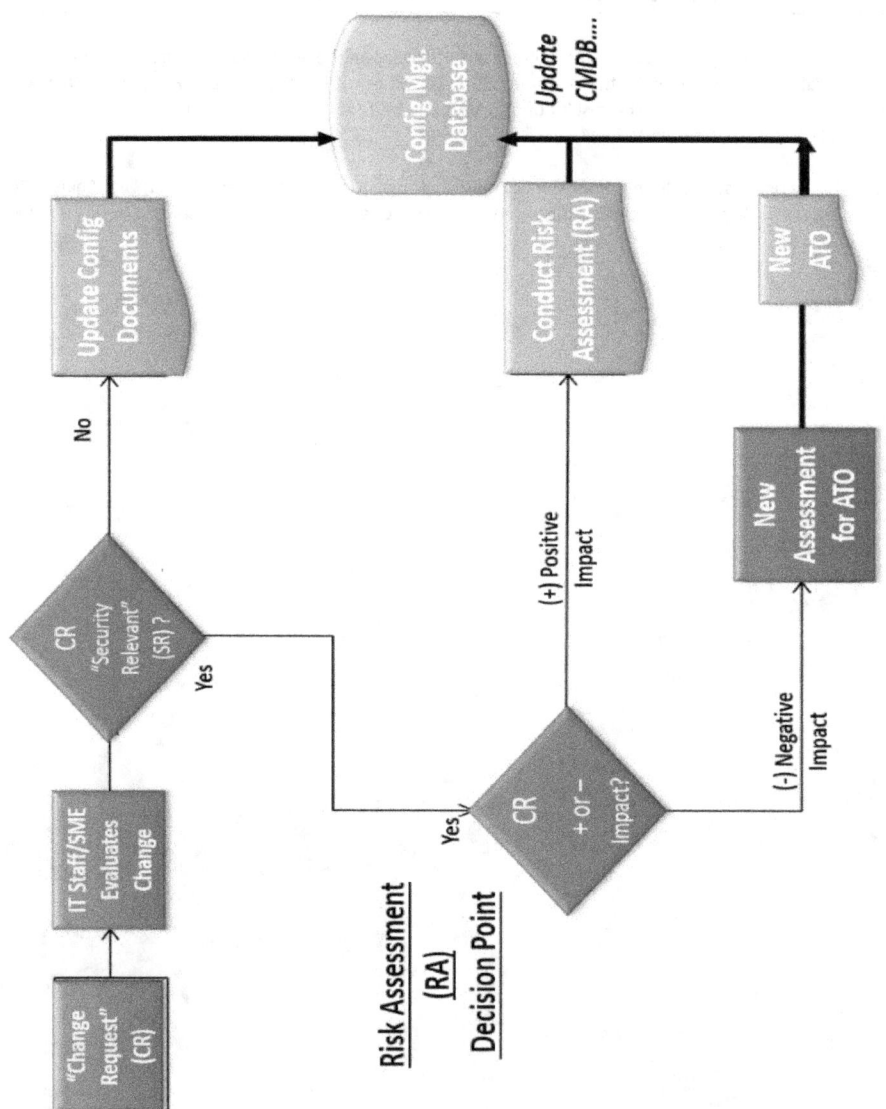

The Risk Assessment Decision Process

Risk Assessment Examples

The differences between a Security Risk Assessment (SRA), a Security Impact Assessment (SIA), and Security Assessment (SA) control.

- An SRA is specific to assessing a systems' security controls and recommendations to correct or mitigate those failed or failing controls. The SRA is part of the organization's corporate governance and risk management processes.

- An SIA is an overall assessment of changes or modifications as part of a formal change management/configuration control process.

- The SA control is about a process that re-assesses the state of all security controls and whether changes have occurred requiring additional mitigations due to new risks or threats to the system.

Example #1: Security Risk Assessment

THRU: Information Systems Security Officer
THRU: Information Systems Security Officer
FOR: System Owner
FROM: System Security Engineer

Executive Summary
A "Security Risk Assessment" SRA was completed on 27 April XXXX according to the Risk Management Framework (RMF) specific to Continuous Monitoring of changes to the DBS software baseline. The determination was that the artifacts provided demonstrated no relationship between functional software development and required secure software processes.

Specifically, NIST 800-53 controls RA-3, and SA-11 has failed the assessment.

Recommendations
- The deployment of the current DBS builds, 3.1, be placed on hold until the vendor can provide substantive evidence of adherence to its government-approved secure software development processes.
- That the **overall** DBS software build process is elevated to a categorization of HIGH RISK.
- Additional regulatory and contractual oversight is exercised, and any enforcing actions are pursued against the vendor-specific to its DODI 8510.01 and RMF responsibilities specific to Step 6 of the RMF process (Continuous Monitoring).

Analysis

Since November 2017, the DBS[10] IPT (Tier III governance), in coordination with DBS Cybersecurity, has sought to streamline and minimize the requirements for constant re-accreditation of current and future DBS baselines.

RMF affords, in general, such flexibilities under RMF controls RA-3 and SA-11 where no "security-relevant" changes have occurred to interim versions/baselines (See Attachment B for background). The agreed approach has been to "walk before running" and only seek a minimal level of affirmation or attestation that the vendor is meeting its approved secure software processes.

To date, the vendor has been dismissive in that pursuit and refuses to meet its regulatory requirements specific to DODI 8510.01.

Attachment A provides a complete review of the documentary evidence and has been assessed as *insufficient* according to the existing RMF ATO issued in 2017. Highlights of those findings include:

- It does not declare, identify, confirm, corroborate, or attest to the secure software development requirement to deliver the current build.
- Does not treat cybersecurity as an integral part of its software development process
- Inadequate to determine whether an assessor can evaluate the security of any software fixes specific to this build.
- There is no context or reference to adherence to secure development, predominantly functional fixes with insufficient information to correlate with any actual or assumed security supporting function or address any open POAM items against the AV.
- It does not identify (implicit or explicit) in terms of assuring that the software development process followed the vendor's established "Trusted Configuration Base."

Also noted was the lack of historical artifacts specific to current and past builds. That categorization would change when the vendor demonstrates current and past adherence to secure software development processes. The presumption is that the vendor has not provided evidence to JPO Cybersecurity to date, and that is the further rationale to place the DBS effort into a HIGH-RISK status.

Of note, the following information was discovered specific to the vendor's **Software Development Plan,** dated 28 September 20XX:

- Software Security, p. 131. "The process requirements for secure software development shall be adhered to and records maintained in the [Software Development Library] SDL as **evidence** [emphasis added] of process compliance. "

Since the vendor did not provide these outputs as part of this "Security Risk Assessment," an assessment of *insufficient* remains in effect. Without access or a reasonable representation of that information, this analysis must conclude there is no evidence to prove that the process was met. If that information is provided, the recommendation would be to place the development effort into a LOW-risk state.

Conclusion

---

[10] DBS is used only as a representational example for the purposes of this control.

The current state of the DBS build effort concerning cybersecurity should be placed in a temporary HIGH-RISK categorization. This categorization results from the vendor's refusal to abide by their regulatory obligations under DODI 8510.01 and RMF.

Example #2: Security Risk Assessment

THRU: Information Systems Security Officer
FOR: DBS IPT
FROM: Systems Security Engineer

Executive Summary
A Risk Analysis was completed on 15 February XXXX for the Backup subsystem. The static code review provided multiple artifacts to include the outputs from its preliminary and final reports. The final report identified near 100% correction (1 open warning) of any software coding weaknesses or vulnerabilities. Recommend approval.

Objective
- Recommend that Security Control Assessors (SCA) conduct a review of provided artifacts and approve and accept this Risk Assessment (RA) following DOD's Risk Management Framework (RMF) specific to the RA-3 control.
- Request approval from SCA's about the current effort to implement and create a formalized RA process supporting the DBS program.

Analysis
The prime contractor and its subcontractor completed an *excellent* "static code" review and artifacts demonstration per RMF Control SA-11. The artifacts provided should become the basis and archetype for any future Risk Assessment (RA) efforts. The quality of the work explicitly completed to the Backup subsystem should be used to develop a more defined RA process. The intent is to increase the security posture and help guide the prime contractor to meet policy and contractual requirements mandated IAW DODI 8510 and RMF (the JSIG).

1. Risk Assessment (RA) Background Information:
    a. Risk Assessments are required throughout the life of the system and are supposed to be updated as risks, and threats change against the specific system. These risks include version or build changes that occur during the normal process of maintaining and enhancing the readiness of the system to meet customer requirements.
    b. System changes are required to be reflected in an updated RA IAW RMF control: RA-3. This includes "… modifications to the information system or environment of operation (including the identification of new threats and vulnerabilities) or other conditions that may impact the security state of the system."
    c. A current process development effort is currently underway with **DBS** and its subsystems. The action requires some level of certainty of secure software development through formal artifacts provided by the developer.
    d. The following documents are considered candidates that address security in whole or part by the developer:
        i. Changes impacting TRUSTED SOFTWARE DEVELOPMENT BASE (TSDB) hardware/components. This should include some form of attestation (signed) artifact by senior software development/quality assurance leadership that such development is in conformance with the Government approved secure process.

ii. Completed Security Technical Implementation Guide (STIG) checklists for the APPLICATION SECURITY DEVELOPMENT STIG for all software. It should be signed and approved by Prime vendor senior software development/quality assurance leadership.

iii. Static code review of source code by government/industry-recognized tool. This should include, at a minimum, the final outputs from the tool to have an executive summary of findings and raw data subject to data rights limitations.

e. Backup Subsystem Software Risk Analysis:

i. The artifact/file, Code-Analysis-Preliminary-Findings-rpt.pdf (See Attachment 1 for a listing of all artifacts), dated 24 March XXXX, identified that the commercial static code analysis tool, CodeSonar ®, (See Attachment 2), was used. The 8-software code sub-modules identified 397 active warnings across 483 total files per submodule. Of concern for cybersecurity purposes are the buffer overruns and integer overflows; the findings and numbers were constant across all submodules.

ii. CodeSonar ® Analysis Report dated 30 June 2017, Code-Analysis-Final-rpt.pdf, identifies 0 active warnings after assuming coding updates were satisfactorily accomplished. In this report, the outputs were parsed based on files versus submodule but identified the file count of 483 in Table 1, Summary for Recent Analyses. There were 483 total files scanned.

iii. In the Final Certification Report, Final-Cert-Review-report.pdf, 15 November XXXX, all false positives were addressed, and only one final warning regarding "uninitialized variables" was identified in the file: oe_core_string.cxx. While uninitialized variables pose a security risk, associated mitigating protections would protect the DBS system from most outside cyber-attacks.

iv. Additionally, a Penetration Test was accomplished against CNI. While not required at the sub-system level, it demonstrates additional due diligence on the developer's part. The results of that effort appear acceptable.

v. Overall, it is reasonable to assume that all code functionality repairs, including high-interest security coding corrections, have been satisfactorily accomplished. Any risk to the Backup subsystem is suggested to be low.

f. (NOTE: The developer may provide additional information regarding this development effort's security processes and practices. They would be a supplement to this Risk Analysis and will be delivered separately, if available, NLT 22 February XXXX)

Conclusion

Request approval of a favorable RA for the **DBS** Backup sub-system.

Suggested specific files for review:

1. Code-Analysis-Preliminary-Findings.pdf
2. Code-Analysis-Final-rpt.pdf
3. SSOW-D1-53.pdf
4. System-Security-Plan-SSPFINAL-20XX1130.docx

5. Final-Cert-Review-report.pdf
6. Pentest-Preliminary-rpt.pdf
7. Pentest-Test-Results.pdf

ANNEX Q – Continuous Monitoring Procedure for NIST 800-171 Security Controls [3.12.1- 3.12.4]

The E-Government Act of 2002 (Public Law 107-347) recognized the importance of information security to the economic and national security interests of the United States. Title III of the E-Government Act, Federal Information Security Management Act of 2002 (FISMA), tasked the National Institute of Standards and Technology (NIST) with responsibilities for standards and guidelines, including the development of:

- Standards to be used by all Federal agencies and supporting contracted workforces to categorize all information and information systems collected or maintained by or on behalf of each agency based on the objectives of providing appropriate levels of information security according to a range of risk levels;
- Guidelines recommending the types of information and information systems to be included in each category; and
- There are minimum information security requirements (i.e., management, operational, and technical controls) for information and information systems in each such category.

Information system owners must select and implement a set of security controls from **NIST 800-171**. Once the controls are implemented and the system authorized to operate, they are monitored continuously under the provisions of the NCF, and every three years, the system undergoes a full reauthorization or, if approved, will comply with a continuous monitoring process. The results of continuous monitoring are reported to the system's Authorizing Official and the organization's Senior Agency Information Security Officer (SAISO) [OR OTHER NAMED, e.g., CISO, CIO, etc.]. The goal of continuous monitoring is to determine if the security controls in the information system continue to be effective over time and, ultimately, to maintain the system's authorization to operate.

The continuous monitoring process is part of Step 6, Monitor Security Controls, of the Risk Management Framework (RMF) defined by NIST. The purpose of this step in the RMF is to provide oversight and monitoring of the security controls in the information system on an ongoing basis and to inform the Authorizing Official when changes occur that may affect the security of the system. The activities in this step of the RMF, described in the Continuous Monitoring Plan, are performed continuously throughout the information system's life cycle. Re-authorization may be required because specific changes to the information system or because federal or agency policies require periodic re-authorization.

Purpose
The purpose of this plan is to document the approach used for continuous monitoring and assessing enabled security controls on the DBS System. This plan includes a listing of security controls to be evaluated, the methodology used to select the controls, the prioritization of the controls, and the frequency and method of assessing the controls. It describes how the selected security controls are to be monitored and assessed for compliance and effectiveness. It also specifies where the results of continuous monitoring are reported.

Scope
The scope of this Continuous Monitoring Plan is defined by the DBS System described in the overall security boundary, as found at Annex W.

Background
A critical aspect of the security authorization process is the post-authorization period involving the continuous monitoring of an information system's security controls (including common controls). Conducting a thorough point-

in-time assessment of the security controls in an organizational information system is a necessary but not sufficient condition to demonstrate security due diligence. Effective information security programs should also include a continuous monitoring program to check the status of subsets of the security controls in an information system on an ongoing basis. The ultimate objective of the continuous monitoring program is to determine if the security controls in the information system continue to be effective over time, given the inevitable changes that occur in the system hardware, software, firmware, or operational environment.

Continuous monitoring involves the participation of individuals in several organizational job roles. It depends on the following: (a) a comprehensive and robust configuration management process; (b) the ability to perform impact analysis of proposed changes to the information system; (c) the ongoing assessment of security controls, which may identify the need for remediation actions; and (d) the reporting of findings.

The continuous monitoring of security controls, as defined for the RMF, overlaps with "conventional" system performance monitoring and security monitoring that many organizations and system owners use to support operations and operational security. Many of the (existing or planned) system monitoring functions provided by automated tools or monitoring systems will support the continuous monitoring process defined by RMF.

Roles and Responsibilities for Continuous Monitoring
This section defines the roles and responsibilities of key personnel associated with the continuous monitoring of security for the DBS system.

The Authorizing Official has an approving role and shall:
- Approve the Continuous Monitoring Plan,
- Accept the residual risk of vulnerabilities found, when deemed appropriate,
- Approve the addition of vulnerabilities to the Plan of Action & Milestones (POAM),
- Approve closure of POAM items, or
- Conduct an Authorization Review for the system and determine whether reauthorization is required.

An Authorizing Official Designated Representative (AODR) may be designated to act on behalf of an Authorizing Official in carrying out and coordinating the required activities associated with security authorization. The AODR may perform the Authorizing Official duties except for making the authorization decision and signing the associated authorization decision document (i.e., the acceptance of risk to organizational operations and assets, individuals, and other organizations).

The Senior Agency Information Security Officer (SAISO) [OR LIKE SENIOR CYBERSECURITY POSITION] has responsibilities that assist in achieving compliance with the NCF. The SENIOR CYBERSECURITY POSITION] has a coordinating role in continuous monitoring and shall:

- Establish, implement, and maintain the organization's continuous monitoring program
- Develop organizational guidance for continuous monitoring of information systems
- Develop configuration guidance for the organization's information technologies
- Consolidate and analyze POAM to determine organizational security weaknesses and deficiencies
- Acquire/develop and maintain automated tools to support security authorization and continuous monitoring
- Provide training on the organization's continuous monitoring process
- Provide support to information owners/information system owners on how to develop and implement continuous monitoring strategies for their information systems, and
- Coordinate organizational common control providers (e.g., external service providers) to ensure that they apply required security controls, assess those controls and share the assessment results with the clients of the common controls (i.e., the system owners).

The Security Control Assessor (SCA) [AKA, AUDITOR, ASSESSOR, ETC.] shall:
- Participate in the development of the Continuous Monitoring Plan,
- Review the Continuous Monitoring Plan and approve for its submission,
- Assist the ISSO to ensure Continuous Monitoring activities are conducted,
- Conduct the assessment of security controls as defined in the Continuous Monitoring Plan,
- Update the Security Assessment Report (SAR) regularly with the continuous monitoring assessment results, and
- Assist the ISSO to ensure vulnerabilities discovered during the security controls assessment are either corrected or mitigated and that system risk is determined.

The Information System Security Officer (ISSO) monitors system security and supports other roles. The ISSO shall:
- Assist in the development of the Continuous Monitoring Plan,
- Approve the Continuous Monitoring Plan for submission to the Authorizing Official,
- Ensure Continuous Monitoring assessment is conducted, and
- Ensure that vulnerabilities discovered during the security controls assessment are either corrected or mitigated and tracked to closure and that system risk is determined,
- Assist the Information System Owner in updating the selection of security controls for the information system when events occur that indicate the baseline set of security controls is no longer adequate to protect the system.

The Information System Owner is responsible for the monitoring process and shall:
- Develop and document a continuous monitoring strategy for each information system with assistance from the ISSO and Security Control Assessor,
- With help from the ISSO and Security Control Assessor, assess risk as needed, such as when system/network/environment changes are proposed or implemented, or when new vulnerabilities are discovered,
- Document vulnerabilities and remediation of vulnerabilities,
- With assistance from the ISSO, update the selection of security controls for the information system when events occur that indicate the baseline set of security controls is no longer adequate to protect the system,
- Update authorization documentation package based on continuous monitoring results,
- Prepare and submit security status reports at the organization-defined frequency,
- Review reports from common control providers to verify that the common controls provide adequate protection for the information system.

Configuration Management

Documenting information system changes and evaluating the potential impact those changes may have on the system's security state is an essential aspect of continuous monitoring. Both continuous monitoring and CM should work harmoniously to ensure that the goals of each process are achieved. The CM process can benefit from constant system monitoring to ensure that the system is operating as intended. That implemented changes do not adversely impact either the performance or security posture of the system. One activity of continuous system monitoring is to perform configuration verification tests to ensure that the configuration for a given system has not been altered outside of the established CM process. In addition to configuration verification tests, agencies should also perform system audits. Both configuration verification tests and system audits entail an examination of characteristics of the system and supporting documentation to verify that the configuration meets user needs and to ensure the current design is the approved system configuration baseline.

It is essential to document the proposed or actual changes to the information system or its operational environment and subsequently determine the impact of those proposed or actual changes on the overall security state of the system. Information systems will typically be in a constant state of change with upgrades to hardware, software, or firmware and possible modifications to the surrounding environments where the systems reside.

Risk Assessment

A change to a system may introduce new vulnerabilities or may interfere with existing security controls. Therefore, an impact analysis should be conducted before system modifications to determine if there will be a significant impact on the system security posture caused by the changes. If the investigation reveals that there will be a substantial impact if the proposed change(s) is made, then additional analysis or testing of the modification may be required, or a security reauthorization may be warranted. If the changes do not significantly impact security status, then the changes should still be assessed (e.g., tested) before moving into production. Continuous monitoring testing priority should be given to controls that have changed.

The general steps of the security impact analysis are as follows:
- Understand the change in a system change request.
- Identify vulnerabilities that the proposed change may introduce.
- Assess risks to the information system, system users, and the organization's mission/business functions.
- Assess security controls impacted by the proposed change; for instance, there may be a cascade effect or interference on other security controls.
- Plan safeguards and countermeasures to the identified impacts; and
- Update critical security documentation to reflect the changes made to the information system.

When continuous monitoring identifies a potential problem that needs to be examined (for example, an intrusion prevention system (IPS) detects an attempted change to a data stream not defined in a threat signature database), the following items should be considered:
- Identify the impact on other security controls that the problem may be causing.
- Identify any inconsistency(ies) between security policy, procedures, and IT practices that the problem may have uncovered.

If such an examination indicates that a system must change, then the security impact analysis steps above must be followed. Once the impact analysis has validated the need for a change in the system, the system owner may consider doing the following:

- Determine the risk level of making the change.
- Identify the cost of an incident if a threat actor exploited the vulnerability.
- Identify the cost of mitigating a vulnerability.
- Identify any compensatory controls that may enhance and augment controls.

The results obtained during continuous monitoring should be considered concerning any necessary updates to the System Security Plan (SSP) and the POAM, since the Authorizing Official, Information System Owner, and Security Control Assessor will use these plans to guide future security assessment activities.

Continuous Monitoring

Continuous monitoring is not identical for all security controls, nor is it performed simultaneously or with the same frequency for all controls. The various activities of the ongoing continuous monitoring process may be executed in the following timeframes:

(1) Near real-time, which uses automated mechanisms such as a security operations center or Security Event Information Manager (SIEM) to process output from security "watchdog" components (e.g., firewall, IDS/IPS, security event monitors/security information monitors) and from security-aware system components (that may produce security-relevant notifications, audit records, or SYSLOG records), and to process audit trail data

from all sources. Results of this processing must be sent, at a minimum, to the designated point of contact (such as an operation center analyst) for further consideration.

(2) Periodic. This is the analysis of data collected at a predetermined frequency specified in the Continuous Monitoring Plan. Assessments of controls may require the collection and analysis of system operations data. The group of data and analysis for periodic monitoring may be facilitated (i.e., scheduled and executed) by an automated tool(s).

(3) On-demand or ad hoc as needed. Controls to be monitored on an on-demand basis should be listed in the set of controls identified. Data collection and analysis may be performed by any qualified individual or job role acceptable to the organization and system owner. The actual security control assessments should be completed by the Security Control Assessor, however. If the ISSO does not assist in data collection, analysis, or control assessments, the ISSO should also review the results.

Common security controls, which are not under the direct supervision of the system owner, system managers, and administrators, must be monitored similarly to the information system controls. They are outside the system's authorization boundary (e.g., external networks, facilities management offices, human resources offices, shared/external service providers). They may be controlled by a different part of the same organization or controlled by a foreign organization. They may be provided by an organizational infrastructure supporting the system. Common security controls inherited from other systems or connected networks need to be monitored, and the results of monitoring must be made available to the system owner. This monitoring is the responsibility of the common control provider and must be coordinated by the authorizing official and the organization's SAISO [SENIOR CYBERSECURITY LEADER] or other senior officials.

Assessment of Security Controls
The assessment of security controls is part of the ongoing continuous monitoring process.

Security controls may be assessed by manual techniques or automated or semi-automated mechanisms. Manual techniques consist of:

- Examination or inspection of system documentation, physical environment facilities, or system configuration data.
- Interviews with knowledgeable personnel; and
- Manual execution of system applications or software-implemented functions from a graphical user interface or an operating system command line.

Some of the controls of the Technical and Operational classes may be capable of being assessed in part by automated or semi-automated mechanisms that cause the controls to be executed, which test the controls—for example, implementing a software application or hardware appliance to analyze audit data tests the control to review and analyze audit data. Semi-automated mechanisms are typically manually invoked and execute a system function that implements a security control(s).

The system information collected during continuous monitoring, and the information collected by automated mechanisms, must be analyzed for the specific NCF security controls being monitored. The data collected may not map cleanly to individual security controls and may need to be (1) analyzed, (2) decomposed into a finer granularity of data, and then (3) further analyzed concerning the appropriate controls. For instance, collected audit data may be used to assess several Audit (AU) family controls.

Summary
The Monitoring Security Controls step of the RMF consists of four focus areas: (i) configuration management and control; (ii) risk or impact analysis; (iii) ongoing security control monitoring; and (iv) status reporting and documentation. In summary, an effective continuous monitoring program includes:

- Configuration management and control processes for the information system, including documenting changes to the information system, network, environment, or operational procedures,
- Security impact analysis on actual or proposed changes to the information system and operational environments,
- Assessment of selected security controls following predetermined priorities and frequencies specified in the Continuous Monitoring Plan,
- Security status reporting to appropriate organizational individuals,
- Active involvement by authorizing officials in the ongoing management of information system-related security risks, and
- Active participation of the system owner, information owner(s)/steward(s), and ISSO in the ongoing management and awareness of the security aspects of the information system and the information maintained on the network.

Security Controls Selection Process
The authorization process for an information system provides two essential elements for the continuous monitoring activity: (a) a required set of security controls that must be maintained, and (b) a set of known weaknesses that must be corrected or monitored (and documented in the POAM), which determines the level of controls assessment needed to evaluate the system security posture. These three elements can serve as a starting point for the selection of security controls to be monitored.

The controls currently identified in the POAM may be selected for monitoring because they are:
- Partially implemented or incomplete.
- Missing or not implemented due to one of the following reasons:
    - The risk-based decision[11], which means that the Authorizing Official has accepted the risk of not achieving all the security controls fully implemented.
    - New requirement for control because of (a) a risk assessment indicating new threat(s), system vulnerabilities, or organizational vulnerabilities or (b) newly discovered system vulnerabilities or deficiencies.
    - Compensated control mitigates risk by other means. The compensating control must be tracked and assessed concerning the control it replaces.
- It is deferred due to resource unavailability or technology constraints.

Also, controls identified in the POAM but resolved within the current year must be selected for monitoring.

The top priority for control monitoring should be directed at:
- The security controls that have the most significant potential for change after implementation (i.e., volatility) or
- The controls that have been implemented based on the organization's POAM for the information system, or
- Mitigating controls implemented due to a POAM item.

---

[11] In certain instances, the system may not have the technical capability to implement a security control or the system owner may make a risk-based decision not to implement a control based on the cost or feasibility of implementing the control relative to risk.

Security control volatility is a measure of how often control is likely to change during the system lifecycle. Some controls must be assessed more frequently because of frequent changes or other reasons, as described in this section. Instability may result from the need to apply software patches or to implement risk mitigations. More significant resources need to be used to security controls deemed to be of higher volatility. There is a higher return on investment for assessing security controls of this type.

In addition to the security controls selected based on the criteria above, security controls may be selected for Continuous Monitoring based on:

- Controls that have changed but did not warrant a complete system re-authorization, and
- Controls that were not tested for the previous one-year period of Continuous Monitoring activity.

With the concurrence of the Authorizing Official, the system owner and ISSO shall select and schedule continuous monitoring activities based on the factors presented above. The Authorizing Official and the SAISO or other senior officials must approve the selection of these controls. The Security Control Assessor is responsible for evaluating the effectiveness of the controls.

In the selection process, the system owner and ISSO shall ensure that the assessment subset that has been selected includes controls that meet the following guidelines:

- Selected controls should represent the managerial class, operational class, and technical class of security controls.
- Selected controls should represent each of the NCF security control families; and
- An organization-specified minimum number of controls should be assessed each year, such as at least 33% of the controls set for the information system.

Common security controls must also be continuously monitored, as explained in Table 1 presents the format of selected controls for continuous monitoring as presented in ATTACHMENT A.

Security Controls Monitoring
Each selected control should have a monitoring method identified for it. The process for each control may be specified in ATTACHMENT A. The methods for monitoring security controls may encompass manual techniques, automated system monitoring computer platforms, such as system/network management centers or consoles, and manually invoked tools, such as test tools and configuration management tools. For most of the Management and Operational classes of security controls defined in the NCF, the methods for monitoring them will be the same as those used for assessment for the initial authorization to operate. These methods are, for the most part, manual and consist of:

- Examination of the information system, network, organization, and common control providers' documentation.
- Interviews with key personnel who are familiar with the operation of the security control being evaluated; and
- Manual invocation of operational class controls for testing purposes by operating certain system functions or executing from an operating system command line.

It will be possible for the Technical class controls and some operational controls to use automated or semi-automated (manually invoked) mechanisms rather than manual methods to monitor their effectiveness. Several automated means are currently available and employed in information systems and networks that can provide the information needed to evaluate the effectiveness of many of the controls.

The outcome of continuous monitoring may be a need to remediate identified deficiencies or vulnerabilities in security control. Remediation involves changes to the system software or hardware, or operational procedures. All changes require that an impact analysis be performed to determine any impact on the system or organization. Proposed changes to the system must be submitted to the configuration management process. After remediation, additional controls may need to be monitored as well as the remedied control.

Analysis of Results of Continuous Monitoring
The system information collected during continuous monitoring, and the information collected by automated mechanisms, must be analyzed concerning the NCF security controls selected for monitoring. The data collected may not map cleanly to individual security controls and may need to be examined, decomposed into a finer granularity of data, and then further analyzed for the appropriate controls. Information analysis is typically performed using the assessment methods used for the initial controls assessment for the approval to operate.

Assessment of security controls shall represent an independent, qualitative, and objective assessment of the stated controls within the system's defined operational and security environment under review.

All security controls applicable to an information system and its environment must be assessed before the initial authorization, and subsets of controls must be re-assessed during each year of the authorization period. Security control assessment methods include:

(1) Examination includes:
   a. Information system and organization documentation, including security policy and procedures documents, system design and architecture documents and diagrams, system operations and administration manuals, and SSP.
   b. Observing System components hardware and cabling and through infrastructure and network-oriented diagrams.
   c. System settings by observing system configuration files and administration displays; and
   d. Physical environment,

(2) Interviews with key personnel to discuss concerns or questions developed during the document analysis and determine the extent of compliance with the security control(s) being assessed.

(3) Active security controls include testing (e.g., functional and penetration testing) and system operation and operational environment observation. When reporting the testing results through vulnerability or penetration testing, the system functions tested and published must be mapped into the appropriate security controls.

After the assessment, tentative changes to the system should be formulated, and an Impact Analysis performed on them. If the interim modifications or other variations (e.g., compensating controls) are implemented, a Risk Assessment should be undertaken. The risk will be assessed for each issue identified from continuous monitoring. An organization-defined procedure will track each discovered deficiency or vulnerability (e.g., by using a tool or approach that documents whether the item is open or closed, how it was resolved when it was resolved, and whether it required a POAM entry). The ISSO and Authorizing Official (or Authorizing Official Designated Representative) will review and approve the issues resolved and issues open and tracked.

UR will hold the final records for the assessment of continuous monitoring activities based on the Continuous Monitoring strategy. Approval of the Continuous Monitoring Plan acknowledges agreement with selected security controls and results from continuous monitoring activities. As stated above, the resolution of security control deficiencies identified will be approved via the organization's review and approval procedure. The System Assessment Report must also be updated, as described in the next section.

Reporting Results of Continuous Monitoring
[This section specifies where the results of Continuous Monitoring are documented and delivered.]
The results of continuous monitoring, including security controls assessments, impact analyses, risk analyses, and recommendations, are presented in the form of security status reports to the authorizing official and Agency senior managers by the system owner. Additionally, these reports may be sent to the ISSO, Information System Security Manager (ISSM), system administrator, system owner, organization/enterprise security officer or POC, organizational security function (e.g., help desk or incident response team), or repository of security issues. At a minimum, the security status report should summarize critical changes to the SSP, SAR, and POAM.

The results of security control re-assessments should be documented in the SAR. The results of continuous monitoring of common controls must also be included (or referenced) in the updated SAR produced during the system's continuous monitoring process. Common security controls implemented by the service provider (i.e., the owner of the system or network) that do not apply to the system do not need to be monitored or documented.

As the security authorization process becomes more dynamic, relying to a higher degree on the continuous monitoring aspects of the process, the ability to update the SAR frequently based on the assessment results of security controls from the Technical and Operational classes becomes a critical aspect of an organization's information security program. The essential information contained in the accreditation package (i.e., the SSP, the SAR, and the POAM) should be updated on an ongoing basis providing the authorizing official and senior Agency officials with a status of the security state of the information system.

With the use of automated support tools and effective organization-wide security program management practices, authorizing officials should be able to access the most current documentation in the authorization package at any time to determine the current security state of the information system, to help manage risk, and to provide essential information for reauthorization decisions.

Plan Approval
[This section provides the form for the signatures of approving authorities of this Continuous Monitoring Plan.]

Signatory Authority

This Continuous Monitoring Plan was prepared for exclusive use and in support of [COMPANY/ORGANIZATION]. This plan has been reviewed and approved, as indicated by the signatures below. Approval of this plan acknowledges agreement with selected security controls and results from any continuous monitoring activities captured within the [ORGANIZATION'S-IDENTIFIED TOOL OR REPOSITORY].

This document will be updated on an annual basis as part of continuous monitoring activities.

_____   _____
[NAME], Information System Security Officer   Date

_____   _____
[Name], Security Control Assessor   Date

_____   _____
[Name], Authorizing Official   Date
[Agency]

[A signature line may also be present for the Authorizing Official Designated Representative if applicable.]

ANNEX R – NIST 800-171 Compliance Checklist

ANNEX R will be used to select the 1/3 controls as part of active continuous monitoring activity.

Unicorn Red will reassess 1/3 of the security controls upon approval of Authority to Operate by the customer's designated Authorizing Official (AO).

The following controls will be assessed as follows:

Year 1: Controls 3.1.1 through 3.4.9
Year 2: Controls 3.5.1 through 3.9.2
Year 3: Controls 3.10.1 through 3.14.7

The following compliance checklist is intended to provide a guide to conduct a "self-assessment" of a cybersecurity posture as required by NIST 800-171.

*Assessment Method: Refer to NIST 800-171A, **Assessing Security Requirements for Controlled Unclassified Information**, which describes types and means to self-validate the control. The three assessment methods are examine, interview, and test.

Control #	Description	Assessment Method*	Document (e.g., SSP or Co. Procedure Guide)	Page #	Reviewed By	Validated By
Access Control (AC)						
3.1.1	**Limit information system access to authorized users, processes acting on behalf of authorized users, or devices (including other information systems)**					
3.1.1[a]	Authorized users are identified.					
3.1.1[b]	Processes acting on behalf of authorized users are identified.					
3.1.1[c]	Devices (and other systems) authorized to connect to the system are identified.					
3.1.1[d]	System access is limited to authorized users.					
3.1.1[e]	System access is limited to processes acting on behalf of authorized users.					
3.1.1[f]	System access is limited to authorized devices (including other systems).					
3.1.1[a]	Authorized users are identified.					
3.1.2	**Limit information system access to the types of transactions and functions that authorized users are permitted to execute**					
3.1.2[a]	The types of transactions and functions that authorized users are permitted to execute are defined.					
3.1.2[b]	System access is limited to the defined types of transactions and functions for authorized users.					
3.1.3	**Control the flow of CUI in accordance with approved authorizations**					
3.1.3[a]	Information flow control policies are defined.					
3.1.3[b]	Methods and enforcement mechanisms for controlling the flow of CUI are defined.					
3.1.3[c]	Designated sources and destinations (e.g., networks, individuals, and devices) for CUI within the system and between interconnected systems are identified.					

3.1.3[d]	Authorizations for controlling the flow of CUI are defined.	
3.1.3[e]	Approved authorizations for controlling the flow of CUI are enforced.	
3.1.4	**Separate the duties of individuals to reduce the risk of malevolent activity without collusion**	
3.1.4[a]	The duties of individuals requiring separation are defined.	
3.1.4[b]	Responsibilities for duties that require separation are assigned to separate individuals.	
3.1.4[c]	Access privileges that enable individuals to exercise the duties that require separation are granted to separate individuals.	
3.1.5	**Employ the principle of least privilege, including for specific security functions and privileged accounts**	
3.1.5[a]	Privileged accounts are identified.	
3.1.5[b]	Access to privileged accounts is authorized in accordance with the principle of least privilege.	
3.1.5[c]	Security functions are identified.	
3.1.5[d]	Access to security functions is authorized in accordance with the principle of least privilege.	
3.1.6	**Use non-privileged accounts or roles when accessing nonsecurity functions**	
3.1.6[a]	Nonsecurity functions are identified.	
3.1.6[b]	Users are required to use non-privileged accounts or roles when accessing nonsecurity functions.	
3.1.7	**Prevent non-privileged users from executing privileged functions and audit the execution of such functions**	
3.1.7[a]	Privileged functions are defined.	
3.1.7[b]	Non-privileged users are defined.	
3.1.7[c]	Non-privileged users are prevented from executing privileged functions.	
3.1.7[d]	The execution of privileged functions is captured in audit logs.	

3.1.8	**Limit unsuccessful logon attempts**	
3.1.8[a]	The means of limiting unsuccessful logon attempts is defined.	
3.1.8[b]	The defined means of limiting unsuccessful logon attempts is implemented.	
3.1.9	**Provide privacy and security notices consistent with applicable CUI rules**	
3.1.9[a]	Privacy and security notices required by CUI-specified rules are identified, consistent, and associated with the specific CUI category.	
3.1.9[b]	Privacy and security notices are displayed.	
3.1.10	**Use session lock with pattern-hiding displays to prevent access/viewing of data after period of inactivity**	
3.1.10[a]	The period of inactivity after which the system initiates a session lock is defined.	
3.1.10[b]	Access to the system and viewing of data is prevented by initiating a session lock after the defined period of inactivity.	
3.1.10[c]	Previously visible information is concealed via a pattern-hiding display after the defined period of inactivity.	
3.1.11	**Terminate (automatically) a user session after a defined condition**	
3.1.11[a]	Conditions requiring a user session to terminate are defined.	
3.1.11[b]	A user session is automatically terminated after any of the defined conditions occur.	

Control #	Description	Assessment Method*	Document (e.g., SSP or Co. Procedure Guide)	Page #	Reviewed By	Validated By
Access Control (AC)						
3.1.12	**Monitor and control remote access sessions**					
3.1.12[a]	Remote access sessions are permitted.					
3.1.12[b]	The types of permitted remote access are identified.					
3.1.12[c]	Remote access sessions are controlled.					
3.1.12[d]	Remote access sessions are monitored.					
3.1.13	**Employ cryptographic mechanisms to protect the confidentiality of remote access sessions**					
3.1.13[a]	Cryptographic mechanisms to protect the confidentiality of remote access sessions are identified.					
3.1.13[b]	Cryptographic mechanisms to protect the confidentiality of remote access sessions are implemented.					
3.1.14	**Route remote access via managed access control points**					
3.1.14[a]	Managed access control points are identified and implemented.					
3.1.14[b]	Remote access is routed through managed network access control points.					
3.1.15	**Authorize remote execution of privileged commands and remote access to security-relevant information**					
3.1.15[a]	Privileged commands authorized for remote execution are identified.					
3.1.15[b]	Security-relevant information authorized to be accessed remotely is identified.					
3.1.15[c]	The execution of the identified privileged commands via remote access is authorized.					
3.1.15[d]	Access to the identified security-relevant information via remote access is authorized.					

3.1.16	**Authorize wireless access prior to allowing such connections**	
3.1.16[a]	Wireless access points are identified.	
3.1.16[b]	Wireless access is authorized prior to allowing such connections.	
3.1.17	**Protect wireless access using authentication and encryption**	
3.1.17[a]	Wireless access to the system is protected using authentication.	
3.1.17[b]	Wireless access to the system is protected using encryption.	
3.1.18	**Control connection of mobile devices**	
3.1.18[a]	Mobile devices that process, store, or transmit CUI are identified.	
3.1.18[b]	Mobile device connections are authorized.	
3.1.18[c]	Mobile device connections are monitored and logged.	
3.1.19	**Encrypt CUI on mobile devices**	
3.1.19[a]	Mobile devices and mobile computing platforms that process, store, or transmit CUI are identified.	
3.1.19[b]	Encryption is employed to protect CUI on identified mobile devices and mobile computing platforms.	
3.1.20[a]	Connections to external systems are identified.	
3.1.20[b]	The use of external systems is identified.	
3.1.20[c]	Connections to external systems are verified.	
3.1.20[d]	The use of external systems is verified.	
3.1.20[e]	Connections to external systems are controlled/limited.	
3.1.20[f]	The use of external systems is controlled/limited.	
3.1.20[a]	Connections to external systems are identified.	
3.1.21	**Limit use of organizational portable storage devices on external systems**	
3.1.21[a]	The use of portable storage devices containing CUI on external systems is identified and documented.	

3.1.21[b]	Limits on the use of portable storage devices containing CUI on external systems are defined.	
3.1.21[c]	The use of portable storage devices containing CUI on external systems is limited as defined.	
3.1.22	**Control CUI posted or processed on publicly accessible systems**	
3.1.22[a]	Individuals authorized to post or process information on publicly accessible systems are identified.	
3.1.22[b]	Procedures to ensure CUI is not posted or processed on publicly accessible systems are identified.	
3.1.22[c]	A review process is in place prior to posting of any content to publicly accessible systems.	
3.1.22[d]	Content on publicly accessible systems is reviewed to ensure that it does not include CUI.	
3.1.22[e]	Mechanisms are in place to remove and address improper posting of CUI.	
3.1.22[a]	Individuals authorized to post or process information on publicly accessible systems are identified.	

Control #	Description	Assessment Method*	Document (e.g., SSP or Co. Procedure Guide)	Page #	Reviewed By	Validated By
Awareness & Training (AT)						
3.2.1	**Ensure that managers, systems administrators, and users of organizational information systems are made aware of the security risks associated with their activities and of the applicable policies, standards, and procedures related to the security of organizational information systems**					
3.2.1[a]	Security risks associated with organizational activities involving CUI are identified.					
3.2.1[b]	Policies, standards, and procedures related to the security of the system are identified.					
3.2.1[c]	Managers, systems administrators, and users of the system are made aware of the security risks associated with their activities.					
3.2.1[d]	Managers, systems administrators, and users of the system are made aware of the applicable policies, standards, and procedures related to the security of the system.					
3.2.2	**Ensure that organizational personnel are adequately trained to carry out their assigned information security-related duties and responsibilities**					
3.2.2[a]	Information security-related duties, roles, and responsibilities are defined.					
3.2.2[b]	Information security-related duties, roles, and responsibilities are assigned to designated personnel.					
3.2.2[c]	Personnel are adequately trained to carry out their assigned information security-related duties, roles, and responsibilities.					
3.2.3	**Provide security awareness training on recognizing and**					

	reporting potential indicators of insider threat
3.2.3[a]	Potential indicators associated with insider threats are identified.
3.2.3[b]	Security awareness training on recognizing and reporting potential indicators of insider threat is provided to managers and employees.

Control #	Description	Assessment Method*	Document (e.g., SSP or Co. Procedure Guide)	Page #	Reviewed By	Validated By
Audit & Accountability (AU)						
3.3.1	**Create, protect, and retain information system audit records to the extent needed to enable the monitoring, analysis, investigation, and reporting of unlawful, unauthorized, or inappropriate information system activity**					
3.3.1[a]	Audit logs needed (i.e., event types to be logged) to enable the monitoring, analysis, investigation, and reporting of unlawful or unauthorized system activity are specified.					
3.3.1[b]	The content of audit records needed to support monitoring, analysis, investigation, and reporting of unlawful or unauthorized system activity is defined.					
3.3.1[c]	Audit records are created (generated).					
3.3.1[d]	Audit records, once created, contain the defined content.					
3.3.1[e]	Retention requirements for audit records are defined.					
3.3.1[f]	Audit records are retained as defined.					
3.3.2	**Ensure that the actions of individual information system users can be uniquely traced to those users, so they can be held accountable for their actions**					
3.3.2[a]	The content of the audit records needed to support the ability to uniquely trace users to their actions is defined.					
3.3.2[b]	Audit records, once created, contain the defined content.					
3.3.3	**Review and update audited events**					
3.3.3[a]	A process for determining when to review logged events is defined.					

3.3.3[b]	Event types being logged are reviewed in accordance with the defined review process.	
3.3.3[c]	Event types being logged are updated based on the review.	
3.3.4	**Alert in the event of an audit process failure**	
3.3.4[a]	Personnel or roles to be alerted in the event of an audit logging process failure are identified.	
3.3.4[b]	Types of audit logging process failures for which alert will be generated are defined.	
3.3.4[c]	Identified personnel or roles are alerted in the event of an audit logging process failure.	
3.3.5	**Correlate audit review, analysis, and reporting processes for investigation and response to indications of inappropriate, suspicious, or unusual activity**	
3.3.5[a]	Audit record review, analysis, and reporting processes for investigation and response to indications of unlawful, unauthorized, suspicious, or unusual activity are defined.	
3.3.5[b]	Defined audit record review, analysis, and reporting processes are correlated.	
3.3.6	**Provide audit reduction and report generation to support on-demand analysis and reporting**	
3.3.6[a]	An audit record reduction capability that supports on-demand analysis is provided.	
3.3.6[b]	A report generation capability that supports on-demand reporting is provided.	
3.3.7	**Provide an information system capability that compares and synchronizes internal system clocks with an authoritative source to generate time stamps for audit records**	
3.3.7[a]	Internal system clocks are used to generate time stamps for audit records.	

3.3.7[b]	An authoritative source with which to compare and synchronize internal system clocks is specified.	
3.3.7[c]	Internal system clocks used to generate time stamps for audit records are compared to and synchronized with the specified authoritative time source.	
3.3.8	**Protect audit information and audit tools from unauthorized access, modification, and deletion**	
3.3.8[a]	Audit information is protected from unauthorized access.	
3.3.8[b]	Audit information is protected from unauthorized modification.	
3.3.8[c]	Audit information is protected from unauthorized deletion.	
3.3.8[d]	Audit logging tools are protected from unauthorized access.	
3.3.8[e]	Audit logging tools are protected from unauthorized modification.	
3.3.8[f]	Audit logging tools are protected from unauthorized deletion.	
3.3.9	**Limit management of audit functionality to a subset of privileged users**	
3.3.9[a]	A subset of privileged users granted access to manage audit logging functionality is defined.	
3.3.9[b]	Management of audit logging functionality is limited to the defined subset of privileged users.	

Control #	Description	Assessment Method*	Document (e.g., SSP or Co. Procedure Guide)	Page #	Reviewed By	Validated By
Configuration Management (CM)						
3.4.1	Establish and maintain baseline configurations and inventories of organizational information systems (including hardware, software, firmware, and documentation) throughout the respective system development life cycles					
3.4.1[a]	A baseline configuration is established.					
3.4.1[b]	The baseline configuration includes hardware, software, firmware, and documentation.					
3.4.1[c]	The baseline configuration is maintained (reviewed and updated) throughout the system development life cycle.					
3.4.1[d]	A system inventory is established.					
3.4.1[e]	The system inventory includes hardware, software, firmware, and documentation.					
3.4.1[f]	The inventory is maintained (reviewed and updated) throughout the system development life cycle.					
3.4.2	Establish and enforce security configuration settings for information technology products employed in organizational information systems					
3.4.2[a]	Security configuration settings for information technology products employed in the system are established and included in the baseline configuration.					
3.4.2[b]	Security configuration settings for information technology products employed in the system are enforced.					
3.4.3	Track, review, approve/disapprove, and audit					

		changes to information systems
	3.4.3[a]	Changes to the system are tracked.
	3.4.3[b]	Changes to the system are reviewed.
	3.4.3[c]	Changes to the system are approved or disapproved.
	3.4.3[d]	Changes to the system are logged.
3.4.4		Analyze the security impact of changes prior to implementation
3.4.5		Define, document, approve, and enforce physical and logical access restrictions associated with changes to the information system
	3.4.5[a]	Physical access restrictions associated with changes to the system are defined.
	3.4.5[b]	Physical access restrictions associated with changes to the system are documented.
	3.4.5[c]	Physical access restrictions associated with changes to the system are approved.
	3.4.5[d]	Physical access restrictions associated with changes to the system are enforced.
	3.4.5[e]	Logical access restrictions associated with changes to the system are defined.
	3.4.5[f]	Logical access restrictions associated with changes to the system are documented.
	3.4.5[g]	Logical access restrictions associated with changes to the system are approved.
	3.4.5[h]	Logical access restrictions associated with changes to the system are enforced.
3.4.6		Employ the principle of least functionality by configuring the information system to provide only essential capabilities

3.4.6[a]	Essential system capabilities are defined based on the principle of least functionality.	
3.4.6[b]	The system is configured to provide only the defined essential capabilities.	
3.4.7	**Restrict, disable, and prevent the use of nonessential programs, functions, ports, protocols, and services**	
3.4.7[a]	Essential programs are defined.	
3.4.7[b]	The use of nonessential programs is defined.	
3.4.7[c]	The use of nonessential programs is restricted, disabled, or prevented as defined.	
3.4.7[d]	Essential functions are defined.	
3.4.7[e]	The use of nonessential functions is defined.	
3.4.7[f]	The use of nonessential functions is restricted, disabled, or prevented as defined.	
3.4.7[g]	Essential ports are defined.	
3.4.7[h]	The use of nonessential ports is defined.	
3.4.7[i]	The use of nonessential ports is restricted, disabled, or prevented as defined.	
3.4.7[j]	Essential protocols are defined.	
3.4.7[k]	The use of nonessential protocols is defined.	
3.4.7[l]	The use of nonessential protocols is restricted, disabled, or prevented as defined.	
3.4.7[m]	Essential services are defined.	
3.4.7[n]	The use of nonessential services is defined.	
3.4.7[o]	The use of nonessential services is restricted, disabled, or prevented as defined.	
3.4.8	**Apply deny-by-exception (blacklist) policy to prevent the use of unauthorized software or deny all, permit-by-exception (whitelisting) policy**	

		to allow the execution of authorized software	
3.4.8[a]		A policy specifying whether whitelisting or blacklisting is to be implemented is specified.	
3.4.8[b]		The software allowed to execute under whitelisting or denied use under blacklisting is specified.	
3.4.8[c]		Whitelisting to allow the execution of authorized software or blacklisting to prevent the use of unauthorized software is implemented as specified.	
3.4.9		Control and monitor user-installed software	
3.4.9[a]		A policy for controlling the installation of software by users is established.	
3.4.9[b]		Installation of software by users is controlled based on the established policy.	
3.4.9[c]		Installation of software by users is monitored.	

Control #	Description	Assessment Method*	Document (e.g., SSP or Co. Procedure Guide)	Page #	Reviewed By	Validated By
Identification & Authentication (IA)						
3.5.1	**Identify information system users, processes acting on behalf of users, or devices**					
3.5.1[a]	System users are identified.					
3.5.1[b]	Processes acting on behalf of users are identified.					
3.5.1[c]	Devices accessing the system are identified.					
3.5.2	**Authenticate (or verify) the identities of those users, processes, or devices, as a prerequisite to allowing access to organizational information systems**					
3.5.2[a]	The identity of each user is authenticated or verified as a prerequisite to system access.					
3.5.2[b]	The identity of each process acting on behalf of a user is authenticated or verified as a prerequisite to system access.					
3.5.2[c]	The identity of each device accessing or connecting to the system is authenticated or verified as a prerequisite to system access.					
3.5.3	**Use multifactor authentication for local and network access to privileged accounts and for network access to non-privileged accounts**					
3.5.3[a]	Privileged accounts are identified.					
3.5.3[b]	Multifactor authentication is implemented for local access to privileged accounts.					
3.5.3[c]	Multifactor authentication is implemented for network access to privileged accounts.					
3.5.3[d]	Multifactor authentication is implemented for network access to non-privileged accounts.					

3.5.4	Employ replay-resistant authentication mechanisms for network access to privileged and nonprivileged accounts	
3.5.5	Prevent reuse of identifiers for a defined period	
3.5.5[a]	A period within which identifiers cannot be reused is defined.	
3.5.5[b]	Reuse of identifiers is prevented within the defined period.	
3.5.6	Disable identifiers after a defined period of inactivity	
3.5.6[a]	A period of inactivity after which an identifier is disabled is defined.	
3.5.6[b]	Identifiers are disabled after the defined period of inactivity.	
3.5.7	Enforce a minimum password complexity and change of characters when new passwords are created	
3.5.7[a]	Password complexity requirements are defined.	
3.5.7[b]	Password change of character requirements are defined.	
3.5.7[c]	Minimum password complexity requirements as defined are enforced when new passwords are created.	
3.5.7[d]	Minimum password change of character requirements as defined are enforced when new passwords are created.	
3.5.8	Prohibit password reuse for a specified number of generations	
3.5.8[a]	The number of generations during which a password cannot be reused is specified.	
3.5.8[b]	Reuse of passwords is prohibited during the specified number of generations.	
3.5.9	Allow temporary password use for system logons with an immediate change to a permanent password	

3.5.10	**Store and transmit only encrypted representation of passwords**	
3.5.10[a]	Passwords are cryptographically protected in storage.	
3.5.10[b]	Passwords are cryptographically protected in transit.	
3.5.11.	**Obscure feedback of authentication information**	

Control #	Description	Assessment Method*	Document (e.g., SSP or Co. Procedure Guide)	Page #	Reviewed By	Validated By
Incident Response (IR)						
3.6.1	**Establish an operational incident-handling capability for organizational information systems that includes adequate preparation, detection, analysis, containment, recovery, and user response activities**					
3.6.1[a]	An operational incident-handling capability is established.					
3.6.1[b]	The operational incident-handling capability includes preparation.					
3.6.1[c]	The operational incident-handling capability includes detection.					
3.6.1[d]	The operational incident-handling capability includes analysis.					
3.6.1[e]	The operational incident-handling capability includes containment.					
3.6.1[f]	The operational incident-handling capability includes recovery.					
3.6.1[g]	The operational incident-handling capability includes user response activities.					
3.6.2	**Track, document, and report incidents to appropriate officials and/or authorities both internal and external to the organization**					
3.6.2[a]	Incidents are tracked.					
3.6.2[b]	Incidents are documented.					
3.6.2[c]	Authorities to whom incidents are to be reported are identified.					
3.6.2[d]	Organizational officials to whom incidents are to be reported are identified.					
3.6.2[e]	Identified authorities are notified of incidents.					
3.6.2[f]	Identified organizational officials are notified of incidents.					

3.6.3 **Test the organizational incident response capability.**

Control #	Description	Assessment Method*	Document (e.g., SSP or Co. Procedure Guide)	Page #	Reviewed By	Validated By
Maintenance (MA)						
3.7.1	Perform maintenance on organizational information systems					
3.7.2	Provide effective controls on the tools, techniques, mechanisms, and personnel used to conduct information system maintenance					
3.7.2[a]	Tools used to conduct system maintenance are controlled.					
3.7.2[b]	Techniques used to conduct system maintenance are controlled.					
3.7.2[c]	Mechanisms used to conduct system maintenance are controlled.					
3.7.2[d]	Personnel used to conduct system maintenance are controlled.					
3.7.3	Ensure equipment removed for off-site maintenance is sanitized of any CUI					
3.7.4	Check media containing diagnostic and test programs for malicious code before the media are used in the information system					
3.7.5	Require multifactor authentication to establish nonlocal maintenance sessions via external network connections and terminate such connections when nonlocal maintenance is complete					
3.7.5[a]	Multifactor authentication is used to establish nonlocal maintenance sessions via external network connections.					
3.7.5[b]	Nonlocal maintenance sessions established via external network connections are terminated when nonlocal maintenance is complete.					

3.7.6	Supervise the maintenance activities of maintenance personnel without required access authorization.	

Control #	Description	Assessment Method*	Document (e.g., SSP or Co. Procedure Guide)	Page #	Reviewed By	Validated By
Media Protection (MP)						
3.8.1	**Protect (i.e., physically control and securely store) information system media containing CUI, both paper and digital**					
3.8.1[a]	Paper media containing CUI is physically controlled.					
3.8.1[b]	Digital media containing CUI is physically controlled.					
3.8.1[c]	Paper media containing CUI is securely stored.					
3.8.1[d]	Digital media containing CUI is securely stored.					
3.8.2	**Limit access to CUI on information system media to authorized users**					
3.8.3	**Sanitize or destroy information system media containing CUI before disposal or release for reuse**					
3.8.3[a]	System media containing CUI is sanitized or destroyed before disposal.					
3.8.3[b]	System media containing CUI is sanitized before it is released for reuse.					
3.8.4	**Mark media with necessary CUI markings and distribution limitations**					
3.8.4[a]	Media containing CUI is marked with applicable CUI markings.					
3.8.4[b]	Media containing CUI is marked with distribution limitations.					
3.8.5	**Control access to media containing CUI and maintain accountability for media during transport outside of controlled areas**					
3.8.5[a]	Access to media containing CUI is controlled.					
3.8.5[b]	Accountability for media containing CUI is maintained during transport outside of controlled areas.					

3.8.6	Implement cryptographic mechanisms to protect the confidentiality of CUI stored on digital media during transport unless otherwise protected by alternative physical safeguards
3.8.7	Control the use of removable media on information system components
3.8.8	Prohibit the use of portable storage devices when such devices have no identifiable owner
3.8.9	Protect the confidentiality of backup CUI at storage locations.

Control #	Description	Assessment Method*	Document (e.g., SSP or Co. Procedure Guide)	Page #	Reviewed By	Validated By
Personnel Security (PS)						
3.9.1	**Screen individuals prior to authorizing access to information systems containing CUI**					
3.9.2	**Ensure that CUI and information systems containing CUI are protected during and after personnel actions such as terminations and transfers**					
3.9.2[a]	A policy and/or process for terminating system access and any credentials coincident with personnel actions is established.					
3.9.2[b]	System access and credentials are terminated consistent with personnel actions such as termination or transfer.					
3.9.2[c]	The system is protected during and after personnel transfer actions.					

Control #	Description	Assessment Method*	Document (e.g., SSP or Co. Procedure Guide)	Page #	Reviewed By	Validated By
Physical Security (PP)						
3.10.1	**Limit physical access to organizational information systems, equipment, and the respective operating environments to authorized individuals**					
3.10.1[a]	Authorized individuals allowed physical access are identified.					
3.10.1[b]	Physical access to organizational systems is limited to authorized individuals.					
3.10.1[c]	Physical access to equipment is limited to authorized individuals.					
3.10.1[d]	Physical access to operating environments is limited to authorized individuals.					
3.10.2	**Protect and monitor the physical facility and support infrastructure for those information systems**					
3.10.2[a]	The physical facility where organizational systems reside is protected.					
3.10.2[b]	The support infrastructure for organizational systems is protected.					
3.10.2[c]	The physical facility where organizational systems reside is monitored.					
3.10.2[d]	The support infrastructure for organizational systems is monitored.					
3.10.3	**Escort visitors and monitor visitor activity**					
3.10.3[a]	Visitors are escorted.					
3.10.3[b]	Visitor activity is monitored.					
3.10.4	**Maintain audit logs of physical access**					
3.10.5	**Control and manage physical access devices**					
3.10.5[a]	Physical access devices are identified.					

3.10.5[b]	Physical access devices are controlled.	
3.10.5[c]	Physical access devices are managed.	
3.10.6	**Enforce safeguarding measures for CUI at alternate work sites (e.g., telework sites)**	
3.10.6[a]	Safeguarding measures for CUI are defined for alternate work sites.	
3.10.6[b]	Safeguarding measures for CUI are enforced for alternate work sites.	

Control #	Description	Assessment Method*	Document (e.g., SSP or Co. Procedure Guide)	Page #	Reviewed By	Validated By
Risk Assessments (RA)						
3.11.1	**Periodically assess the risk to organizational operations (including mission, functions, image, or reputation), organizational assets, and individuals, resulting from the operation of organizational information systems and the associated processing, storage, or transmission of CUI**					
3.11.1[a]	The frequency to assess risk to organizational operations, organizational assets, and individuals is defined.					
3.11.1[b]	Risk to organizational operations, organizational assets, and individuals resulting from the operation of an organizational system that processes, stores, or transmits CUI is assessed with the defined frequency.					
3.11.2	**Scan for vulnerabilities in the information system and applications periodically and when new vulnerabilities affecting the system are identified**					
3.11.2[a]	The frequency to scan for vulnerabilities in organizational systems and applications is defined.					
3.11.2[b]	Vulnerability scans are performed on organizational systems with the defined frequency.					
3.11.2[c]	Vulnerability scans are performed on applications with the defined frequency.					
3.11.2[d]	Vulnerability scans are performed on organizational systems when new vulnerabilities are identified.					

3.11.2[e]	Vulnerability scans are performed on applications when new vulnerabilities are identified.	
3.11.3	**Remediate vulnerabilities in accordance with assessments of risk**	
3.11.3[a]	Vulnerabilities are identified.	
3.11.3[b]	Vulnerabilities are remediated in accordance with risk assessments.	

Control #	Description	Assessment Method*	Document (e.g., SSP or Co. Procedure Guide)	Page #	Reviewed By	Validated By
Security Assessments (SA)						
3.12.1	Periodically assess the security controls in organizational information systems to determine if the controls are effective in their application					
3.12.1[a]	The frequency of security control assessments is defined.					
3.12.1[b]	Security controls are assessed with the defined frequency to determine if the controls are effective in their application.					
3.12.2	Develop and implement plans of action designed to correct deficiencies and reduce or eliminate vulnerabilities in organizational information systems					
3.12.2[a]	Deficiencies and vulnerabilities to be addressed by the plan of action are identified.					
3.12.2[b]	A plan of action is developed to correct identified deficiencies and reduce or eliminate identified vulnerabilities.					
3.12.2[c]	The plan of action is implemented to correct identified deficiencies and reduce or eliminate identified vulnerabilities.					
3.12.3	Monitor information system security controls on an ongoing basis to ensure the continued effectiveness of the controls					
3.12.4	Develop, document, and periodically update system security plans that describe system boundaries, system environments of operation, how security requirements are implemented, and the					

		relationships with or connections to other systems	
3.12.4[a]	A system security plan is developed.		
3.12.4[b]	The system boundary is described and documented in the system security plan.		
3.12.4[c]	The system environment of operation is described and documented in the system security plan.		
3.12.4[d]	The security requirements identified and approved by the designated authority as non-applicable are identified.		
3.12.4[e]	The method of security requirement implementation is described and documented in the system security plan.		
3.12.4[f]	The relationship with or connection to other systems is described and documented in the system security plan.		
3.12.4[g]	The frequency to update the system security plan is defined.		
3.12.4[h]	System security plan is updated with the defined frequency.		

Control #	Description	Assessment Method*	Document (e.g., SSP or Co. Procedure Guide)	Page #	Reviewed By	Validated By
System & Communications Protection (SC)						
3.13.1	**Monitor, control, and protect organizational communications (i.e., information transmitted or received by organizational information systems) at the external boundaries and key internal boundaries of the information systems**					
3.13.1[a]	The external system boundary is defined.					
3.13.1[b]	Key internal system boundaries are defined.					
3.13.1[c]	Communications are monitored at the external system boundary.					
3.13.1[d]	Communications are monitored at key internal boundaries.					
3.13.1[e]	Communications are controlled at the external system boundary.					
3.13.1[f]	Communications are controlled at key internal boundaries.					
3.13.1[g]	Communications are protected at the external system boundary.					
3.13.1[h]	Communications are protected at key internal boundaries.					
3.13.2	**Employ architectural designs, software development techniques, and systems engineering principles that promote effective information security within organizational information systems**					
3.13.2[a]	Architectural designs that promote effective information security are identified.					
3.13.2[b]	Software development techniques that promote effective information security are identified.					
3.13.2[c]	Systems engineering principles that promote effective information security are identified.					

3.13.2[d]	Identified architectural designs that promote effective information security are employed.	
3.13.2[e]	Identified software development techniques that promote effective information security are employed.	
3.13.2[f]	Identified systems engineering principles that promote effective information security are employed.	
3.13.3	**Separate user functionality from information system management functionality**	
3.13.3[a]	User functionality is identified.	
3.13.3[b]	System management functionality is identified.	
3.13.3[c]	User functionality is separated from system management functionality.	
3.13.4	**Prevent unauthorized and unintended information transfer via shared system resources**	
3.13.5	**Implement subnetworks for publicly accessible system components that are physically or logically separated from internal networks**	
3.13.5[a]	Publicly accessible system components are identified.	
3.13.5[b]	Subnetworks for publicly accessible system components are physically or logically separated from internal networks.	
3.13.6	**Deny network communications traffic by default and allow network communications traffic by exception (i.e., deny all, permit by exception)**	
3.13.6[a]	Network communications traffic is denied by default.	
3.13.6[b]	Network communications traffic is allowed by exception.	
3.13.7	**Prevent remote devices from simultaneously establishing non-remote connections with the information system and**	

communicating via some other connection to resources in external networks.

Control #	Description	Assessment Method*	Document (e.g., SSP or Co. Procedure Guide)	Page #	Reviewed By	Validated By
System & Communications Protection (SC)						
3.13.8	**Implement cryptographic mechanisms to prevent unauthorized disclosure of CUI during transmission unless otherwise protected by alternative physical safeguards**					
3.13.8[a]	Cryptographic mechanisms intended to prevent unauthorized disclosure of CUI are identified.					
3.13.8[b]	Alternative physical safeguards intended to prevent unauthorized disclosure of CUI are identified.					
3.13.8[c]	Either cryptographic mechanisms or alternative physical safeguards are implemented to prevent unauthorized disclosure of CUI during transmission.					
3.13.9	**Terminate network connections associated with communications sessions at the end of the sessions or after a defined period of inactivity**					
3.13.9[a]	A period of inactivity to terminate network connections associated with communications sessions is defined.					
3.13.9[b]	Network connections associated with communications sessions are terminated at the end of the sessions.					
3.13.9[c]	Network connections associated with communications sessions are terminated after the defined period of inactivity.					
3.13.10	**Establish and manage cryptographic keys for cryptography employed in the information system**					
3.13.10[a]	Cryptographic keys are established whenever cryptography is employed.					
3.13.10[b]	Cryptographic keys are managed whenever cryptography is employed.					

3.13.11	Employ FIPS-validated cryptography when used to protect the confidentiality of CUI	
3.13.12	Prohibit remote activation of collaborative computing devices and provide indication of devices in use to users present at the device	
3.13.12[a]	Collaborative computing devices are identified.	
3.13.12[b]	Collaborative computing devices provide indication to users of devices in use.	
3.13.12[c]	Remote activation of collaborative computing devices is prohibited.	
3.13.13	Control and monitor the use of mobile code	
3.13.13[a]	Use of mobile code is controlled.	
3.13.13[b]	Use of mobile code is monitored.	
3.13.14	Control and monitor the use of Voice over Internet Protocol (VoIP) technologies	
3.13.14[a]	Use of Voice over Internet Protocol (VoIP) technologies is controlled.	
3.13.14[b]	Use of Voice over Internet Protocol (VoIP) technologies is monitored.	
3.13.15	Protect the authenticity of communications sessions	
3.13.16	Protect the confidentiality of CUI at rest.	

Control #	Description	Assessment Method*	Document	Page #	Reviewed By	Validated By
System & Information Integrity (SI)						
3.14.1	**Identify, report, and correct information and information system flaws in a timely manner**					
3.14.1[a]	The time within which to identify system flaws is specified.					
3.14.1[b]	System flaws are identified within the specified time frame.					
3.14.1[c]	The time within which to report system flaws is specified.					
3.14.1[d]	System flaws are reported within the specified time frame.					
3.14.1[e]	The time within which to correct system flaws is specified.					
3.14.1[f]	System flaws are corrected within the specified time frame.					
3.14.2	**Provide protection from malicious code at appropriate locations within organizational information systems**					
3.14.2[a]	Designated locations for malicious code protection are identified.					
3.14.2[b]	Protection from malicious code at designated locations is provided.					
3.14.3	**Monitor information system security alerts and advisories and take appropriate actions in response**					
3.14.3[a]	Response actions to system security alerts and advisories are identified.					
3.14.3[b]	System security alerts and advisories are monitored.					
3.14.3[c]	Actions in response to system security alerts and advisories are taken.					
3.14.4	**Update malicious code protection mechanisms when new releases are available**					
3.14.5	**Perform periodic scans of the information system and real-time scans of files from**					

		external sources as files are downloaded, opened, or executed.
3.14.5[a]		The frequency for malicious code scans is defined.
3.14.5[b]		Malicious code scans are performed with the defined frequency.
3.14.5[c]		Real-time malicious code scans of files from external sources as files are downloaded, opened, or executed are performed.
3.14.6		**Monitor the information system including inbound and outbound communications traffic, to detect attacks and indicators of potential attacks**
3.14.6[a]		The system is monitored to detect attacks and indicators of potential attacks.
3.14.6[b]		Inbound communications traffic is monitored to detect attacks and indicators of potential attacks.
3.14.6[c]		Outbound communications traffic is monitored to detect attacks and indicators of potential attacks.
3.14.7		**Identify unauthorized use of the information system**
3.14.7[a]		Authorized use of the system is defined.
3.14.7[b]		Unauthorized use of the system is identified.

ANNEX S – Acceptable Encryption Policy

Purpose
The purpose of this policy is to provide guidance that limits the use of encryption to those algorithms that have received substantial public review and have been proven to work effectively. Additionally, this policy ensures that Federal regulations are followed, and legal authority is granted to disseminate and use encryption technologies outside of the United States.

Scope
This policy applies to all Unicorn Red Solutions employees and affiliates.

Policy

4.1 Algorithm Requirements

    4.1.1 Ciphers in use must meet or exceed the set defined as "AES-compatible" or "partially AES-compatible" according to the IETF/IRTF Cipher Catalog, or the set defined for use in the United States National Institute of Standards and Technology (NIST) publication FIPS 140-2, or any superseding documents according to the date of implementation. The use of the Advanced Encryption Standard (AES) is strongly recommended for symmetric encryption.

    4.1.2 Algorithms in use must meet the standards defined for use in NIST publication FIPS 140-2[12] or any superseding document, according to the date of implementation. The use of the RSA and Elliptic Curve Cryptography (ECC) algorithms is strongly recommended for asymmetric encryption.

    4.1.3 Signature Algorithms

Algorithm	Key Length (min)	Additional Comment
ECDSA	P-256	Cisco Legal recommends RFC6090 compliance to avoid patent infringement.
RSA	2048	Must use a secure padding scheme. PKCS#7 padding scheme is recommended. Message hashing required.
LDWM	SHA256	Refer to LDWM Hash-based Signatures Draft

4.2 Hash Function Requirements

---

[12] NOTE: FIPS 140-2 will expire in 2021 and be replaced by FIPS 140-3.

In general, Unicorn Red Solutions adheres to the NIST Policy on Hash Functions.

4.3 Key Agreement and Authentication

- **4.1.4** Key exchanges must use one of the following cryptographic protocols: Diffie-Hellman, IKE, or Elliptic curve Diffie-Hellman (ECDH).
- **4.1.5** Endpoints must be authenticated before the exchange or derivation of session keys.
- **4.1.6** Public keys used to establish trust must be authenticated before use. Examples of authentication include transmission via cryptographically signed messages or manual verification of the public key hash.
- **4.1.7** All servers used for authentication (for example, RADIUS or TACACS) must have installed a valid certificate signed by a known trusted provider.
- **4.1.8** All servers and applications using TLS must have the certificates signed by a known, trusted provider.

4.4 Key Generation

- **4.4.1** Cryptographic keys must be generated and stored securely that prevents loss, theft, or compromise.
- **4.4.2** Key generation must be seeded from an industry-standard random number generator (RNG). For examples, see NIST Annex C: Approved Random Number Generators for FIPS PUB 140-2.

Policy Compliance

5.1 Compliance Measurement
The Infosec team will verify compliance to this policy through various methods, including but not limited to business tool reports, internal and external audits, and feedback to the policy owner.

5,2 Exceptions
The Infosec team must approve any exception to the policy in advance.

5.3 Non-Compliance
An employee found to have violated this policy may be subject to disciplinary action, up to and including termination of employment.

Related Standards, Policies, and Processes

National Institute of Standards and Technology (NIST) publication FIPS 140-2,
NIST Policy on Hash Functions

Definitions and Terms

The following definition and terms can be found in the SANS Glossary located at:
https://www.sans.org/security-resources/glossary-of-terms/
- Proprietary Encryption

ANNEX T – Separation of Duties for System Security Administration and Auditing

1. PURPOSE
This document establishes an operational policy for separating duties among the personnel responsible for security administration, system administration, database administration, system operation, and auditing of Unicorn Red security management infrastructure.

2. BACKGROUND
Unicorn Red operates and maintains a complex, distributed security management infrastructure. The security management infrastructure encompasses server security (e.g., Windows and UNIX), database security (e.g., Oracle, DB2, and SQL), firewall security, router security, and other security devices maintained within the Unicorn Red network and infrastructures.

The control and management of Unicorn Red security management infrastructure necessitate separation of duties among the key administrative components, such as:
- System administration of the physical devices (including the operating systems and all components running under the operating systems);
- Database administration of development, test, and production database systems.
- Security administration of distributed security management devices; and
- Auditing of security management devices and administrative activities.

Separation of job duties and responsibilities ensures that no one person has the authority and the ability to circumvent routine checks and balances. Separation of duties can help prevent malicious actions from occurring and help catch those that do occur. For example, separating administrative tasks from auditing functions is necessary to avoid tampering with critical system log files.

3. SCOPE
This operational policy applies to all Unicorn Red infrastructure devices, systems, and databases controlled and operated by Unicorn Red or its designated IT Infrastructure Implementation Agent(s) or Contractor(s). This policy does not cover security devices, systems, and databases controlled and operated by other Unicorn Red contractors not previously designated.

4. OPERATIONAL POLICY
Separate and distinct responsibilities and privileges must be associated with particular security-relevant operations. However, security personnel must work closely with all system and database administration personnel to maximize system performance and security.

Security administration is an independent responsibility and shall not be assigned to a system/ application programmer, database administrator, system operator, or security auditor. Functions performed by security administrators shall be entirely separated from the tasks performed by system/application programmers, database administrators, system administrators, system operators, and security auditors.

Functions performed by security administrators shall be separated from the tasks performed by personnel charged with auditing the security of Unicorn Red infrastructure, systems, and databases to reduce the likelihood of fraudulent actions being taken, not detected, and/or not reported.

Security auditors shall have complete administrative control over all security audits and log files. These personnel, however, will not have the data-altering capability for security devices, security management devices, audit and security logs, or Unicorn Red infrastructure devices.

5. ROLES AND RESPONSIBILITIES
The following entities have responsibilities related to the implementation of this operational policy:

A - IT Infrastructure System Administrators
IT Infrastructure System Administrators are responsible for the following activities:

- Daily operation of the Unicorn Red data and security systems, including administration of infrastructure operating systems.
- Designing, testing, installing, maintaining, and upgrading Unicorn Red infrastructure devices (hardware and software);
- Performing setup and configuration of the audit system and security log files.
- Daily, ensuring that the system job that collects security and system log audit data from all Unicorn Red system devices are transferred to one of the following central collection points: Syslog Server, Nagios, or other defined collection point);
- Maintaining and generating reports and journals on all audit reviews.
- Configuring and scheduling daily audit log runs, including the backup of all security log data based on the current backup and archiving strategy.
- Restoring security audit data at the request of the Office of Information Services (OIS) / Information Technology Operations (UNICORN RED) Information System Security Officer (ISSO) or other security entities; and
- Reviewing system log and security audit files for anomalies daily and reporting all identified anomalies as appropriate.

B - IT Infrastructure Security Administrators
IT Infrastructure Security Administrators are responsible for the following activities:
- Managing all UNICORN RED distributed security management devices.
- Reviewing system logs and security audit files for anomalies daily, and reporting all identified anomalies as appropriate; and
- Maintaining and generating reports and journals on all audit reviews.

C - Unicorn Red Security Auditors
Unicorn Red Security Auditors are responsible for the following activities:

- Defining and maintaining procedures for auditing infrastructure and contractor-maintained systems and security management log and audit files.
- Performing continuous in-depth security audits and penetration tests on all Unicorn Red systems and infrastructure devices.
- Controlling access to all Unicorn Red security audit and log file systems and devices.
- Reviewing security audit logs on an ongoing basis ensures that security processes are followed and that security anomalies are identified, reported, and corrected.
- Ensuring that security log data are appropriately retained and archived.
- Maintaining and generating reports and journals on all audit reviews.
- Researching all identified security anomalies or vulnerabilities, and generating associated CAPs as appropriate; and
- Recording all security audit findings and maintaining their associated CAPs in the CISS Database.

6. EFFECTIVE DATES

This operational policy becomes effective when the Unicorn Red Chief Information Officer (CIO) signs it and remains in effect until officially superseded or canceled by the CIO.

7. INFORMATION AND ASSISTANCE

Contact the Director of the Information Technology Operations (UNICORN RED) for further information regarding this operational policy.

8. APPROVED

ANNEX U – Incident Response Procedures

Purpose
The purpose of this Procedure is to provide step-by-step instructions for responding to an actual or suspected compromise of Unicorn Red computing resources.

Applies To
This Procedure applies to anyone using Unicorn Red computing resources that suspects that the security or privacy of these resources has been compromised. This procedure also applies to situations with no compromise, but someone suspects their computing resources are actively being attacked. This Procedure does not apply to computing resources owned by employees.

Definitions
A *Compromised Computer* is defined as any computing resource whose confidentiality, integrity, or availability has been adversely impacted by an untrusted source, either intentionally or unintentionally. A compromise can occur either through manual interaction by the untrusted source or through automation. Gaining unauthorized access to a computer by impersonating a legitimate user or conducting a brute-force attack would constitute a compromise. Exploiting a loophole in a computer's configuration would also include a compromise. Depending on the circumstances, a computer infected with a virus, worm, trojan, or other malicious software may be considered a compromise. If the malicious software is detected and removed by antivirus software promptly, it is probably not necessary to follow this process. Some level of judgment will need to be used in these situations. Symptoms of a Compromised Computer include, but are not limited to, the following:

- The computer is experiencing unexpected and unexplainable disk activity
- The computer is experiencing random and inexplicable performance degradation
- The computer's logs (e.g., system logs, application logs, etc.) contain suspicious entries that indicate repeated login failures or connections to unfamiliar services
- A complaint is received from a third party regarding suspicious activity originating from the computer

Non-public Information is defined as any information classified as Private or Restricted information according to the Guidelines for Data Classification.

Personally, Identifiable Information is a subset of Non-public Information defined by various state and federal regulations. Examples of Personally Identifiable Information include, but at not limited to, social security numbers, driver's license numbers, health information, and certain types of financial account information.

Regulatory Requirements
Various state and federal regulations require unicorn Red to investigate any incident that may involve the breach of personally identifiable information. Unicorn Red is also required to notify an individual if the privacy of their personally identifiable information has been breached. Failure to preserve evidence or investigate a compromised computer could result in unnecessary financial costs for the institution. It is also essential that the details of a compromise and the ensuing investigation remain confidential. All communications related to a compromise should be coordinated with the Information Security Office and the Office of General Counsel. Any contact with law enforcement should be immediately referred to or authorized by the Office of General Counsel.

Procedure

The following steps should be taken to respond to an actual or suspected compromised computer:

1. **Disconnect the computer from the network**
   Disconnecting the computer from the network prevents a potentially untrusted source from taking further actions on the compromised computer. This also prevents any further leakage of non-public information if that is a potential concern. Shutting down the computer would also have this effect but could destroy evidence essential to investigating the compromise. Similarly, rebuilding the computer would destroy all evidence pertinent to an investigation.

2. **Contact the Information Security Office**
   Before taking any additional action on the compromised computer, the Information System Security Office should be contacted. Continuing to use the compromised computer or attempting to investigate the compromise could result in the destruction of evidence pertinent to an investigation. The Information Security Office can be contacted by phone at **123-555-2044** or by email at XXXXX. If the ISSO is unavailable to take your call, emergency contact information will be provided in the voice message.

3. **Notify users of the computer, if any, of a temporary service interruption**
   Suppose the compromised computer provides some service. In that case, users of this service will likely be impacted by the interruption brought on by disconnecting the computer from the network. These users should be notified in some manner of the interruption. Options for notification may include emailing the user base or posting a notice to a frequently visited website. As stated previously, the details of a compromise and the ensuing investigation should be kept confidential. Therefore, the notification of service interruption should not indicate that there has been a compromise.

4. **Preserve any log information not resident on the compromised computer**
   All log files about a compromised computer stored on a secondary computer or external media should be preserved immediately. Preservation may include making a copy of the log files and burning them to a CD. If there is no immediate risk of the logs being deleted or overwritten, this step can occur following Step 5. Log files stored locally on the compromised computer will be collected as part of a forensic investigation coordinated by the Information Security Office. This will help ensure that no evidence is destroyed or altered during the collection process.

5. **Wait for further instructions from the Information Security Office**
   The Information Security Office will conduct some preliminary investigation before determining the best course of action for the Compromised Computer. While waiting for further instructions, do not share any details related to the compromise unless necessary. Additionally, do not attempt to contact law enforcement officials. Such communication must be coordinated with the Information Security Office and the Office of General Counsel due to the potential legal implications of a compromised computer.

Additional Information

If you have any questions or comments related to this Procedure, please email Unicorn Red Information Security Office at XXXXX.

Additional information can also be found using the following resource(s):
- Information Security Policy
  http://www.cmu.edu/iso/governance/policies/information-security.html
- Information Security Roles and Responsibilities
  http://www.cmu.edu/iso/governance/roles/

- Guidelines for Data Classification http://www.cmu.edu/iso/governance/guidelines/data-classification.html
- Guidelines for Data Protection http://www.cmu.edu/iso/governance/guidelines/data-protection/

ANNEX V – Disaster Recovery Procedures

Overview
Since disasters happen so rarely, management often ignores the disaster recovery planning process. It is essential to realize that having a contingency plan in the event of a disaster gives Unicorn Red a competitive advantage. This policy requires management to support and diligently attend to disaster contingency planning efforts financially. Disasters are not limited to adverse weather conditions. Any event that could likely cause an extended delay of service should be considered. The Disaster Recovery Plan is often part of the Business Continuity Plan.

Purpose
This policy defines the requirement for a baseline disaster recovery plan to be developed and implemented by Unicorn Red that will describe the process to recover IT Systems, Applications, and Data from any disaster that causes a significant outage.

Scope
This policy is directed to the IT Management Staff, who ensures the plan is developed, tested, and kept up to date. This policy is sole to state the requirement to have a disaster recovery plan. It does not provide requirements around what goes into the plan or sub-plans.

Policy
4.1 Contingency Plans
The following contingency plans must be created:
- Computer Emergency Response Plan: Who is to be contacted, when, and how? What must immediate actions be taken in the event of certain occurrences?
- Succession Plan: Describe the flow of responsibility when normal staff is unavailable to perform their duties.
- Data Study: Detail the data stored on the systems, its criticality, and its confidentiality.
- Criticality of Service List: List all the services provided and their order of importance.
- It also explains the order of recovery in both short-term and long-term timeframes.
- Data Backup and Restoration Plan: Detail which data is backed up, the media to which it is saved, where that media is stored, and how often the backup is done. It should also describe how that data could be recovered.
- Equipment Replacement Plan: Describe what equipment is required to begin to provide services, list the order in which it is necessary, and note where to purchase the equipment.
- Mass Media Management: Who oversees giving information to the mass media?
- Also, provide some guidelines on what data is appropriate to be provided.

After creating the plans, it is essential to practice them to the extent possible. Management should set aside time to test the implementation of the disaster recovery plan. Tabletop exercises should be conducted annually. During these tests, issues that may cause the plan to fail can be discovered and corrected in an environment with few consequences.

The plan, at a minimum, should be reviewed and updated on an annual basis.

Policy   Compliance

Compliance Measurement
The IT Ops team will verify compliance to this policy through various methods, including but not limited to periodic walk-throughs, video monitoring, business tool reports, internal and external audits, and feedback to the policy owner.

Exceptions
The IT Ops must approve any exception to the policy in advance.

Non-Compliance
An employee found to have violated this policy may be subject to disciplinary action, up to and including termination of employment.

Related Standards, Policies, and Processes
None.

Definitions and Terms
N/A

ANNEX W – DEFENSE BUSINESS SOLUTION Architecture Documents (as of Jan 30, 20xx)

1. **Architecture Diagrams (Security Boundary)**

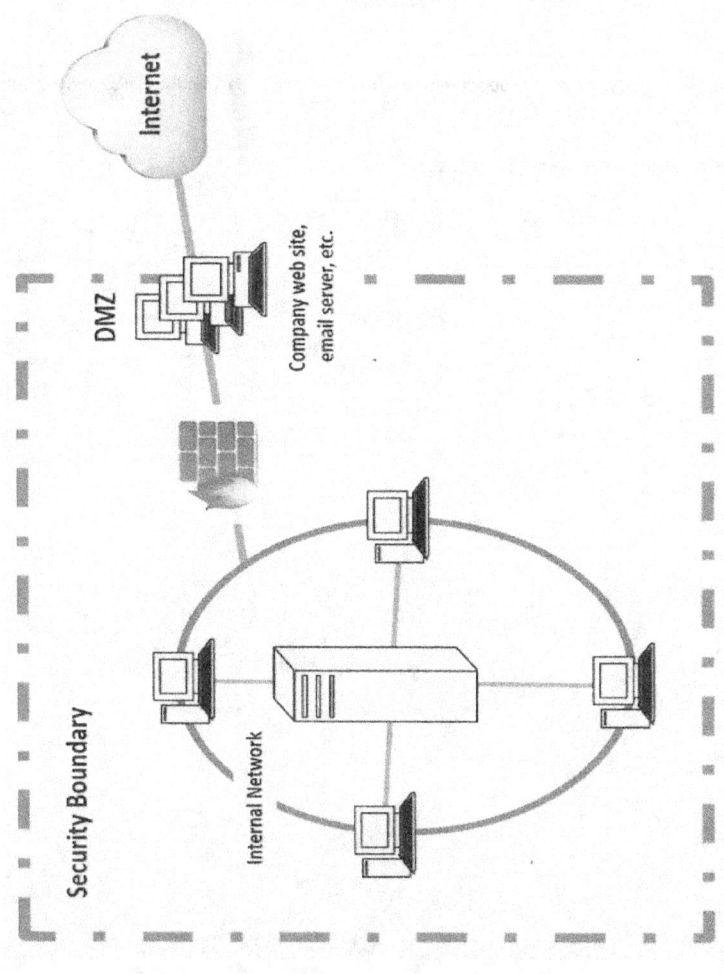

SIMPLIFIED NETWORK TOPOLOGY DIAGRAM

Overall Security Boundary

Sub-Security Segments

Security Segments to include Cloud Providers

2. Hardware Listing (PLACE HARDWARE LISTING HERE)

3. Software Listing(PLACE SOFTWARE LISTING HERE)

ANNEX X – Preliminary Security Assessment Report (July 20XX)

This report documents critical observations, findings, and mitigations of the *DBS* application, while under development. This is a supplemental report to the vulnerability assessment and other security assessments yet to be conducted against the platform. The testing has been conducted on the *DBS* test environment (test.blind-moto.net) in parallel with development. A full vulnerability assessment of the capability should be performed on the final version before deployment.

Section 1: Initial overview of the web application

Passive observation of the *DBS* web application without supplying user credentials or attempting to interact with the site allowed access to all of the JavaScript files that run the platform. The main.js and styles.js files revealed sensitive information about the capability, including (but not limited to) references to "DBS" project name, 'SMS,' 'SMS messages,' 'Phone number,' 'voicemail,' 'voicemail alert,' 'SMS alert,' 'assigned functions,' user management settings and parameters, vendor references ('NCS'), and local directory paths (c:\users\...\...\...), etc.

Initial Mitigation: An IP address whitelist was created to disallow non-whitelisted IPs to reach the landing page of the *DBS* application. This may suffice for a short-term mitigation strategy but is ultimately not recommended for a long-term solution by itself.

Section 2: Web application IP allocation [observation]

IP addresses of this capability are dynamically assigned by the provider (Zeta Internet Services ZIS). During one of the testing phases, the following IP address assignments were observed:

test.blin.net has address 19.86.280.32
test.blin.net has address 19.86.2380.33
test.blin.net has address 19.86.2308.74
test.blin.net has address 19.86.2380.xx

Section 3: Web application security headers

The following security headers were found to be not present or not set in the *DBS* web application:
- X-Frame-Options header is not included in the HTTP response to protect against 'ClickJacking' attacks.
- The cache-control and pragma HTTP header have not been set correctly or are missing allowing the browser and proxies to cache content.
- Web Browser XSS Protection is not enabled or disabled by configuring the 'X-XSS-Protection' HTTP response header.
- The Anti-MIME-Sniffing header X-Content-Type-Options was not set to 'nosniff.'

Mitigation: The headers were successfully set to deter these issues in the *DBS* application.

Section 4: Ports and services [observation]

The following ports and running services were observed on the *DBS* application:

```
PORT     STATE    SERVICE   VERSION
80/tcp   open     http      Zeta Internet Services CloudFront httpd
|_http-server-header: Front
|_http-title: ERROR: The request could not be satisfied
443/tcp  open     ssl/https Front
|_http-server-header: Front
|_http-title: ERROR: The request could not be satisfied
3306/tcp filtered mydbm
```

Section 5: *DBS* application hierarchy

The following assets to the *DBS* web application were observable and reachable during testing:

https://test.blind-moto.net
https://test.blind-moto.net/assets
https://test.blind-moto.net/assets/DBS_icon.ico
https://test.blind-moto.net/env.js
https://test.blind-moto.net/es2015-polyfills.7e65c9559769cd8b8.js
https://test.blind-moto.net/main.7e2b7ed3f05bc513.js
https://test.blind-moto.net/polyfills.ac7dc07fb27dfe0e.js
https://test.blind-moto.net/robots.txt
https://test.blind-moto.net/runtime.2620bfa8dc87a77c.js
https://test.blind-moto.net/sitemap.xml
https://test.blind-moto.net/styles.833a5c8d2070.css

This does not include out-of-scope assets (e.g., bootstrap, googleapis, etc.)

Some JavaScript files (env.js, main.7e2b7ed3f8e913.js) can be read or obtained without authentication with a simple GET request or via a web browser. These files reveal sensitive information related to the capability (see Section 1).

<u>Initial Mitigation</u>: An IP address whitelist was created to disallow non-whitelisted IPs to reach the landing page of the *DBS* application. This may suffice for a short-term mitigation strategy but is ultimately not recommended for a long-term solution by itself.

Section 6: Man-in-the-Middle (MitM) attack on DBS application

The *DBS* web application is susceptible to a MitM attack. By presenting the DBS application with a fake certificate, traffic between the web application/servers can be intercepted, captured, and observed.

```
{"username":"test.manager1","timestamp":15625387310,"action":"test.manager1 successful login"}
HTTP/1.1 200 OK
Content-Type: application/json; charset=utf-8
Content-Length: 32
Connection: close
Date: Tue, 09 Jul 20XX 15:16:41 GMT
x-zis-RequestId: 8a20b3-a25c-1e9-80f4-3dd3
```

```
access-control-allow-origin: *
access-control-allow-headers: Origin, X-Requested-With, Content-Type, Accept
x-zis-Remapped-content-length: 20
x-zis-Remapped-connection: close
x-zis-apigw-id: ckBppGpMFWeQ=
etag: W/"14-Y53wuE/mmbSikKcT/WualL1N65U"
x-powered-by: Express
X-Zs-Trace-Id: Root=1-5d24afd7-52494a6f0542b7c40;Sampled=0
x-zis-Remapped-date: Tue, 09 Jul 2019 15:16:41 GMT
X-Cache: Miss from cloudfront
Via: 1.1 443f14332247174145b9ac2efe4.ront.net (CloudFront)
X-Zis-Cf-Pop: IAD89-C2
X-Zis-Cf-Id: AxL3MWXwEZZNw5tRQ0o4m4kypR8awBY8qWfyyVjLGk391PQuA==

{"status":"success"}
```

Initial mitigation: Since the *DBS* application is using an IP whitelist, this may offer a short-term solution to this issue. Certificate validation/Certification pinning may be a consideration to provide a more robust solution to prevent MitM attacks against the service.

Further testing would be required to determine if exploitation, such as replay attacks, token sidejacking, etc., is possible.

Section 7: TLS 1.2 observed in network traffic [observation]

During passive network capture, the TLS v1.2 protocol was observed during all communication to the *DBS* application.

ANNEX Y – CUI Marking, Handling & Storage Guide

CONTROLLED UNCLASSIFIED INFORMATION (CUI)/ CRITICAL DEFENSE INFORMATION (CUI) MARKING, HANDLING & STORAGE GUIDE

Defense Business Solution System v1.0

[DATE]

PREPARED BY: _____, ISSO/ISSE

APPROVED BY: _____, Program Manager (PENDING)

Proper Marking, Handling, and Storage of CUI

Proper markings alert information holders to the presence of CUI. Markings ensure that CUI is identified and the information is appropriately marked for protection. They alert CUI holders to any dissemination and safeguarding control requirements.

Introduction

This information involves privacy, security, proprietary, and law enforcement-related information. Before implementation of a Controlled Unclassified Information (CUI)/Controlled Defense Information (CUI) Program, organizations have employed ad hoc, agency-specific policies, procedures, and markings to safeguard and control such information. This was highly inefficient and confusing. Subsequent guidance resulted in inconsistent marking and safeguarding of documents, leading to unclear or unnecessarily restrictive dissemination policies.

Specifically, a CUI Program standardizes how the Executive branch handles unclassified information[13] that does not meet the criteria required for classification under E.O. 13526, "Classified National Security Information," December 29, 2009, or the Atomic Energy Act. Such information must be protected based upon law, regulation, or government-wide policy. Protections involve the safeguards employed while this information is stored or handled by the Executive branch departments or its subordinate agencies and includes all contractors and sub-contractors supporting federal contracts.

Companies, businesses, organizations, agencies, and employees must review their organization's policy before marking any CUI or CUI. The handling of CUI must be per **E.O. 13556, "Controlled Unclassified Information," November 4, 2010**, 32 CFR Part 2002 (this link provides a full version https://www.govinfo.gov/content/pkg/CFR-2017-title32-vol6/pdf/CFR-2017-title32-vol6-part2002.pdf). This guide contains direction on what each marking is, where and

---

[13] While the Legislative and Judicial Branch should defer to the Executive Branch for all matters regarding national security protections and markings, it cannot be guaranteed for vendors working with the other two branches of the US government.

how to apply it, and which items are mandatory or optional based on government (primary) and Unicorn Red security policy (secondary). Supplemental guidance will be published by the government's overall CUI Executive Agent (EA), the National Archive and Records Administration (NARA).

Security markings and safeguarding are a significant part of successfully applying NIST 800-171. This guide delineates how to mark forms of written and electronic media to protect sensitive CUI. **Unicorn Red Solutions** and its employees are responsible for safeguarding all designated information. They are accountable for any administrative, civil, or criminal implications of failing to care for this information correctly.

For the Defense Business Solution System, data created in support of operations will be marked at CONTROLLED DEFENSE INFORMATION (CUI). They will follow the customer's Security Classification Guide (SCG) or like approved security direction.

CUI Banner Markings (Reference 32 CFR 2002.20(b))

Banner markings are necessary header and footer designations alerting individuals with a need-to-know the mandatory restrictions to protect the information. Individuals should see banner markings to ensure maximum protection if the information is exposed or inadvertently visible to unauthorized individuals. The following is a list of basic knowledge required by **Unicorn Red** personnel supporting **Defense Business Solution** and vendors and sub-contractors.

- The initial marking for all CUI is the CUI Banner Marking. This is the central marking that appears at the top and bottom of each page of any document that contains CUI.

- This marking is MANDATORY for all documents containing CUI. The content of the CUI Banner Marking must be inclusive of all CUI within the document and must be the same on each page.

- The Banner Marking should appear as bold capitalized black text and be centered. It will be at least **four (4) sizes larger** than the base font used in the document (recommended fonts include Times New Roman or Arial at 12-point font) for visual prominence.

- The CUI Banner Marking may include up to three elements:
    1. The CUI Control Marking (mandatory) will consist of either the word "CONTROLLED" or the acronym "CUI."
    2. CUI Category or Subcategory Markings (mandatory for CUI-Specified). These are separated from the CUI Control Marking by a double forward-slash (//). When including multiple categories or subcategories in a Banner Marking, they must be alphabetized and separated by a single forward-slash (/).
    3. A double forward-slash precedes Limited Dissemination (LIMDIS) Control Markings (//) to separate them from the rest of the CUI Banner Marking. *(LIMDIS is currently not approved for use as of the publication of this guide.)*

    A sample CUI Banner Marking:

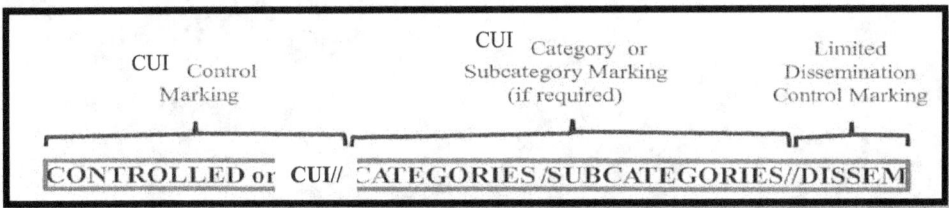

*The above example uses the words "CATEGORIES" and "SUBCATEGORIES" as substitutes for CUI Category or Subcategory Markings and the word "DISSEM" as a substitute for Limited Dissemination Control Marking. Consult the CUI Registry for actual markings.

 The CUI Registry – What do you need to know?

The CUI Registry provides the primary guidance for the proper marking, handling, and storage of information, NOT national security information; this includes confidential, secret, and top secret. While the CUI Registry is discussed throughout this guide, it only provides the basis of security of information created to support this effort. Overall, the customer, their respective Security Classification Guide (SCG), and Unicorn Red Solutions' security policies will contribute to the overall security and protection of the Defense

Business Solution system in that priority order. Questions should be referred to the Unicorn Red Program Manager, Security Officer, or Information Security Officer.

The CUI Registry may be found at https://www.archives.gov/cui/registry/category-list

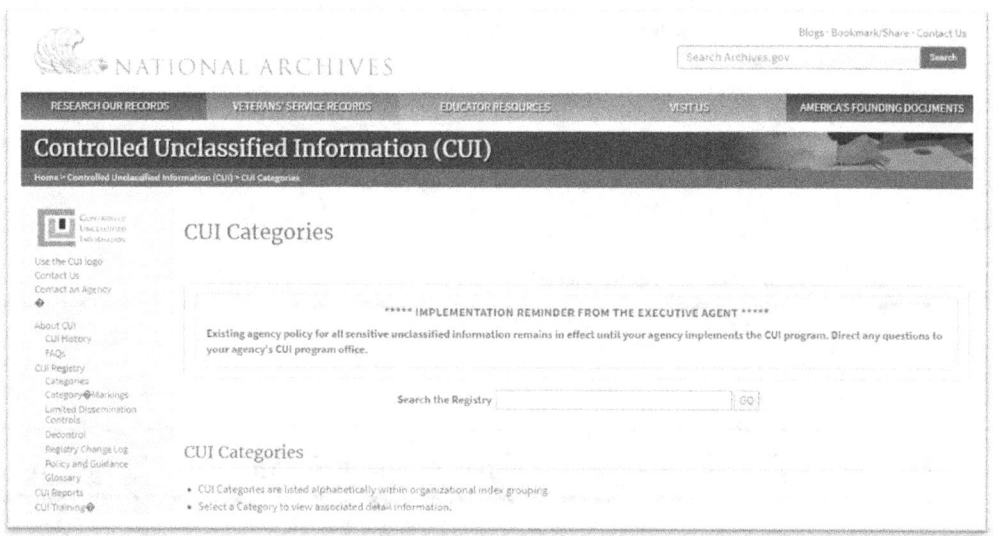

CUI Banner Control Markings (Reference 32 CFR 2002.20(b)(1))

The CUI Control Marking is mandatory for all CUI and may consist of either the word "CONTROLLED" or the acronym "CUI." A best practice for CUI Banner Marking includes it being placed at the top and bottom of each document page. Below are two examples showing the options for the CUI Banner Marking.

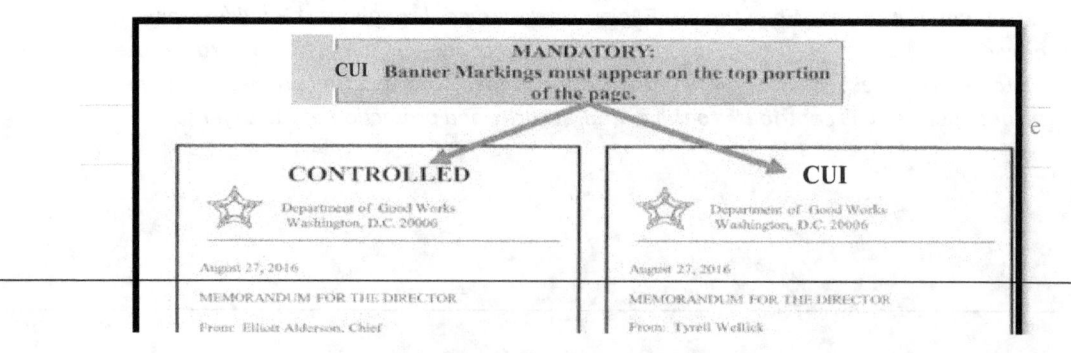

CUI Categories and Subcategories (Reference 32 CFR 2002.12)

A CUI Program is founded on the precondition that only information requiring protection based on law, federal regulation, or government-wide policy *is* CUI. *CUI Categories and Subcategories are necessarily different.* CUI Categories and Subcategories are based on at least one or more laws, regulations, or government-wide policies; these are also referred to as *Authorities*[14] that require a specific type of information to be protected or restricted in its dissemination.

There are two types of CUI Categories and Subcategories: CUI-Basic and CUI-Specified.

1. ***CUI-Basic*** is the standard CUI category. All rules of CUI apply to CUI-Basic Categories and Subcategories. This ensures the proper creation and handling of properly marked CUI.
2. ***CUI-Specified*** is different since the requirements for how users must treat each type of information vary with each Category or Subcategory.

---

[14] Consider Authorities as local security rules or policies that are unique to the Federal agency or UR. Typically, the Contract Officer should be able to assist in information briefings with the agency to ensure full compliance by the vendor.

Some authorities have specialized needs for handling varied CUI information; the Defense Business Solution customer will typically designate this through an SCG. *(NOTE: It is not likely that CUI-Specified will be used with the Defense Business Solution system; however, it is provided here based upon the existing NARA direction for CUI protection).*

CUI-Specified is NOT a "higher level" of CUI; it is *merely different*. Its differences are dictated by law, federal regulation, or government-wide policy; they cannot be ignored. Some CUI Categories and Subcategories are only CUI-Specified, sometimes based upon the Authorities local rules or policies. The reason these differences exist is caused by various laws or regulations about the same information types; however, only *some* may include additional or alternate handling requirements for standard CUI-Basic protections.

Only CUI created under government Authorities would be CUI-Specified. Suppose the law, regulation, or Government-wide policy pertains to the supported federal agency. In that case, they have listed in the National Archives and Repository Administration (NARA) CUI Registry as a Specified Authority. **Unicorn Red** personnel are required to mark the CUI based on that Authority and direction provided by the customer. These changes will be reflected in all updates to this guide.

Banner Markings for Category and Subcategory Markings (Reference 32 CFR 2002.20(b)(2))

Unicorn Red approves the use of CUI-Basic Category or Subcategory Markings through this CUI guide. All CUI-Basic Category or Subcategory Markings must be included in the CUI Banner Marking. When including multiple CUI Category or Subcategory Markings in the CUI Banner Marking, they must be separated by a single forward-slash (/). A double forward-slash separates CUI Category or Subcategory Markings (//) from the CUI Control Marking. When a document contains CUI-Specified, all CUI-Specified Category or Subcategory Markings must be included in the CUI Banner Marking.

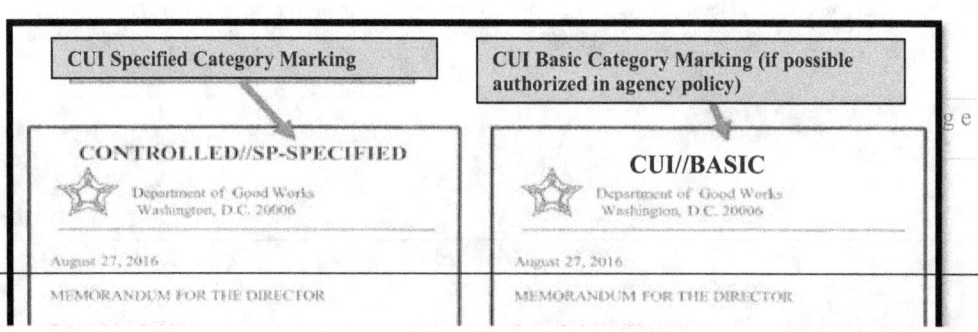

Banner Markings

The above examples use "SP-SPECIFIED" and "BASIC" as substitutes for CUI Category and Subcategory Markings. Consult the CUI Registry for actual CUI markings.

Since CUI-Specified Categories and Subcategories are different – both from CUI-Basic and from each other – CUI-Specified must always be included in the CUI Banner. This is done to ensure that authorized CUI holders and end-users who receive a document containing CUI-Specified knows that the document must be treated in a manner that differs from CUI-Basic. This is accomplished in two ways:

1. All CUI-Specified documents must include the Category or Subcategory marking for all the CUI-Specified contained in that document in the CUI Banner Marking. This ensures that initially, a user in receipt of that document is aware of the CUI Banner. This permits the user to be mindful of whether they have something other than ordinary CUI-Basic. It also allows the user to meet any additional or alternative requirements for the CUI-Specified they hold.

2. To ensure that it is evident that a Category or Subcategory is Specified, the marking has "SP-" added to the beginning of the marking after the CUI or Controlled designation.

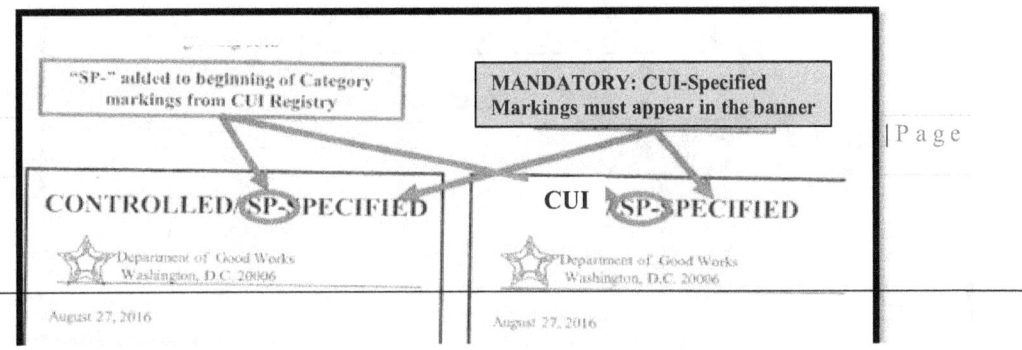

The above examples use the word "SPECIFIED" as a substitute for CUI Category and Subcategory Markings. Consult the CUI Registry for actual CUI markings.

Banner Markings with Multiple of Subcategory Markings (Reference 32 CFR 2002.20)

CUI-Specified Markings must precede CUI-Basic Markings where authorized for use by the agency head in the CUI Banner. Consult the **Unicorn Red** security or CUI policy for guidance on using CUI-Basic Category or Subcategory Markings. Additionally, CUI Category and Subcategory Markings should be alphabetized within CUI type (Basic or Specified). Alphabetized Specified CUI categories and subcategories must precede alphabetized Basic CUI categories and subcategories.

Below are examples of CUI Banner Markings used in a document that contains both CUI-Specified and CUI-Basic.

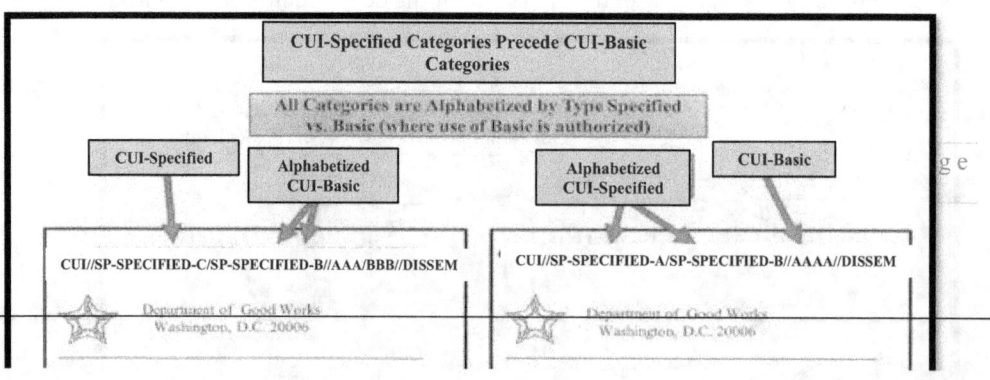

Multiple Category or Subcategory Markings

The above examples use "AAAA" and "BBBB" as substitutes for CUI-Basic Category and Subcategory Markings, "SP-SPECIFIED-X" as a substitute for a CUI-Specified Category and Subcategory Markings, and "DISSEM" as a substitute for a Limited Dissemination Control Marking. Consult the CUI Registry for actual CUI markings.

Banner Markings (Limited Dissemination Controls) (Reference 32 CFR 2002.20(b)(3))

LIMDIS designates restricted distribution by the government or **Unicorn Red** to only specified individuals or organizations. At this time, ***LIMDIS is not used or authorized.*** Only Limited Dissemination (LIMDIS) Control Markings found in the CUI Registry are permitted for use. Limited Dissemination Control Markings are separated from preceding sections of the CUI Banner Marking by double forward-slash *(//)*. When a document contains multiple Limited Dissemination Control Markings, those Limited Dissemination Control Markings must be alphabetized and separated from each other with a single forward-slash (/).

Below are examples that show the proper use of Limited Dissemination Control Markings in the CUI Banner Marking in a letter-type document or a slide presentation.

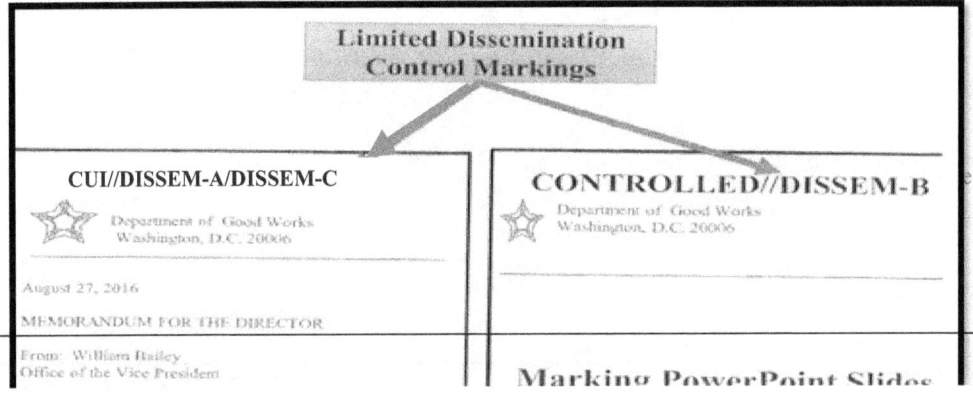

LIMDIS Controls

The above example uses "DISSEM-X" as a substitute for Limited Dissemination Control Markings. Consult the CUI Registry for actual CUI markings.

Designation Indicator (Reference 32 CFR 2002.20(a)(3)(d))

All documents containing CUI must indicate the designator's company or agency, i.e., **Unicorn Red Solutions**, only *if created in the course of duties supporting the Defense Business Solution mission.* This will be accomplished using a "Controlled by" line. Points of contact, branches, or divisions within **Unicorn Red** will be applied to all CUI documents created by **Unicorn Red** in the performance of its support t INFINITI.

Below are examples of designation indicators in a slide presentation and a letter-type document.

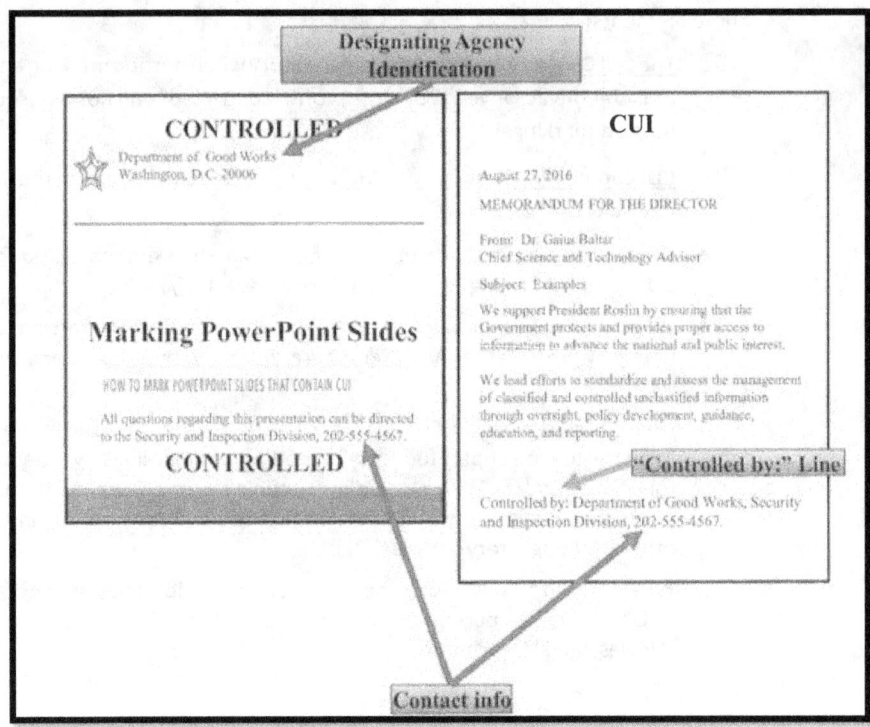

Designation Indicators

Portion Markings (Reference 32 CFR 2002.20(f))
   Portion marking of CUI is *optional* for documents not containing national security information or markings (See the chapter on classified markings). However, **Unicorn Red** encourages portion markings of documents over three or more pages[15].
   When CUI Portion Markings are used, these rules will be followed:

1. CUI Portion Markings are placed at the beginning of the portion (e.g., beginning of sentence or segment of the CUI).

2. Apply markings throughout the entire document.

3. CUI Portion Markings are contained within parentheses and may include up to

---

[15] Portion markings help when providing reports and responding to requests for information from the public; this provides clear boundaries for information release in accordance with the law.

three elements:

    a. <u>The CUI Control Marking</u>: This is mandatory when portion marking and must be the acronym "CUI" (the word "Controlled" will not be used in portion markings).

    b. <u>CUI Category or Subcategory Markings:</u> These can be found in the CUI Registry.

    c. When used, CUI Category or Subcategory Markings are separated from the CUI Control Marking by a double forward-slash (//).

    d. When including multiple categories or subcategories in a portion, CUI Category or Subcategory Markings are separated by a single forward-slash (/).

    e. Limited Dissemination Control Markings: These can be found in the CUI Registry and are separated from preceding CUI markings by a double forward-slash (//). When including multiple Limited Dissemination Control Markings, they must be alphabetized and separated from each other by a single forward-slash (/).

    f. When CUI Portion Markings are used, and a portion does not contain CUI, a "U" is placed in parentheses to indicate that the portion contains "Unclassified" Information.

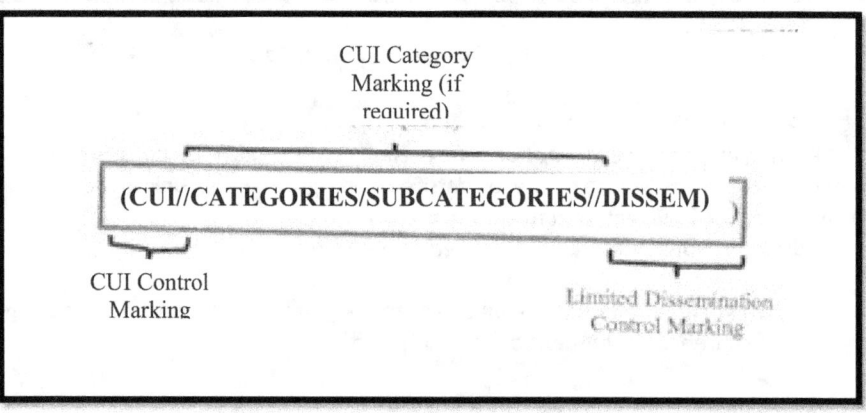

Portion Marking Standards

The above example uses the words "CATEGORIES" and "SUBCATEGORIES" as substitutes for CUI Category or Subcategory Markings and the word "DISSEM" as a substitute for a Limited Dissemination Control Marking. Consult the CUI Registry for actual CUI markings.

The presence of at least one item categorized as CUI in a document requires CUI marking of the entire document. CUI Portion Markings are of significant assistance in determining if a document contains CUI and therefore must be marked appropriately. Additionally, when portion markings are used, and any portion does not have CUI, a "(U)" is placed in front of that portion to indicate that it contains Uncontrolled or non-CUI - Unclassified[16] Information.

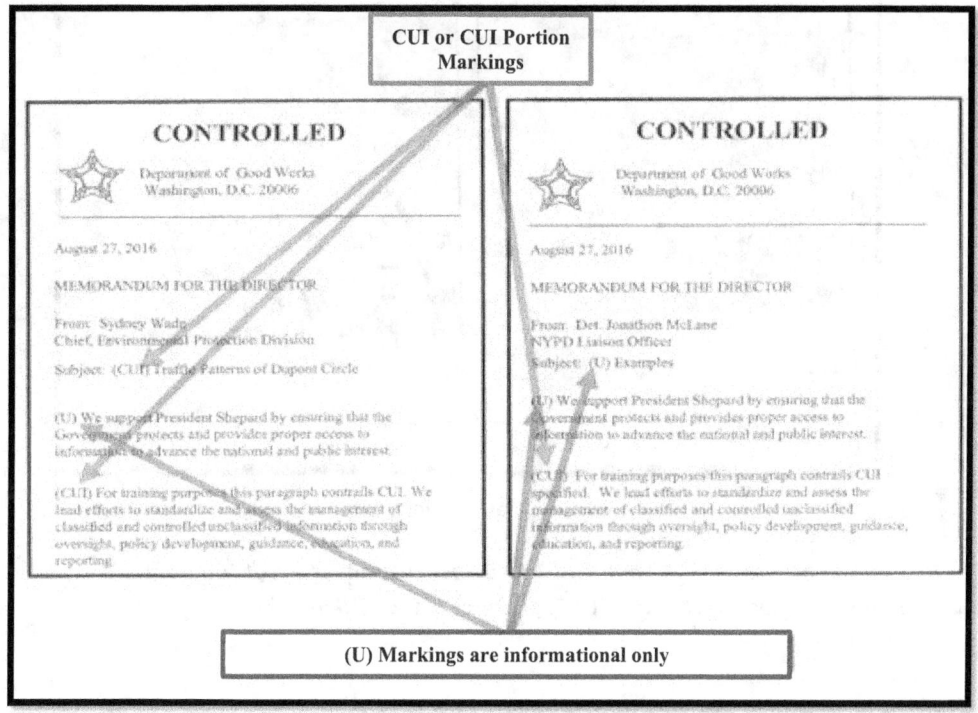

"Parenthetical" Portion Marking Examples

---

[16] Uncontrolled appears to be an ambiguous statement from NARA; it is best considered as UNCLASSIFIED information for the purposes of this guide.

Portion Markings with Category Only (Reference 32 CFR 2002.20(f))

    This example shows how to portion mark a document using the CUI Control Marking and CUI Category or Subcategory Markings. When a record contains CUI-Specified, all CUI-Specified Category or Subcategory Markings must be included in the CUI Banner Marking. When CUI Portion Markings are used, and a portion does not contain CUI, a "U" is placed in parentheses to indicate that the portion includes Uncontrolled-Unclassified Information.

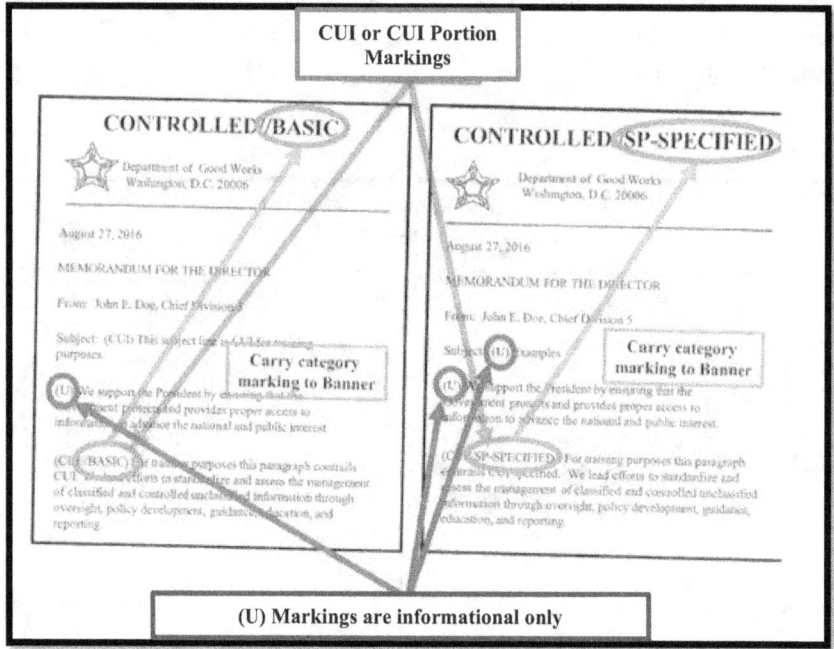

Portion Marking with Category Only

The above example uses "BASIC" and "SPECIFIED" as substitutes for CUI Category or Subcategory Markings. Consult the CUI Registry for actual CUI markings.

Portion Markings with Category and Dissemination Caveats (Reference 32 CFR 2002.20(f))

    The example below shows how to portion mark a document using all three components of the CUI Banner Marking. When a document contains CUI-Specified, CUI-Specified Category or Subcategory Markings must be included in the CUI Banner Marking.

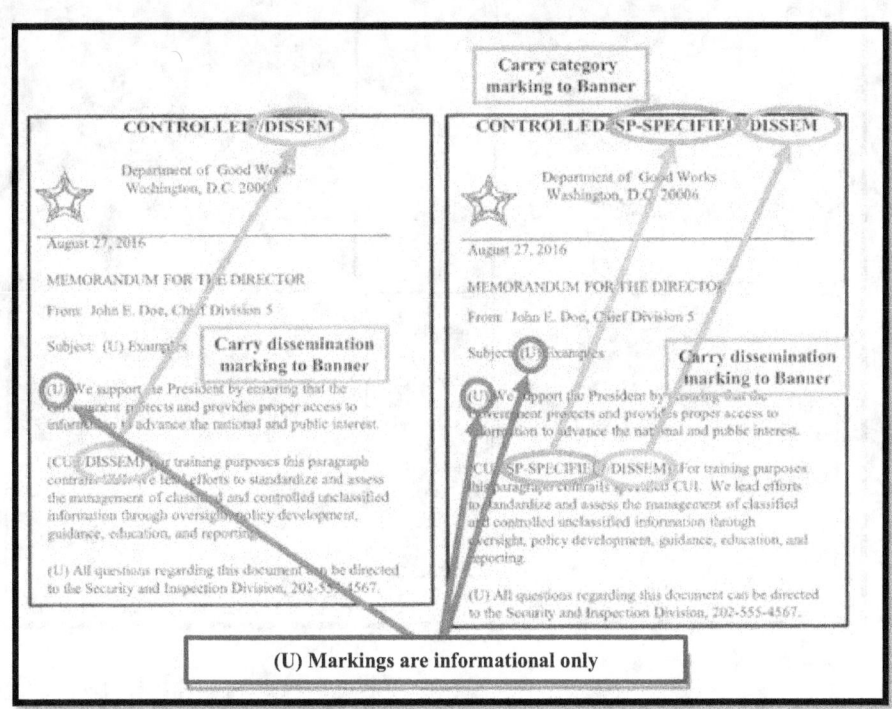

Portion Markings with Category and Dissemination

The above example uses "SP-SPECIFIED" as a substitute for a CUI Category or Subcategory Marking and "DISSEM" as a substitute for Limited Dissemination Control Markings. Consult the CUI Registry for actual CUI markings.

Marking of Multiple Pages (Reference 32 CFR 2002.20(c))

The composition of the CUI Banner Marking for a multi-page document is essentially the totality of all the CUI markings in the document; if any portion of the document contains CUI-Specified or a Limited Dissemination Control Marking, then the CUI Banner Marking must reflect all warnings or *caveats*.

Below is an example of one multi-page document with CUI Portion Marking.

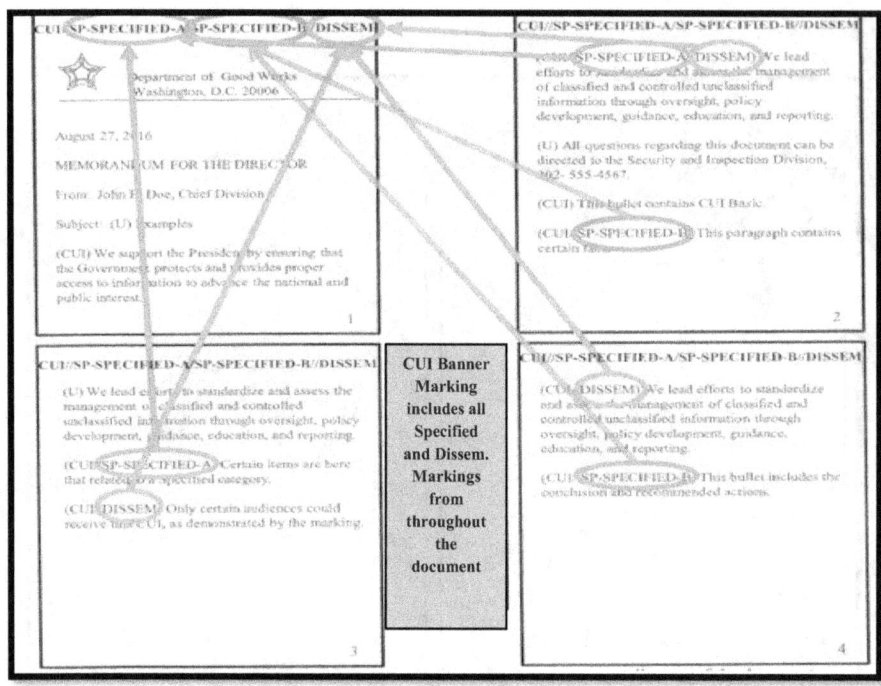

The overall CUI Banner Marking for the document must appear on all pages of the document.

Required Indicators as directed by Authorities (Reference 32 CFR 2002.20 (b)(2)(iii))
Required indicators that include informational, warning, or dissemination statements may be mandated by the law, Federal regulation, or Government-wide policy that makes a specific item of information CUI. These indicators shall not be included in the CUI Banner or portion markings but must appear in a manner readily apparent to authorized personnel. This shall be consistent with the requirements of a governing document to include the customer's SCG or **Unicorn Red's** company-wide security policy.

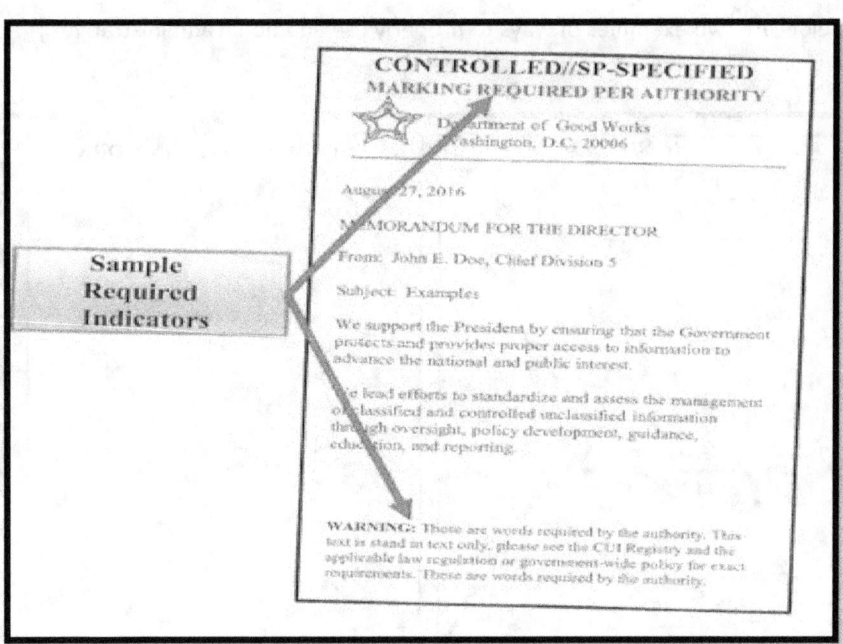

The above example uses "SPECIFIED" as a substitute for a CUI-Specified Category or Subcategory Marking. Consult the CUI Registry for actual CUI markings.

Supplemental Administrative Markings (Reference 32 CFR 2002.20(l))
    Unicorn Red employees may use supplemental administrative markings (e.g., Draft, Deliberative, Pre- decisional, Provisional) and CUI to inform recipients of the non-final status of documents. All such records will be dated on the front page of the main document and must be converted to final or destroyed **within 180-days of creation** by the owner. Supplemental administrative markings may not be used to control CUI and may not be commingled with other CUI Banner Marking or Portion Markings. *Additional administrative markings may not duplicate any marking in the CUI Registry.*

Below are two examples of ways to properly use additional administrative markings.

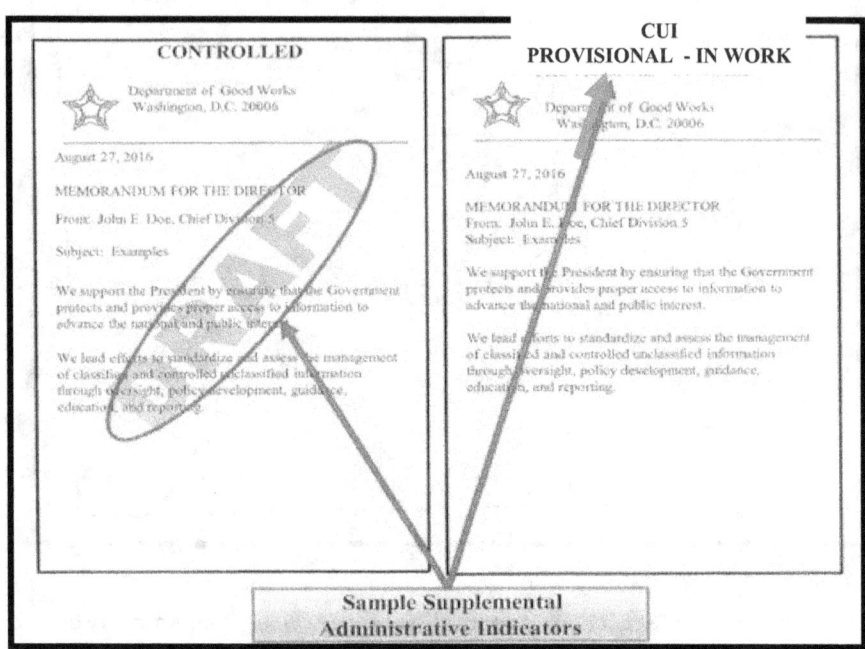

Common Mistakes for Supplemental Administrative Markings

Below are two examples of how to **NOT** use administrative markings.

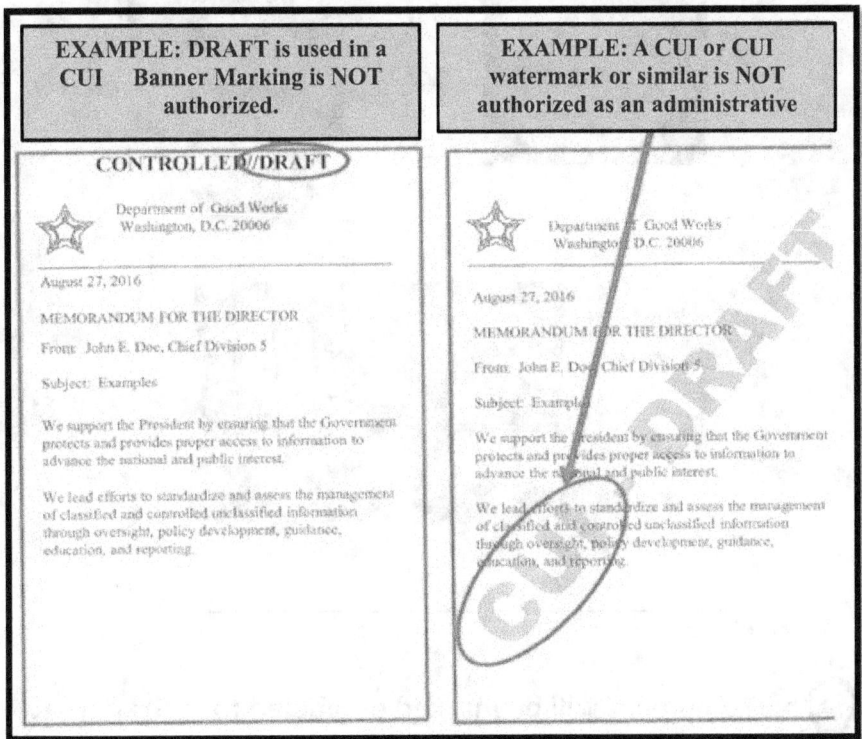

Electronic Media Storage and Marking Procedures (Reference 32 CFR 2002.20)

Media such as USB sticks, hard drives, and CD ROMs must be marked to alert CUI holders to the presence of CUI stored on the device. Due to space limitations, it may not be possible to include Category, Subcategory, or Limited Dissemination Control Markings on the given surface. At a minimum, mark the media with the CUI Control Marking ("CONTROLLED" or "CUI"), who created it, and the date of creation of the media. Computer equipment and devices with data storage capacity will also be marked or labeled to indicate that CUI is stored on the device.

NOTE: DOGW is an acronym for Department of Good Works.

 Equipment will be marked or labeled to indicate that CUI is stored on the device.

Marking Forms (Reference 32 CFR 2002.20)

Forms that contain CUI will be marked accordingly when completed. If space on the form is limited, cover sheets can be used. As forms are updated during the implementation of the CUI Program, they should be modified to include a statement that indicates the form is CUI when finalized.

CUI Coversheets (Reference 32 CFR 2002.32)

The use of CUI or CUI coversheets is required when transporting this material outside of controlled spaces to include transit to other physical locations. Coversheets can be downloaded from the CUI Registry or obtain printed copies through the General Services Administration (GSA) Global Supply Centers or the GSAAdvantage online service (https://www.gsa.gov/buying-selling/purchasing-programs/requisition-programs/gsa-global-supply/easy-ordering/gsa-global-supply-online-ordering).

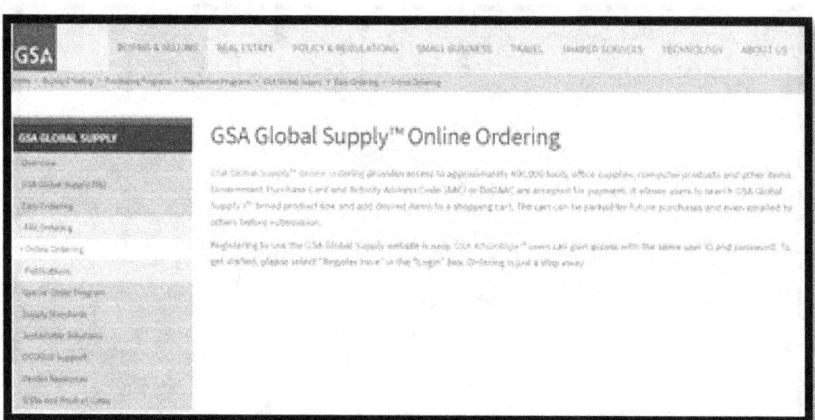

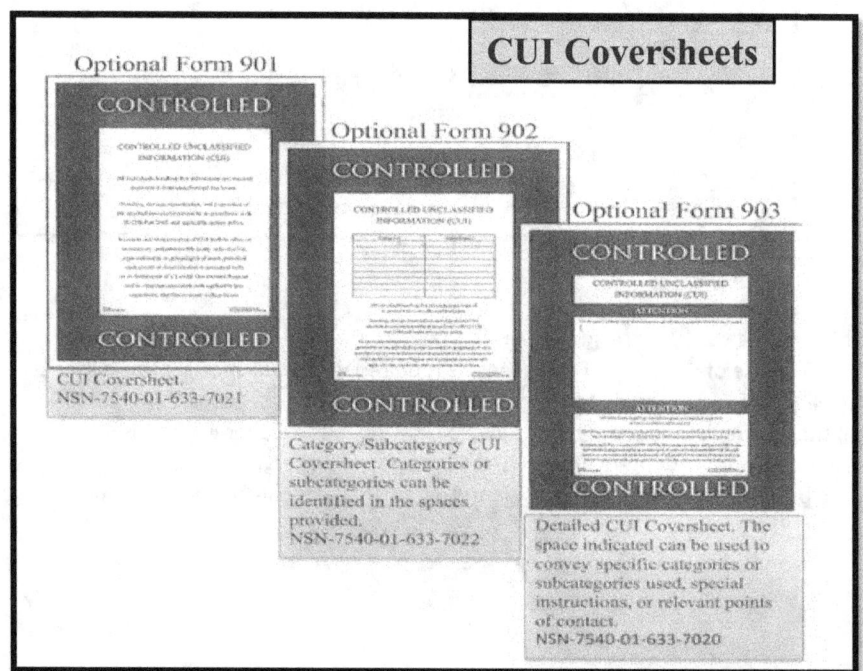

Marking Transmittal Documents (Reference 32 CFR 2002.20)

When a transmittal document accompanies CUI, the transmittal document must indicate that CUI is attached or enclosed. The transmittal document must also include the following or similar instructions, as appropriate:

- "When the enclosure is removed, this document is "Unclassified Information"; or
- "When the enclosure is removed, this document is (CUI Control Level); or
- "Upon removal, this document does not contain CUI."

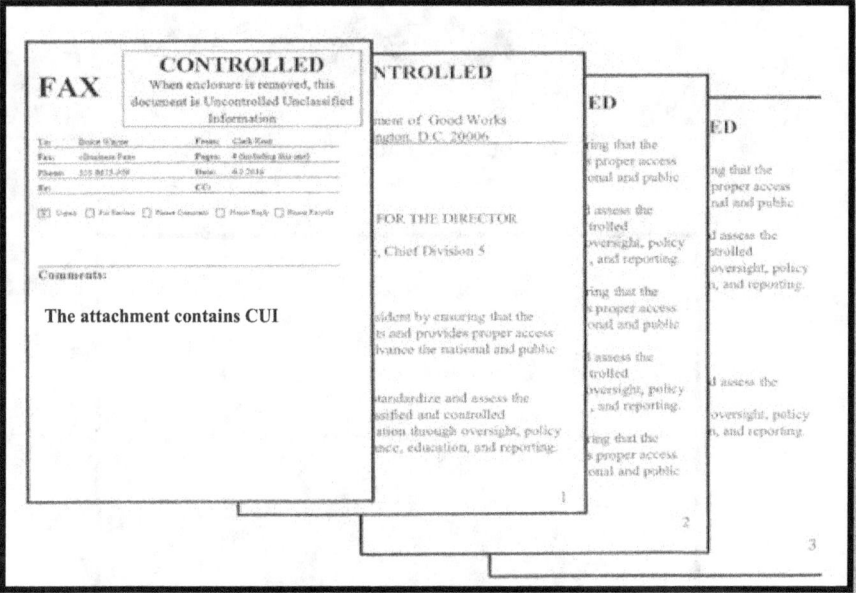

Alternate Marking Methods (Reference 32 CFR 2002.20)

Unicorn Red will authorize alternate marking methods on IT systems, websites, browsers, or databases through customer SCG and CUI policy. These may be used to alert users to the presence of CUI where the agency head has issued a limited CUI marking waiver for CUI designated within the agency. These warnings may take multiple forms and include the examples below.

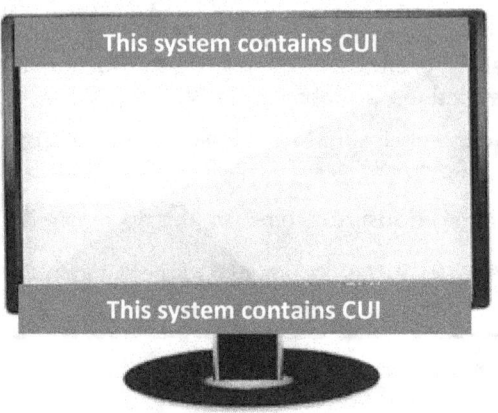

Computer Monitor CUI Banners

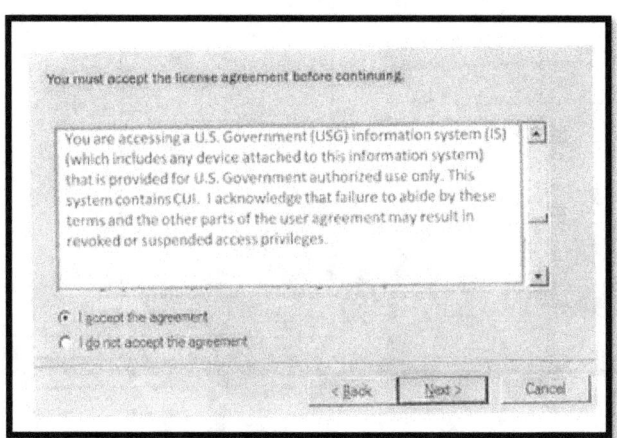

Agency or Company Legal Warning Notification for CUI or CUI

Room or Area Markings (Reference 32 CFR 2002.20)
It is essential to alert personnel who are not authorized to access the area or information in areas containing CUI. This may be accomplished by several means to include signs posted exterior to the room or rooms, on entry doors, and in any ante-room designated to verify clearances or need-to-know status of a group or individual.

Below is a sample of a sign that indicates the presence of CUI.

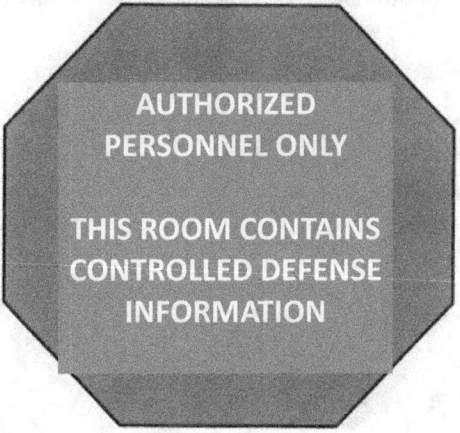

Example Exterior Door and Interior Rooms Sign

Container Markings (Reference 32 CFR 2002.20)

All CUI storage containers of CUI will be marked to indicate that it contains CUI.

Below are some basic examples.

Shipping and Mailing (Reference 32 CFR 2002.20)

When shipping CUI:

- Address packages that contain CUI for delivery only to a specific recipient.
- DO NOT put CUI markings on the outside of an envelope or package for

mailing/shipping.
- Use in-transit automated tracking and accountability tools where possible.

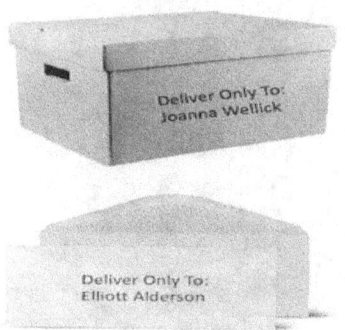

Re-marking Legacy Information (Reference 32 CFR 2002.36)

Legacy information is *unclassified* information marked as *restricted* (or similar markings) from access or dissemination in some way or otherwise controlled before the CUI Program was established. This may include, for example, such designations as:

- For Official Use Only (FOUO)
- Unclassified but Sensitive
- Sensitive
- Restricted

All legacy information is not automatically assumed to be CUI. The **Unicorn Red** security officer will be notified and determine what legacy information qualifies as CUI and mark accordingly.

LEGACY MARKING

Department of Good Works
Washington, D.C. 20006

August 27, 2016

MEMORANDUM FOR THE DIRECTOR

From: John E. Doe, Chief Division 5

Subject: Examples

We support the President by ensuring that the Government protects and provides proper access to information to advance the national and public interest.

We lead efforts to standardize and assess the management of classified and controlled unclassified information through oversight, policy development, guidance, education, and reporting.

"LEGACY MARKING" is used as a substitute for ad hoc, agency markings used to label unclassified information before creating the CUI Program.

When legacy information is to be re-used and incorporated into another document of any kind, it must undergo the process described below.

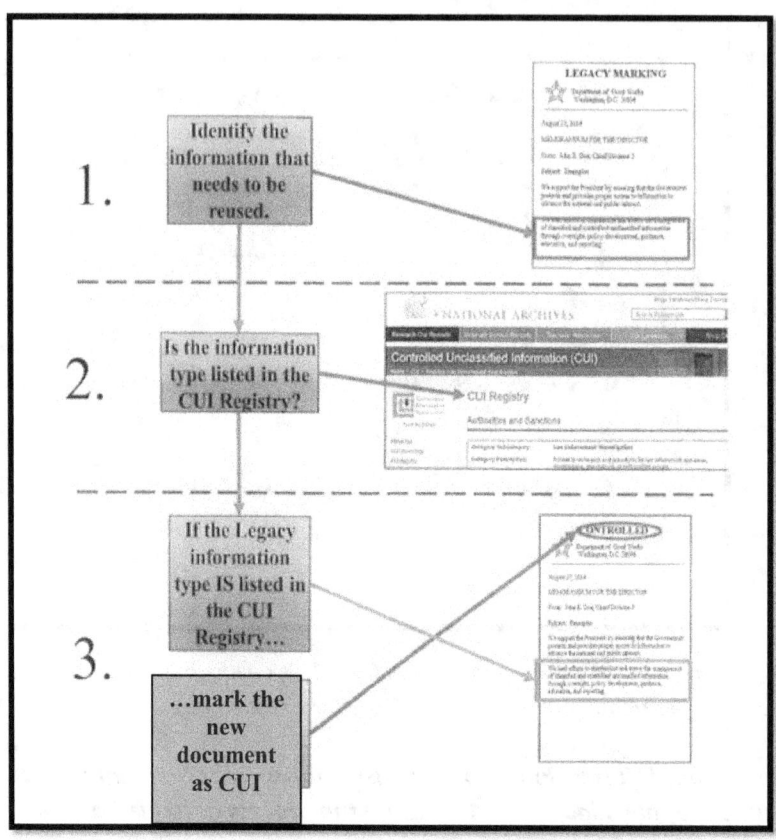

Legacy Marked Document Marking Decision-tree

When possible, contact the originator of the information for guidance in remarking and protecting the legacy information in the CUI Program.

ANNEX Z--CUI MARKINGS IN CLASSIFIED ENVIRONMENTS

Marking Commingled Information (Reference 32 CFR 2002.20(g))

When CUI is included in a document that contains any classified information, that document is referred to as ***commingled***. Commingled documents are subject to the requirements of the CUI and Classified National Security Information (CNSI) Programs. As a best practice, keep the CUI and classified information in separate and designated areas and security containers to the greatest extent possible[17]. Mark all paragraphs (portion markings) to ensure that authorized holders can distinguish CUI from information containing CNSI or Unclassified Information; the de-controlling provisions for CUI apply only to portions marked as CUI. CNSI portions remain classified based on their declassification requirements and require protections as directed under **Executive Order 13526.**

Executive Order 13526 - Classified National Security Information

In the overall marking banner's CUI section, double forward slashes (//) are used to separate significant elements, and single forward slashes (/) are used to separate sub-elements. The CUI Control Marking ("CUI") appears in the overall banner marking directly before the CUI category and subcategory markings. When CUI-Specified is in the document, the category and subcategory marking(s) must appear in the overall banner marking. Optional CUI-Basic category and subcategory markings would appear next. Both CUI-Specified and CUI-

---

[17] Typically, classified facilities should be partitioned to include designated drawers, safes, and folders specific to CUI storage.

Basic markings are separately alphabetized. The limited dissemination control markings (if used) apply to the entire document and the CUI and classified information. Placeholders are not used for missing elements or sub-elements.

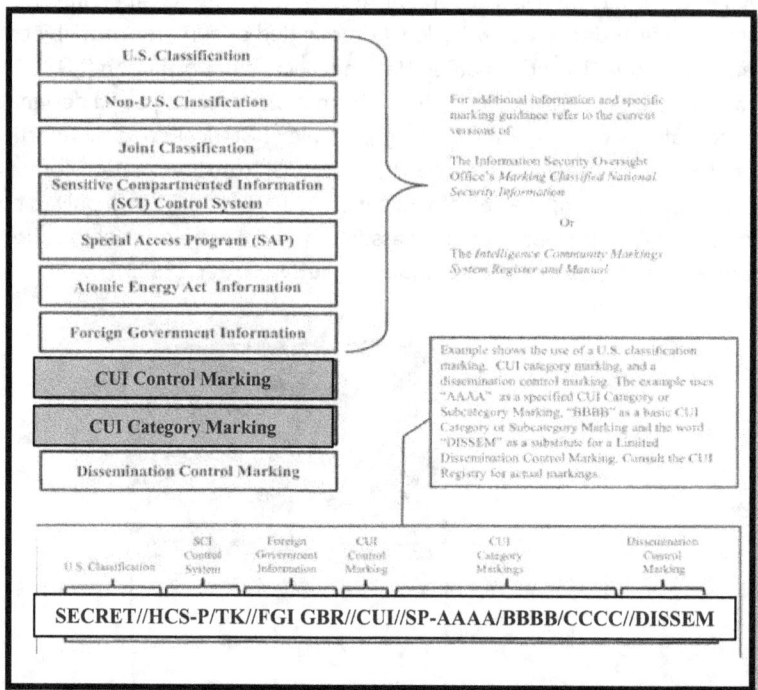

Commingling in the same paragraph is not recommended. Where sections contain CUI and CNSI commingled, portion marking elements follow a similar syntax to the banner marking.

REMINDER: The paragraph, AKA "portion," always takes the HIGHEST classification of the information contained in that paragraph.

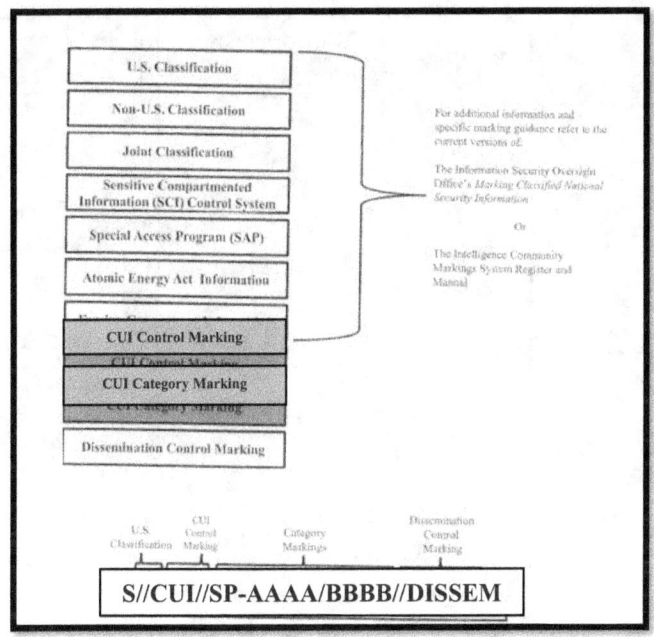

For additional information and specific marking, the guidance refers to the current versions of The Information Security Oversight Office's *Marking Classified National Security Information*.

Commingling Example 1

In cases where CUI is commingled with classified information, the following applies:

- The CUI Control Marking is used only in its abbreviated form ("CUI"). The longer form ("CONTROLLED") is not used. Either the classification marking, CUI control marking ("CUI"), or the Unclassified Marking ("U") must be used in every portion.

- Limited Dissemination Control Markings must appear in the banner line and in all portions to which they apply.

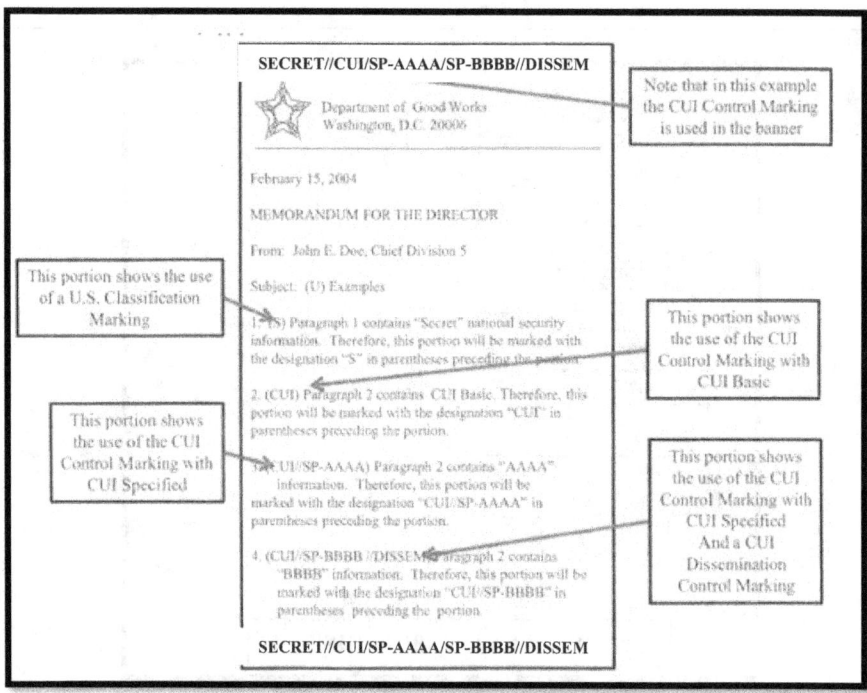

The above examples use "SP-AAAA" or "SP-BBBB" as CUI-Specified Category or Subcategory Markings and the word "DISSEM" as a substitute for a Limited Dissemination Control Marking. Consult the CUI Registry for actual markings. (*All CUI markings above should be replaced with CUI).

Commingling Example 2

These examples show the various ways CUI may be identified in a document.

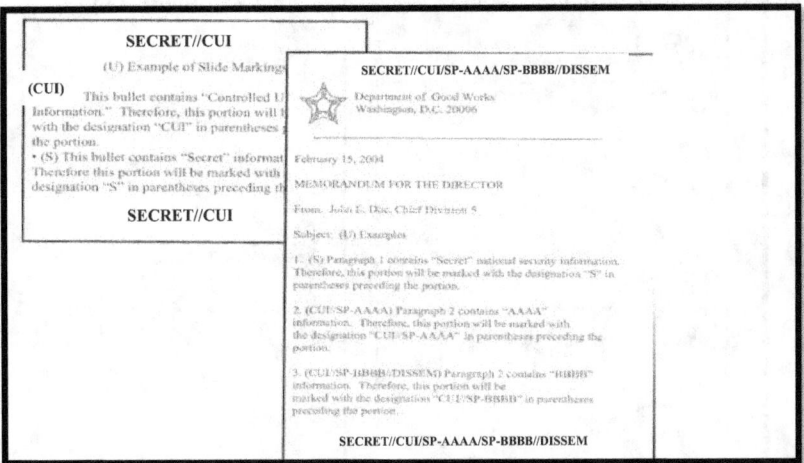

The above examples use "SP-AAAA" or "SP-BBBB" as CUI-Specified Category or Subcategory Markings and the word "DISSEM" as a substitute for a Limited Dissemination Control Marking. (*All CUI markings above should be replaced with CUI).

Commingling Example 3

Below are two samples of CUI commingled with classified information, specifically with Classified National Security Information (CNSI). The sample on the left has the CUI and CNSI separated into paragraphs allowing for more natural future separation to accommodate differing access requirements. The example on the right has CUI and CNSI in the same section.

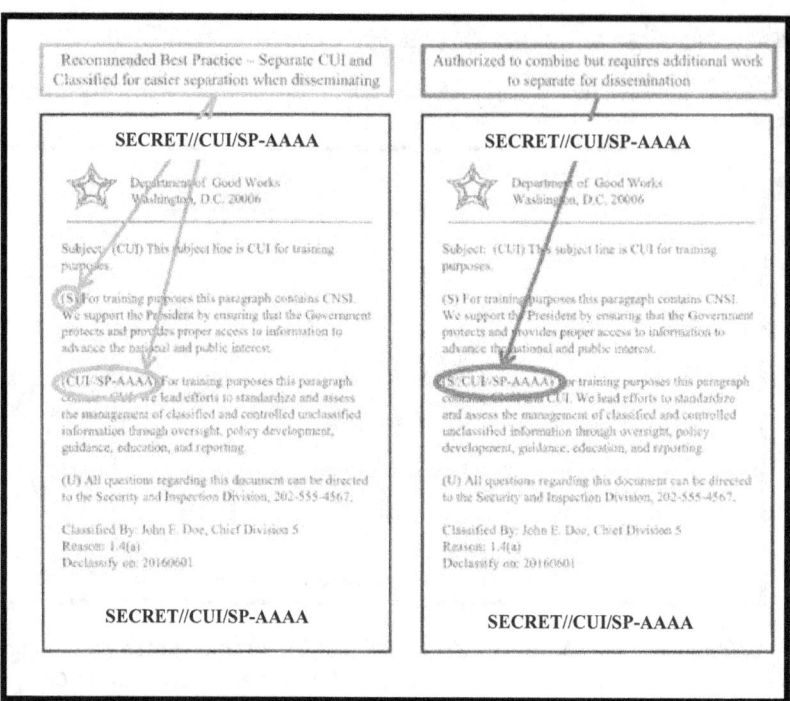

The above examples use the word "SP-AAAA" as a substitute for a CUI-Specified Category or Subcategory Marking. Consult the CUI Registry for actual markings.

Commingling Portion Markings (Reference 32 CFR 2002.20(g))

    In a commingled document, when a portion contains both CUI and classified information, the portion marking for the classified information must precede the CUI Portion Marking. When commingling CUI with classified information, the user should retain the CUI and classified portions separate to the greatest extent possible to allow maximum information sharing. Many of the intricate markings seen below can be avoided by following this simple practice. Below are some examples of how to mark portions containing CUI.

Portion Marking	Contents of portions Marked Section – CUI only in portion
(CUI)	This section contains CUI-Basic.
(CUI//AAAA)	This section contains CUI-Basic (with optional category marking).
(CUI//SP-BBBB)	This section contains CUI-Specified.
(CUI//SP-BBBB/SP-CCCC)	This section contains two CUI-Specified Categories in alphabetical order.
(CUI//DISSEM)	This section contains CUI-Basic with a Limited Dissemination Control Marking.
(CUI//AAAA//DISSEM)	This section contains CUI-Basic with a Limited Dissemination Control Marking.
(CUI//SP-BBBB//DISSEM)	This section contains CUI-Specified Categories with a Limited Dissemination Control Marking.
Portion Marking	**Contents of portions Marked Section – WITH COMMINGLED PORTION MARKINGS**
(S//CUI)	This section contains Secret information and CUI-Basic.
(S//CUI//AAAA)	This section contains Secret information and CUI-Basic (with optional category marking).
(S//CUI//SP-BBBB)	This section contains Secret information and CUI-Specified.
(S//CUI//SP-BBBB/SP-CCCC)	This section contains Secret information and has two CUI-Specified Categories in alphabetical order.
(S//CUI//SP-BBBB//DISSEM)	This section contains Secret information and CUI-Specified with a Limited Dissemination Control Marking.

Examples of CUI Security Portion Markings

APPENDICES

APPENDIX A -- RELEVANT REFERENCES[18]

Federal Information Security Modernization Act of 2014 (P.L. 113-283), December 2014.
http://www.gpo.gov/fdsys/pkg/PLAW-113publ283/pdf/PLAW-113publ283.pdf

Executive Order 13556, *Controlled Unclassified Information*, November 2010.
http://www.gpo.gov/fdsys/pkg/FR-2010-11-09/pdf/2010-28360.pdf

Executive Order 13636, *Improving Critical Infrastructure Cybersecurity*, February 2013.
http://www.gpo.gov/fdsys/pkg/FR-2013-02-19/pdf/2013-03915.pdf

National Institute of Standards and Technology Federal Information Processing Standards Publication 200 (as amended), *Minimum Security Requirements for Federal Information and Information Systems*.
http://csrc.nist.gov/publications/fips/fips200/FIPS-200-final-march.pdf

National Institute of Standards and Technology Special Publication 800-53 (as amended), *Security and Privacy Controls for Federal Information Systems and Organizations*.
http://dx.doi.org/10.6028/NIST.SP.800-53r4

National Institute of Standards and Technology Special Publication 800-171, rev. 1, *Protecting Controlled Unclassified Information in Nonfederal Information Systems and Organizations*. https://nvlpubs.nist.gov/nistpubs/SpecialPublications/NIST.SP.800-171r1.pdf

National Institute of Standards and Technology Special Publication 800-171A, *Assessing Security Requirements for Controlled Unclassified Information*
https://csrc.nist.gov/CSRC/media/Publications/sp/800-171a/draft/sp800-171A-draft.pdf

National Institute of Standards and Technology *Framework for Improving Critical Infrastructure Cybersecurity* (as amended).
http://www.nist.gov/cyberframework

---

[18] Also, see references in the beginning of the G-CSP for other guiding documents and policies.

APPENDIX B -- TERMS & GLOSSARY

Audit log. A chronological record of information system activities, including records of system accesses and operations performed in a given period.

Authentication. Verifying the identity of a user, process, or device, often a prerequisite to allowing access to resources in an information system.

Availability. Ensuring timely and reliable access to and use of information.

Baseline Configuration. A documented set of specifications for an information system, or a configuration item within a system, has been formally reviewed and agreed on at a given point in time, which can be changed only through change control procedures.

Blacklisting. The process used to identify: (i) software programs that are not authorized to execute on an information system; or (ii) prohibited websites.

Confidentiality. Preserving authorized restrictions on information access and disclosure, including means for protecting personal privacy and proprietary information.

Configuration Management. A collection of activities focused on establishing and maintaining the integrity of information technology products and information systems through control of processes for initializing, changing, and monitoring the configurations of those products and systems throughout the system development life cycle.

Controlled Unclassified Information (CUI/FCI). Information that law, regulation, or governmentwide policy requires has safeguarding or disseminating controls, excluding information classified under Executive Order 13526, Classified National Security Information, December 29, 2009, or any predecessor or successor order, or the Atomic Energy Act of 1954, as amended.

External network. A network not controlled by the company.

FIPS-validated cryptography. The Cryptographic Module Validation Program (CMVP) validated a cryptographic module to meet requirements specified in FIPS Publication 140-2 (as amended). As a prerequisite to CMVP validation, the cryptographic module must employ a cryptographic algorithm implementation that has successfully passed validation testing by the Cryptographic Algorithm Validation Program (CAVP).

Hardware. The physical components of an information system.

Incident. An occurrence that actually or potentially jeopardizes the confidentiality, integrity, or availability of an information system or the information the system processes, stores, or transmits or constitutes a violation or imminent threat of a breach of security policies, security procedures, or acceptable use policies.

Information Security. Protecting information and information systems from unauthorized access, use, disclosure, disruption, modification, or destruction to provide confidentiality, integrity, and availability.

Information System. A discrete set of information resources is organized for collecting, processing, maintenance, use, sharing, dissemination, or disposition of information.

Information Technology. Any equipment or interconnected system or subsystem of equipment used in the automatic acquisition, storage, manipulation, management, movement, control, display, switching, interchange, transmission, or reception of data or information by the executive agency. It includes computers, ancillary equipment, software, firmware, and similar procedures, services (including support services), and related resources.

Integrity. Guarding against improper information modification or destruction and includes ensuring information non-repudiation and authenticity.

Internal Network. A network where: (i) the establishment, maintenance, and provisioning of security controls are under the direct control of organizational employees or contractors; or (ii) cryptographic encapsulation or similar security technology implemented between organization-controlled endpoints provides the same effect (at least concerning confidentiality and integrity).

Malicious Code. Software intended to perform an unauthorized process that will hurt an information system's confidentiality, integrity, or availability; a virus, worm, Trojan horse, or other code-based entity that infects a host. Spyware and some forms of adware are also examples of malicious code.

Media. Physical devices or writing surfaces include magnetic tapes, optical disks, magnetic disks, and printouts (including display media) onto which information is recorded, stored, or printed within an information system.

Mobile Code. Software programs or parts of programs obtained from remote information systems, transmitted across a network, and executed on a local information system without explicit installation or execution by the recipient.

Mobile device. A portable computing device that: (i) has a small form factor such that a single individual can easily carry it; (ii) is designed to operate without a physical connection (e.g., wirelessly transmit or receive information); (iii) possesses local, non-removable or removable data storage; and (iv) includes a self-contained power source. Mobile devices may also include voice communication capabilities, onboard sensors that allow the devices to capture information, or built-in features for synchronizing local data with remote locations. Examples include smartphones, tablets, and E-readers.

Multifactor Authentication. Authentication using two or more different factors to achieve authentication. Factors include: (i) something you know (e.g., password/PIN); (ii) something you have (e.g., cryptographic identification device, token); or (iii) something you are (e.g., biometric).

Nonfederal Information System. An information system that does not meet the criteria for a federal information system. Nonfederal organization.

Network. Information system(s) implemented with a collection of interconnected components. Such components may include routers, hubs, cabling, telecommunications controllers, key distribution centers, and technical control devices.

Portable storage device. An information system component that can be inserted into and removed from an information system is used to store data or information (e.g., text, video, audio, or image data). Such components are typically implemented on magnetic, optical, or solid-state devices (e.g., floppy disks, compact/digital video disks, flash/thumb drives, external hard disk drives, and flash memory cards/drives containing nonvolatile memory).

Privileged Account. An information system account with authorizations of a privileged user.

Privileged User. A user who is authorized (and therefore, trusted) performs security-relevant functions that ordinary users cannot achieve.

Remote Access. Access to an organizational information system by a user (or a process acting on behalf of a user) communicating through an external network (e.g., the Internet).

Risk. A measure of the extent to which a potential circumstance or event threatens an entity, and typically a function of (i) the adverse impacts that would arise if the situation or event occurs; and (ii) the likelihood of occurrence. Information system-related security risks are those risks that arise from the loss of confidentiality, integrity, or availability of information or information systems and reflect the potential adverse impacts to organizational operations (including mission, functions, image, or reputation), corporate assets, individuals, other organizations, and the Nation.

Sanitization. Actions were taken to render data written on media unrecoverable by both ordinary and, for some forms of sanitization, extraordinary means. The process of removing information from media such that data recovery is not possible. It includes removing all classified labels, markings, and activity logs.

Security Control. A safeguard or countermeasure is prescribed for an information system or organization designed to protect the confidentiality, integrity, and availability of its information and meet a set of defined security requirements.

Security Control Assessment. The testing or evaluation of security controls determines the extent to which the controls are implemented correctly, operating as intended, and producing the desired outcome concerning meeting the security requirements for an information system or organization.

Security Functions. The information system's hardware, software, or firmware is responsible for enforcing the system security policy and supporting the isolation of code and data on which the protection is based.

Threat. Any circumstance or event with the potential to adversely impact organizational operations (including mission, functions, image, or reputation), corporate assets, individuals, other organizations, or the Nation through an information system via unauthorized access, destruction, disclosure, modification of information, or denial of service.

Whitelisting. The process used to identify: (i) software programs that are authorized to execute an information system.

APPENDIX C – MANAGING THE LIFECYCLE OF A POAM

Intelligence Cycle Approach for the POAM Lifecycle

This section is designed to provide a structure for anyone developing a POAM for their company or agency. It describes how to approach the POAM development process and formulate and track POAMs during their lifecycle. The process has been slightly modified to provide a more pertinent description for POAM creation, but we have found this model to be useful for the novice through professional cybersecurity or IT specialist that regularly works in this arena. We suggest using the US Intelligence Community's Intelligence Lifecycle as a guide to address POAM's from "cradle-to-grave."

This includes the following six stages:

1. **IDENTIFY** Those controls that time, technology, or cost cannot be met to satisfy the unimplemented control.

2. **RESEARCH:** You now have decided the control is not going to meet your immediate CMMC needs. The typical initial milestone is to conduct some form of research or market survey of available solutions. This will include:

    - **The kind or type of solution.** Either as a person (e.g., additional expertise), process (e.g., what established workflow can provide a repeatable solution), or technology (e.g., what hardware/software solution fixes all or part of the control.
    - **How the federal government wants it implemented**? For example, are hard tokens required, or can the company use a soft token solution to address 2FA?
    - **Internal challenges.** What does the company face overall with people, process, or technology perspectives specific to the control?

3. **RECOMMEND:** At this phase, all research and analysis have been done and presumably well-documented. Typically, the cybersecurity team or business IT team will formulate recommended solutions to the System Owner, i.e., the business decision-makers such as the Chief Information or Operations Officer. The recommendations must be technically feasible, but cost and resources should be part of any recommendation.

4. **DECIDE:** At this point, company decision-makers not only approve of the approach to correct the security shortfall but have agreed to resource requirements to authorize the expenditures of funds and efforts.

5. **IMPLEMENT:** Finally, the solution is implemented, and the POAM is updated for closure. This should be reported to the Contract Office or its representative

regularly.

6. **CONTINUAL IMPROVEMENT.** Like any process, it should be regularly reviewed and updated accurately to the needs and capabilities of the company or organization. This could include better templates, additional staffing, or more regular updates to management to ensure a thorough but supportive understanding of how cybersecurity meets the needs and mission of the business.

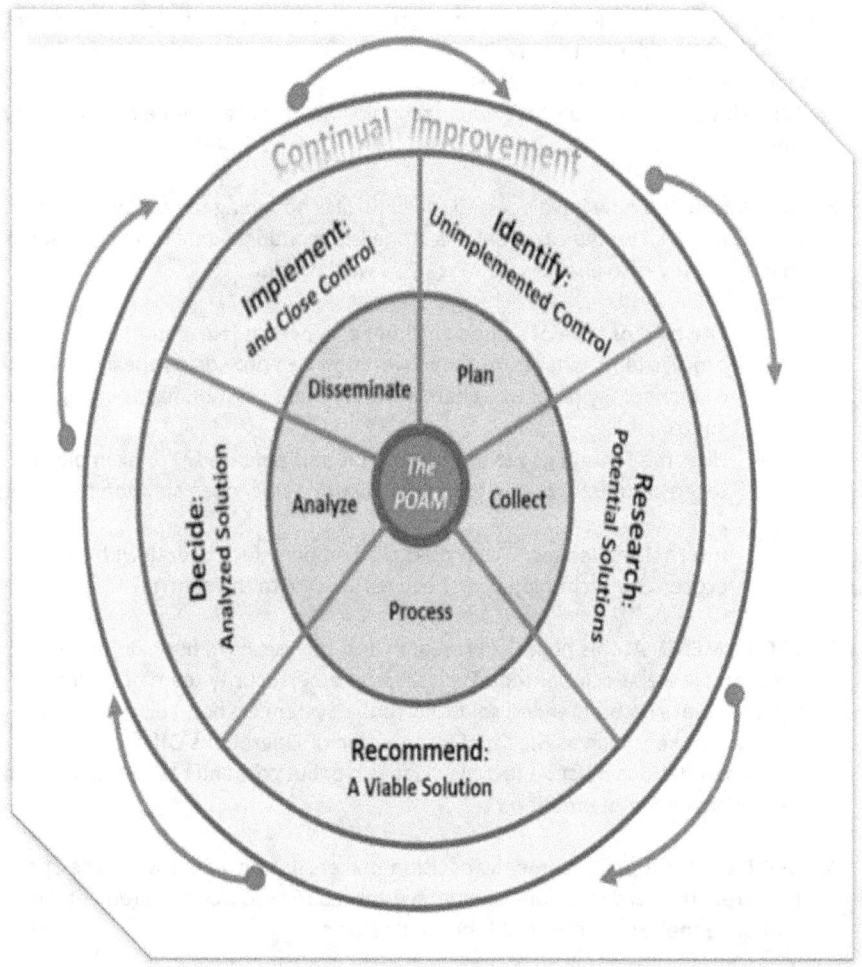

The POAM Lifecycle

We begin in the "Identify" section of the lifecycle process above. At this stage, several things may occur. Either the business owner or IT staff recognizes that the security control is not or cannot be immediately met. Alternatively, they employ an automated security tool, such as ACAS® or Nessus®, that identifies securities vulnerabilities within the IS. This could also include findings such as the default password, like "password," which has not been changed on an internal switch or router. It could also include updated security patching that has not occurred; some automated applications will not only identify but recommend courses of action to mitigate or fix a security finding. Always try to leverage those as soon as possible to secure your IT environment.

Also, assumed in this stage is the act of documenting findings. The finding should be placed in a POAM template as the business moves through the lifecycle. This could be done using documents created in Word®, for example, but recommend using a spreadsheet program that allows the easier filtering and management of the POAM. Spreadsheets afford greater flexibility during the "heavy lift" portion of formulating all POAMs not intended to be fixed immediately because of technical shortfalls. This would include not having in-house technical expertise, such as setting up Two Factor Authentication (2FA), or because of current company financial limitations; this would most likely be reasonable when the costs are currently prohibitive to implement a specific control.

The "research" phase includes technical analysis, Internet searches, market research, etc., regarding viable solutions to address the security control not being "compliant." This activity is typically part of an initial milestone established in the POAM. It may be added in the POAM and could be, for example: "Conduct initial market research of candidate systems that can provide an affordable Two Factor Authentication (2FA) solution to meet security control 3.X.X." Another example might be: "The cybersecurity section will identify at least two candidate Data at Rest (DAR) solutions to protect the company's corporate and CUI data." These initial milestones are a normal part of any initial milestones that clearly describe reasonable actions to address non-compliant controls.

Another part of any milestone establishment action is to identify when a milestone is expected to be complete. Typically, milestones are done for 30 days, but if the complexity of such an activity requires additional time, ensure the company has identified reasonable periods with actual dates of *expected* completion. Never use undefined milestones such as "next version update" or "Calendar Year 2020 in Quarter 4." Real times are mandatory to indeed manage findings supported by, for example, automated workflow or tracking applications the company may acquire in the future to enhance its cybersecurity risk management program.

At the "recommendation" phase, this is the time when the prior research has resulted in at least one solution, be it additional skilled personnel (people), enhanced company policies that manage the security control better (process), or a device that solves the control in part or total (technology). This should be part of this phase and the POAM template as a milestone with the expected completion date.

At the "decide" phase, company or agency decision-makers should approve a recommended solution. That decision should be documented in a configuration change tracking document, configuration management decision memorandum, or in the POAM itself. This should include approved resources, but most importantly, any funding decision should be acted upon as quickly as possible. While many of these suggestions may seem necessary, it is often overlooked to document the decision so future personnel and management can understand how the solution was determined.

The "implementation" phase may become the most difficult. A leader should be designated to coordinate the specific activity to meet the control— it may not necessarily be a technical solution. Still, it may also include, for example, a documentation development activity that creates a process to manage the POAM.

Implementation should also include primary programmatic considerations. This should consist of performance, schedule, cost, and risk:

- Performance: consider what success the solution is attempting to address. Will it send email alerts to users? Will the system shut down automatically once an intrusion is confirmed in the corporate network? Will the Incident Response Plan include notifications to law enforcement? Performance is always a powerful and measurable means to ensure that the solution will address the POAM/security control shortfall. Always try to measure performance specific to the actual control that is being met.

- Schedule: Devise a plan based upon the developed milestones that are reasonable and not unrealistic. Ensure that the POAM template is updated and approved by management as soon as a deviation becomes apparent. This should be a senior management representative with authority to provide extensions to the current plan. This could include, for example, a Senior IT Manager, Chief Information Security Officer, or Chief Operating Officer.

- Cost: While it is assumed that all funding has been provided early in the process, always ensure contingencies are in place to request additional funding. It is common in most IT programs to maintain a 15-20% funding reserve for emergencies. Otherwise, the Project Manager or lead will have to re-justify to management for additional funding late in the implementation portion of the cycle.

- Risk: This is not the risk identified, for example, by the review of security controls or automated scans of the system. This risk is specific to the program's success in accomplishing its goal to close the security finding. Risk should always focus on the performance, cost, and schedule risks as significant concerns. Consider creating a risk matrix or risk log to help during the implementation phase.

Finally, ensure that the company can satisfactorily implement its solution close the control, and notify the Contract Office of the completion. Typically, updates and notifications should occur at least once a quarter, but more often is appropriate for more highly impactful controls. Two-factor authentication and automated auditing, for example, are best updated as quickly as possible. This not only secures the company's network and IT environment but builds confidence with the government that security requirements are being met.

A final area to consider in terms of best practices within cybersecurity, and more specifically, in developing complete POAMs, is the area of **continual improvement**. Leveraging the legacy Intelligence Lifecycle process should be an ongoing model for IT and cybersecurity specialists to emulate. Those supporting this process should always be prepared to make changes or modifications that better represent the state and readiness of the system with its listing of POAMs. The Intelligence Lifecycle provides the ideal model for a business to follow and implement to meet its POAM responsibilities within the CMMC.

ABOUT THE AUTHOR

Dr. Russo is a former Senior Information Security Engineer within the Department of Defense's (DOD) F-35 Joint Strike Fighter program. He has an extensive background in cybersecurity and is an expert in the Risk Management Framework (RMF) and DOD Instruction 8510, which implement RMF throughout the DOD and the federal government. He holds a Certified Information Systems Security Professional (CISSP) certification and a CISSP in information security architecture (ISSAP). He has a 2017 certification as a Chief Information Security Officer (CISO) from the National Defense University, Washington, DC. He retired from the US Army in 2012 as the Senior Intelligence Officer.

He is the former CISO at the Department of Education. In 2016, he led the effort to close over 95% of the outstanding US Congressional and Inspector General cybersecurity shortfall weaknesses spanning as far back as five years.

Dr. Russo is the former Senior Cybersecurity Engineer supporting the Joint Medical Logistics Development Functional Center of the Defense Health Agency (DHA) at Fort Detrick, MD. He led a team of engineering and cybersecurity professionals protecting five major Medical Logistics systems supporting over 200 DOD Medical Treatment Facilities around the globe.

In 2011, Dr. Russo was certified by the Office of Personnel Management as a graduate of the Senior Executive Service Candidate program.

From 2009 through 2011, Dr. Russo was the Chief Technology Officer at the Small Business Administration (SBA). He led a team of over 100 IT professionals in supporting an intercontinental Enterprise IT infrastructure and security operations spanning 12-time zones; he deployed cutting-edge technologies to enhance SBA's business and information sharing operations supporting the small business community. Dr. Russo was the first-ever Program Executive Officer (PEO)/Senior Program Manager in the Office of Intelligence & Analysis at Headquarters, Department of Homeland Security (DHS), Washington, DC. Dr. Russo was responsible for developing and deploying secure Information and Intelligence support systems for OI&A to include software applications and systems to enhance the DHS mission. He was responsible for the program management development lifecycle during his tenure at DHS.

He holds a Master of Science from the National Defense University in Government Information Leadership with a concentration in Cybersecurity and a Bachelor of Arts in Political Science with a minor in Russian Studies from Lehigh University. He holds Level III Defense Acquisition certification in Program Management, Information Technology, and Systems Engineering. He has been a member of the DOD Acquisition Corps since 2001.

Copyright 2021, Cybersentinel, LLC, All Rights Reserved
Washington, DC ∞ Tucson, AZ